P9-EDA-725

OLSON'S *New Deal for California*

OLSON'S

ROBERT E. BURKE

new deal for california

UNIVERSITY OF CALIFORNIA PRESS

BERKELEY AND LOS ANGELES

1953

University of California Press
Berkeley and Los Angeles, California
Cambridge University Press
London, England

Printed in the United States of America
By the University of California Printing Department

Designed by Marion Jackson

For Helen

preface

ONE OF THE GREAT POLITICAL MYSTERIES OF THE PAST TWENTY years has been the Democratic party of California.

Franklin Delano Roosevelt swept the state four elections in a row and Harry S. Truman squeaked through to win in 1948, even though popular Governor Earl Warren was the Republican nominee for vice-president and Henry A. Wallace secured nearly 200,000 votes. Three times Democrats were elected to the United States Senate, William Gibbs McAdoo in 1932 and Sheridan Downey in 1938 and 1944. From 1936 onward the registration figures were about three to two Democratic.

Yet in all this period—indeed, during the whole of the first half of the twentieth century—there has been only one Democratic state administration, that of Culbert L. Olson. Elected in 1938 and defeated in 1942, Olson in many respects personified the leadership—if it could be called that—of the Democratic party—if, indeed, there was such a thing at the state level. A study of his administration may help to promote an understanding of California politics and should help California Democrats to see their situation a little more clearly.

It was Olson's misfortune that, while his enemies early and clearly understood his faults, his friends (and potential friends) never came to understand his virtues. If only—and "if only" is a term that must frequently recur in the minds of those who try to follow Olson's saga sympathetically—Olson had been elected earlier, or had had more patronage to bestow, or had been a better administrator, or even had had better luck! But "not even God can change history."

This book, based upon the author's doctoral dissertation, "The Olson Regime in California," is an attempt to tell the story of the hectic Olson administration in a straightforward manner and for its own sake. For those who prefer to have an early inkling of the author's supposed bias, it might be noted that he cast his first vote for Olson and has never regretted it. However, it is his hope that he has examined the Olson record critically and has found some of the reasons for its lack of success, and for the lack of success of the Democratic party of California at the state level.

This study could not have been made without the aid of Culbert L. Olson. He made his papers fully available, and spent many hours in interviews with the author, answering all questions and recapturing vividly the spirit of his dramatic days at Sacramento. He simply desired that the truth be told, and never suggested that the author do more than study the sources and draw his own conclusions. Thus this is in no sense an "official" history.

The thanks of the author go also to the following Californians active in the politics of the period, who discussed it with him: former Attorney General Robert W. Kenny, Carey McWilliams, former Governor Frank F. Merriam, Superior Judge M. Stanley Mosk, former Congressman Ellis E. Patterson, Justice Paul Peek, and Congressman Samuel William Yorty.

The author is grateful to the great California journalist, Franklin Hichborn, for permission to use quotations from his manuscripts.

The author wishes to thank the members of the staffs of the John Randolph and Dora Haynes Foundation, Los Angeles; and of two notable University of California institutions, the Bureau of Public Administration and the Bancroft Library, for many courtesies. Mrs. Julia Macleod of the Manuscripts Division of the Bancroft Library was especially helpful. He is greatly indebted for advice and criticism to the following friends who read all or parts of the manuscript at some stage in its development: Professors John D. Hicks, Joseph P. Harris, James F. King, and Lawrence Kinnaird, all of the University of California; and Messrs. Paul W. Chamberlain, Ross E. Chichester, David Kasavan, and Robert D. Lundy. Miss Ester Petrik, who typed the manuscript in its final form, saved the author the embarrassment of at least some small errors. Finally, the author is grateful to Jordan Brotman of the University of California Press for much aid.

Of course, no one other than the author can be held responsible for the interpretations and conclusions. Indeed, if it had turned out that his friends and associates had agreed with all of them he would have been exceedingly surprised!

R.E.B.

Berkeley, California
September 15, 1952

acknowledgments

THE AUTHOR EXPRESSES HIS THANKS TO THE FOLLOWING AUTHORS and publishers for permission to quote copyright material:

American Mercury, for Eugene Lyon's article, "Lament for Ham-and-Eggs," January, 1940.

California Alumni Association, for Eric C. Bellquist's article, "Tolerance Needed," *California Monthly,* April, 1942.

California Savings and Loan League, for Neill Davis' article, "Who Won the Budget Battle—and Why," *Building-Loan Journal,* July, 1939.

Catholic University of America Press, for Father August Raymond Ogden's book, *The Dies Committee; a Study of the Special House Committee for the Investigation of Un-American Activities* 1938–1944 (Washington, D.C., 1945).

George Creel, for his book *Rebel at Large: Recollections of Fifty Crowded Years* (New York: Putnam, 1947).

Thomas Y. Crowell Co., for the book *Glory Roads; The Psychological State of California,* by Luther Whiteman and Samuel L. Lewis (New York, 1936).

Curtis Publishing Co. and Mrs. Harold L. Ickes, for Part VI of the series, "My Twelve Years with FDR," by Harold L. Ickes, *Saturday Evening Post,* July 10, 1948.

Curtis Publishing Co. and Frank J. Taylor, for Mr. Taylor's article, "Man With a New Broom: California's Governor Warren," *Saturday Evening Post,* August 7, 1943.

Robert de Roos, for his book *The Thirsty Land* (Stanford, 1948.)

De Vorss and Co., for the book *Out of the Frying Pan,* by Winston and Marian Moore (Los Angeles, 1939).

Clinton T. Duffy and Dean Jennings, for their book *The San Quentin Story* (Garden City: Doubleday, 1950).

Alfred A. Knopf, Inc., for the book *December 7: The First Thirty Hours,* by correspondents of *Time, Life,* and *Fortune* (New York, 1942).

Carey McWilliams, for his books *California: The Great Exception* (New York; A. A. Wyn, 1949); *Prejudice; Japanese-Americans: Symbol of Racial Intolerance* (Boston: Little, Brown, 1944); and *Southern California Country: An Island on the Land* (New York: Duell, Sloan and Pearce, 1946).

Murray and Gee, Inc., for Senator John Phillips' book, *Inside California* (Los Angeles, 1939).

The Nation, for the following articles: Paul Y. Anderson, "Investigate Mr. Dies!" (November 5, 1938) and "What the Election Means" (November 19, 1938); Upton Sinclair, "Future of EPIC" (November 28, 1934); and Alden Stevens, "100,000 Political Footballs" (July 19, 1941).

New Republic, for the following articles: Helen Fuller, "Voting for Victory" (October 12, 1942); Carey McWilliams, "Warren of California" (October 18, 1943); and the unsigned editorial, "Tom Mooney Goes Free" (January 18, 1939).

Newsweek, for Raymond Moley's article, "Chaos in California" (April 15, 1940).

Oakland *Tribune*, for permission to reproduce the picture on the title page of this book.

Kenyon J. Scudder, for his book *Prisoners Are People* (Garden City: Doubleday, 1952).

Upton Sinclair, for his book *I, Candidate for Governor And How I Got Licked* (Pasadena: the author, 1935).

Bradford Smith, for his book *Americans from Japan* (Philadelphia and New York: Lippincott, 1948).

Irving Stone, for his book *Earl Warren; A Great American Story* (New York: Prentice-Hall, 1948).

Anna Louise Strong, for her book *My Native Land* (New York: Viking, 1940).

University of Chicago Press, for Morton Grodzin's book, *Americans Betrayed: Politics and the Japanese Evacuation* (1949).

University of Oklahoma Press, for Cortez A. M. Ewing's book, *Congressional Elections, 1896–1944* (Norman, Okla., 1947).

Vanguard Press, for the book *Our Sovereign State*, edited by Robert S. Allen (New York, 1949).

Jerry Voorhis, for his book *Confessions of a Congressman* (Garden City: Doubleday, 1947).

contents

1 *the rise*
of the california democrats

IN 1930 CALIFORNIA WAS VIRTUALLY A ONE-PARTY STATE. THE Republicans had a better than three-to-one lead in registration, there had been no Democratic United States senator elected since the defeat of Senator James D. Phelan in 1920, and no Democratic state administration since James H. Budd left office in 1899. Occasionally an isolated Democrat was elected to the Legislature, chiefly through a provision in the direct primary law that permitted candidates to appear on all ballots without indicating their party affiliations. But California politics was essentially a Republican party affair, with the several factions so confident of success at the general elections that they could afford to slug it out among themselves at the primaries. Three successive Republican governors were defeated for renomination and yet the Democrats never once came close to winning that office.

The Democrats in the state had long been plagued with bad luck, as well as factionalism. In 1910, when the party began to come back elsewhere in the country, and indeed made a strong bid for the California governorship, its progressivism was rejected in favor of the progressivism of a dramatic and outspoken young Republican attorney, Hiram W. Johnson. During Johnson's term-and-a-half as governor (1911–1917), the

1

Democrats were at a disadvantage in the state—the administration's political reforms (most notably the revision of the direct primary law in 1913, permitting candidates to run for any and all party nominations), its new Progressive party (formed in 1914), and that party's conscious, studied, unrelenting stream of propaganda against all political parties (other than the Progressive, of course), succeeded almost in achieving half of the governor's objective of destroying the "old parties." In 1918 the Democratic voters gave their nomination for governor to Republican Mayor James Rolph, Jr. of San Francisco, who had failed to win his own party's nomination and under the law was thus disqualified from accepting that of the Democrats. In that year the Democratic party had no candidate for governor on the general election ballot—the ultimate in degradation had been reached.

However, the great depression and the consequent reaction against Hoover changed this picture drastically. The chief local beneficiary was William Gibbs McAdoo, former secretary of the treasury and one of the multitude of Easterners and Middle-Westerners who had flocked to California during the boom of the 'twenties. In the 1932 presidential preference primary McAdoo headed the victorious slate pledged to Speaker of the House John Nance Garner and backed by William Randolph Hearst. At the national convention McAdoo swung to Franklin Delano Roosevelt and assured his nomination for the presidency. At the primary election in August 1932 McAdoo won the Democratic nomination for United States senator and at the general election he was victorious over the divided opposition of a "wet" Republican and a Prohibitionist.

During the next two years, the McAdoo machine, based largely upon federal patronage, dominated the Democratic scene in California. Its chief leaders were George Creel, the wartime head of public information, Hamilton Cotton, and Colonel William Neblett, the latter two of Los Angeles. McAdoo himself became a New Deal regular in the Senate.

Unfortunately for the Democratic leaders, the governorship had not been open to contest in 1932, having by law been timed for the "off years." Their candidate in 1934 was Creel himself, and they had the greatest confidence in their ability to turn out Republican Governor Frank F. Merriam.

George Creel's dreams of political glory were not to come true, however, for he ran headlong into one of the most spectacular political movements in California history. The McAdoo machine was never to be the same again and the Democratic party was to be torn by inner strife for years to come.

Upton Sinclair, the famous author and frequent Socialist candidate for office, changed his registration to Democratic in the fall of 1933 and shortly thereafter announced his candidacy by publishing a remarkable pamphlet, *I, Governor of California and How I Ended Poverty.*

Sinclair's plan to "End Poverty in California" (EPIC) has been well summarized by former Congressman Jerry Voorhis, who made his political debut as one of the EPIC candidates for the Assembly:

> It was this: that unemployed people be given an opportunity to produce for their own needs instead of being "cared for" by direct relief. The state was to buy or lease lands on which food products would be grown by some of the unemployed. Factories were to be erected where others among them would turn out such essential manufactured articles as clothing, furniture, and processed foods. The people were to be paid in scrip money, expendable only for goods produced within their cooperative "production-for-use" system.[1]

This plan had an extraordinary appeal. EPIC clubs sprang up throughout the state, although with a heavy concentration in southern California, until they eventually numbered about 800. Sinclair published a weekly paper and a series of little pamphlets, spoke continually to meetings and endorsed through his End Poverty League, Incorporated, a slate of candidates for most state offices and Congress.[2] Sinclair won a clear majority in the August Democratic primary over all eight of his opponents, securing 436,200 votes to 288,106 for Creel, his chief rival. Something of the bewilderment that must have characterized the McAdoo group at the time was expressed years later by George Creel in his autobiography: "Northern California offered no problem, for hard headed, hard-working native sons and daughters were in a majority, but when I crossed the Tehachapi into Southern California, it was like plunging into darkest Africa without gun bearers."[3]

Sinclair's running mate, Sheridan Downey, an attorney of Sacramento and San Francisco, won the nomination for lieutenant governor easily, as did one of the EPIC candidates for State Board of Equalization, three for the State Senate, and thirty-nine for Assembly. The Demo-

cratic state convention meeting in Sacramento in September was dominated by EPIC delegates, and the platform it drew up was a slightly
diluted version of the EPIC plan. Culbert L. Olson, attorney and
Sinclair-endorsed Democratic nominee for state senator from Los Angeles County, was named state chairman for the biennium, winning
over McAdoo's law partner, William H. Neblett.[4]

The EPIC managers had made every effort to get their supporters
to become registered Democrats. "Remember you must be registered
Democratic to vote for Upton Sinclair at the August 28 primaries," ran
an advertisement in *Upon Sinclair's EPIC News* (June 18, 1934). At
the general election in November there were 1,555,705 registered Democrats and 1,430,198 registered Republicans in the state, as compared
with 1,161,482 Democrats and 1,565,264 Republicans at the 1932 general election. If registration figures meant anything, California was now
a Democratic state.

The 1934 campaign was easily the most bitter in California history,
characterized by solid newspaper opposition to Sinclair, clever if unscrupulous quotations out of context from Sinclair's voluminous and
controversial writings by his opponents, failure of the Roosevelt administration to support the Democratic nominee, and many important Democratic defections. The campaign was complicated by the presence in
the race of a third important candidate, in addition to Sinclair and
Merriam, in the person of Raymond L. Haight, Los Angeles attorney
and nominee of the Commonwealth and Progressive parties.

The election resulted in a defeat for the new majority party of California, at a time when the Democrats were achieving great successes
in almost every other state. Sinclair received 879,537 votes, as compared
with 1,138,620 for Merriam and 302,519 for Haight (who had campaigned as a middle-of-the-roader, with the support of the powerful
McClatchy newspapers in the Central Valley). Governor Merriam carried all but nine of the state's fifty-eight counties. Sinclair won six
(Contra Costa, Lassen, Madera, Plumas, Trinity and Tuolumne) and
Haight three (El Dorado, Fresno and Stanislaus). It might be noted that
Sinclairism, in spite of its southern California origin, seems to have
persisted longest in the north.

After proclaiming that he had just begun to fight, Upton Sinclair characteristically retired to his study to write an account of his crusade.
This book, *I, Candidate for Governor And How I Got Licked*, remains

the most lasting of Sinclair's contributions to California politics. Almost as soon as he had boasted, "We are the Democratic Party of California and we are going to stay that,"[5] the EPIC clubs began to vanish and by 1936 there was almost nothing left of his once vigorous organization. In the 1936 presidential preference primary an EPIC slate, pledged to Sinclair on the first ballot and to President Roosevelt thereafter, was defeated almost eight to one by the regulars, headed by Senator McAdoo. Carey McWilliams has noted:

> Sinclairism was Kearneyism and Johnsonism, all over again. Once again a mass revolt, in an amazingly brief period, had risen to great power, with little preparation or formal organization. In each case, popular discontent had quickly crystallized in the form of independent political action. Like the Workingman's Party, the Epic movement swept a number of candidates into office and laid the foundation for important subsequent development; and, like the earlier movement, the Epic organization disappeared almost as quickly as it had emerged.[6]

In spite of its bitter factionalism and its set-back in the 1934 governorship contest, the Democratic party continued to rise in California. In the Legislature, the Democrats increased in strength until they had a clear majority of the Assembly (47 out of 80) at the 1937 session and were able to elect as Speaker William Moseley Jones of Montebello, one of Senator McAdoo's law partners. The State Senate remained Republican, though the Democratic minority rose to 16 (out of 40) at the 1937 session. Only four Republican congressmen were elected in 1936 to the California delegation to the House of Representatives (20 men), and President Roosevelt carried the state by a majority of 900,000 that year.

As 1938 approached, Democratic politicians were confident that they could win the governorship if only they could find a candidate behind whom the party could unite.

2 *the rise of culbert l. olson*

the McAdoo forces demoralized and still groggy from their own defeat, Culbert L. Olson was in an excellent position to assume leadership of the Democrats. Elected to the State Senate to fill the sole seat allotted to Los Angeles County, and with most of his two-year term as chairman of the Democratic state central committee still ahead of him, the tall, white-haired and distinguished-looking attorney had his chance as 1935 opened. While he had not been formally an EPIC himself, he had run with Sinclair's endorsement, and became the natural leader of the EPIC-liberal minority in the Legislature. Not only was Olson the only senator from the state's most populous county, but also he was one of the very few new Democratic legislators with previous experience.

Culbert L. Olson was born in 1876 on a farm in Millard County, Utah Territory, the son of an immigrant Dane.[1] As a boy he worked on the farm and on construction jobs, and as a student at Brigham Young University he worked his way as a railroad brakeman and telegraph operator. In 1896, after a year of pre-legal work, he became reporter and city editor on the Ogden *Standard*. His mother, Delilah King Olson, was an ardent suffragette, school teacher and, after her husband's death,

6

a county office holder. The Utah environment, with its emphasis on social responsibility and coöperative economic endeavor, made a profound impression upon the young Olson, even though he was not himself a Mormon.

In 1896, still too young to vote, Olson was an ardent Bryan Democrat, and in 1897 he moved to the national capital as secretary to his cousin, William H. King, newly elected to the House of Representatives. During the next four years he studied law, acted as correspondent for a newspaper, and worked for King. In 1901 he returned to Utah with his LL.B. from Columbian (later George Washington) University and began the practice of law at Salt Lake City. His legal practice grew rapidly, and in time he branched out as a promoter of mining projects, a builder of hotels in Idaho and Nevada, and a banker. In 1905 Olson married Kate Jeremy, and became the father of a son, Richard, in 1907, and of twins, Dean and John, in 1917.

In 1916 he won a seat in the Utah State Senate where he became chairman of the judiciary committee. As chairman he acted as sponsor of a long list of progressive legislation, including bills to regulate public utilities, to eliminate corrupt practices, to set up the initiative and referendum, to provide workmen's compensation, to limit the use of injunctions in labor disputes, to protect collective bargaining, and to regulate the issuance of securities. Much of this program became law, and in 1920 Olson secured one-third of the votes of the Utah Democratic state convention for the nomination for the United States Senate. In that same year Senator Olson was a delegate to the national convention at San Francisco, and pleaded without success before the platform committee on behalf of a more "advanced" Democratic platform.

In the same year Olson made a momentous decision. He dropped his political career in Utah and moved his family and law practice to Los Angeles. The discouraging signs of a return to conservatism in Utah as elsewhere had much to do with this decision. The Los Angeles to which he came was the great booming city of the 'twenties and his law practice grew. Olson specialized in legal work in behalf of the victims of unscrupulous business promoters and stock manipulators. It is not surprising that he found plenty to do in southern California during the 'twenties.

Olson's interest in political matters did not disappear during the years 1920–1932, but he took no active part except in 1924, when he campaigned throughout southern California for Robert M. LaFollette. In

1932 he was active in the Los Angeles Democratic Club, which he had helped to organize, and he campaigned for the unsuccessful Roosevelt ticket in the presidential preference primary.

Olson's entry into state politics in earnest in 1934 has been described by Upon Sinclair:

> Mr. Olson had come forward early in the EPIC campaign; he was president of the Los Angeles Democratic Club, and he invited me to explain my ideas to this organization. He assured me of his devotion to the idea of production for use and his willingness to go along with our forces; but he did not want to come out definitely as an EPIC man until after the primaries, thinking that he could have more influence over the old-line Democrats by following that course.[2]

Giving up his initial plan of running for governor, Olson filed for the Democratic nomination for the Los Angeles County seat in the State Senate. He was the only one of Sinclair's pre-primary endorsed candidates for the Senate to win election. Chosen state chairman with the support of the EPICs, Olson managed the Democratic campaign in the 1934 general election, and won a wide acquaintance throughout the state. He won his own race for the Senate, although he did not get a majority and in fact secured fewer votes than Upton Sinclair won in Los Angeles County. Bitterly anti-McAdoo, for along with the EPICs he considered that the McAdoo machine had sabotaged the Sinclair-Downey campaign, Olson threw down the gauntlet to all the "conservatives" who had deserted the party in 1934: "Only those who remained loyal to the Democratic Party during the recent campaign will remain in the party and be recognized as Democrats."[3] Just how he expected to make good on this threat is not clear, for he and the EPICs had few weapons at their disposal.

At the 1935 session of the Legislature, Senator Olson assumed the leadership of the EPIC-liberal bloc, a numerous minority in the Assembly and a handful in the predominantly rural Senate. By dint of very hard work on his part, a production-for-use bill which provided for state aid for coöperatives and for state reopening of closed factories, came within two votes of passage in the upper house.[4] New taxes imposed by the 1935 Legislature (establishing of an income tax and increasing of inheritance and bank and corporation franchise taxes) were originally proposed by the Olson-led Democratic minority and eventually accepted as the Merriam administration's own, and resulted in a balanced budget. Olson won what was considered to be the major liberal victory at this session when he secured the elimination of the sales tax on foods for home consumption.[5] His fight against a memorial to Congress asking enactment of the Townsend Pension Plan was a courageous one, for the Townsendites were then at their most powerful in southern California. Franklin Hichborn, the veteran legislative correspondent and old-line progressive, wrote: "I have listened to considerable oratory in the Senate Chamber, but never have I seen there more fearless stand or heard more convincing argument, than Olson's in opposition to the Townsend scheme."[6]

At the close of the 1935 Legislature, Olson became the chairman of a Senate interim committee to investigate tidelands oil. As an attorney he had had considerable experience in petroleum litigation and in the Legislature he had taken the leadership in behalf of the smaller oil operators. In the same year Olson was appointed special assistant to the United States attorney general, in charge of California oil matters.

The tidelands oil question in this period involved the state's oil reserves at Huntington Beach.[7] These reserves were being drained away by Standard Oil wells centered on the "Pacific Electric Strip" between the state highway and the ocean, as well as by "independents" whose wells were dug farther inland and "slanted" through Standard's holdings to the state's tidelands. At the 1935 session a bill giving to the owners of littoral lands (at Huntington Beach this meant only Standard) the exclusive right to apply for and receive leases for slant drilling into the tidelands, passed both houses over Olson's opposition, but was vetoed by Governor Merriam.

In 1936 an initiative measure providing essentially the same thing while cutting down the size of the minimum royalty, qualified for the ballot, and Senator Olson wrote the opposing argument for the voter's handbook.[8] Here he assailed the slogan "Save Our Beaches" being used by proponents of the measure, and pointed out that "where it controls littoral lands, as at Huntington Beach, the Standard Oil Company has itself destroyed the beaches for public purposes as much as they can be destroyed, by innumerable wells drilled and now being operated by it at the water's edge, or by other operations either from the uplands or in the tidelands." This initiative, Proposition 4, was defeated by the voters.

THE RISE OF CULBERT L. OLSON   9

At the 1937 Legislature Olson secured the passage of his own bill on tidelands oil. This measure provided for leasing by the state of rights to drill tidelands oil after competitive bidding on each of eleven parcels,[9] with no company or individual eligible for contiguous parcels. It further provided that if the bids received were not high enough the state would do its own drilling. The Olson oil bill was held up to referendum, however, and was turned down by the voters at the 1938 general election (the same election at which Olson himself won the governorship).

This phase of the tidelands oil question was settled by the 1938 special session of the Legislature with the passage of the State Lands Act of 1938, which forbade tidelands drilling but permitted leasing for slant drilling to the highest bidder without limit to the number of parcels that might be leased and without a minimum royalty. Franklin Hichborn gave full credit to Olson: "That the oil has not gone to Standard during the term of the present Governor is due almost entirely to the effective work of Senator Olson."[10] Olson's activity with tidelands oil had given him experience as an investigator, and a chance to prove his mettle as a legislator, even though he was not to see his own measure become law.

Olson personally desired to enter the race for United States senator in 1938, believing himself better qualified for that post than for the governorship, and anxious to have it out with his old enemy, Senator McAdoo.[11] The San Francisco *Chronicle* of March 13, 1937, reported a plan of liberals to use the new Commonwealth-Progressive Federation as a campaign vehicle for Olson for senator, Raymond L. Haight for governor, Assemblyman Ellis E. Patterson for lieutenant governor, and Sheridan Downey for attorney general. In April Olson resigned his $10,000 post as special assistant attorney general, ostensibly due to the press of his work as state senator, but reportedly due to pressure from the national administration, where McAdoo had much influence.[12] Olson's old friend and Utah Senate colleague, Secretary of War George Dern, was now dead and Olson had lost his most influential friend in Washington. Furthermore, Olson had undoubtedly antagonized some leaders in the national administration by his abortive efforts to set up a Roosevelt slate minus the McAdoo forces in the 1936 presidential preference primary.

The 1938 Democratic Primary

In June 1937 Senator Olson wrote to Everett C. McKeage, San Francisco attorney and friend, that he would make the race for governor if he could have a reasonable assurance that enough means for carrying on a campaign were available.[13] In August McKeage reserved with the secretary of state the name "Culbert L. Olson for Governor Club, Incorporated."[14] Finally, on September 4, 1937, Senator Olson announced publicly his candidacy for governor: "I have seriously considered and carefully analyzed my own utility for further public service, and also prevailing party sentiment. I have found that the predominating sentiment of the Democratic Party is in favor of my becoming a candidate for Governor."[15]

While issuing no platform at this time, Olson pledged "positive policies and honest leadership" to liberal Democrats. After an extremely busy several months of campaigning, Senator Olson issued his platform on April 18, 1938. It was a 6,000-word statement of his principles and proposed policies, as well as an attack on the Merriam administration.[16] His preamble began with a severe indictment:

> A generation of Republican rule in California now culminates under [sic] the moribund Merriam-Hatfield regime, in a political impasse intolerable alike to the taxpayer and the family on relief, to the business man and the worker. The functions of government have been perverted, responsibility has been evaded, the democratic process has been subverted, natural resources, assets of the State, have been given away and public moneys have been wasted. The people have been defrauded, their needs defeated, their requests disregarded.

Olson charged further that "privileged interests" controlled the Merriam regime: "State offices have become their agencies." Olson then asked for his own election with these words:

> There must be a real change—not a mere nominal or partisan change—in the character of our State government.
>
> In presenting myself as a Democratic candidate for Governorship, I ask the people for a mandate to make that change, a mandate to drive out political iniquity, a mandate to give moral leadership, a mandate to apply business methods and elemental honesty to the conduct of the business of the State of California.
>
> I will carry out that mandate pledged to the principles, purposes and policies set forth in the following statement of my platform.

The platform proper listed in some detail Olson's views on most important state questions, and was a frank effort to outline a New Deal for California. First came his pronouncement in favor of public ownership of public utilities, with an endorsement of the Garrison revenue bond bill. This measure, passed by the 1937 Legislature but held up to referendum, proposed to encourage public ownership of power and water by local districts through facilitating the issuance of revenue bonds. Olson charged that the Merriam administration had undermined civil service by failing to secure adequate appropriations for the State Personnel Board. He pledged that his chief concern in tax matters would be ability to pay, and he promised further sales tax exemptions "as rapidly as these exemptions can be accomplished without upsetting the State's budgeting requirements or crippling any of the State's essential or constitutionally mandatory functions." He said that, subject to legislative approval, he would appoint a commission to examine the state's whole financial structure.

The question of unemployment, still the most vital problem in California in 1938, was handled at some length in Olson's primary platform. He stated flatly that he considered unemployment had "come to stay, at least until a more perfect economic order shall evolve," and charged the Republican administration with treating it "as if it were only temporary and therefore did not exist." The chief proposal advanced by Olson was that of more "production-for-use": "Self-help should be encouraged, organized and assisted among the unemployed and the under-employed. This would enable them to fend for themselves, and to make better livings than if on WPA or direct relief. It would rehabilitate them, inspire their self-reliance. At the same time it would reduce both the relief load and the expense of administration."

On other subjects the Olson platform was briefer. Olson favored exclusive federal financing and administering of old age pensions. "Until that is accomplished, I shall favor State aid for the aged to the limit that public finances will permit." He pointed to his support of slum clearance and low-cost housing measures. He pledged his coöperation in solving the "paradox" that a third of the community could not afford the costs of serious illness or accident. He promised to ask for "legislation providing for a State agency to collect information for, and generally serve the consumer." He announced his support for "rigid laws against usury and usurious interest rates and charges." His discussion of "Business Development" was rather vague: he cited the evil effects of monopoly, stated that government would have to concern itself more with the problems of distribution, and proposed that the state "explore the problem of little business in its relation to the larger problem of restoring balance between production and distribution." On "Education," Olson urged the inevitable "adequate training in the fundamentals—reading, writing and arithmetic," "the fullest development of practical vocational education," and full tenure for teachers. He proposed to extend to all veterans the benefits of the Veterans' Welfare Board, then enjoyed only by World War veterans.

The subjects of "Labor," "Law Enforcement" and "Civil Liberties" were the last in the Olson platform, and on them he was frank and clear. He asked for a California Wagner Act to protect labor's rights, and pointed to collective bargaining as the best means of attaining peace between labor and employer. "Violence on the part of either must not be countenanced. The State should be prepared to assist negotiations by acting as intercessor. I shall rely on peaceful methods in the settlement of industrial disputes." Olson charged that the Merriam administration had been lax in its enforcement of minimum wage–maximum hours laws for women and minors. He pledged "honest, speedy law enforcement," and in a significant passage stated: "Persecution under color of prosecution, prosecution without regard to the question of guilt, false imprisonment, these are un-American perversions of justice and tend to undermine confidence in the due process of law." Finally, he affirmed his belief in civil liberties and condemned "the propagation of racial and religious prejudices and discriminations," pledging: "I shall stand firmly for the preservation of our democracy and of representative constitutional government against all attacks from whatever quarter."

In the interval between Olson's announcement of candidacy and the issuance of his platform, others had entered the race for the Democratic nomination for governor. The first was Representative John F. Dockweiler, scion of an old Los Angeles Democratic family and member of Congress since 1933.[17] He used the slogan "It's Time California Elects A Californian," and ran as a consistent supporter of the Roosevelt administration, both as assistant whip of the House Democrats and as one of the two Pacific Coast Democrats on the appropriations committee. He had a substantial amount of support from old-line Democrats of the state, including at least some of the McAdoo group.

Two days after Dockweiler entered the race, Sheriff Daniel C. Murphy of San Francisco became a candidate for the Democratic nomination for governor.[18] He was a former state senator and had long been active in the AFL, as president of the Web Pressmen's Union, and for five years had been president of the California State Federation of Labor. He was endorsed by the AFL Political League in convention at Santa Barbara, winning 304 votes to 179 for Olson and 82 for Dockweiler. He was also endorsed by the San Francisco *News:* "We recommend the nomination of Sheriff Murphy because we have known him longer and better than any other candidate and have implicit faith in his honesty, ability, and progressivism."[19]

Another candidate entering the race for the Democratic nomination for governor was Herbert C. Legg, Los Angeles County supervisor. He had the endorsement of Manchester Boddy, publisher of the chief Democratic newspapers in the state, the Los Angeles *Daily News* and *Evening News.*[20] His campaign emphasized his support of the Roosevelt administration and his practical experience gained while a county supervisor.

J. F. T. O'Connor resigned his post as comptroller of the currency to make the race for governor. He had been a member of the North Dakota Legislature in the years 1917–1921, and had later moved to California and entered William Gibbs McAdoo's law firm. He had managed the campaign of the unsuccessful Roosevelt slate in the 1932 presidential preference primary. He campaigned as Roosevelt's personal candidate, making use of a letter to him from the president which praised his record as comptroller and stated that "I know that the same faithful and intelligent service which you have rendered the nation as Comptroller of the Currency will be cheerfully and successfully given to whatever task you may assume." He was identified by some political writers as the candidate of the McAdoo machine.[21]

The last serious contender for the Democratic nomination for governor in 1938 was not a Democrat at all but Raymond L. Haight of Los Angeles, a registered Progressive who cross-filed on both major party tickets. He had been the third candidate in the race for the governorship at the 1934 general election, when he had polled a substantial vote. A native son, Haight was an attorney in Los Angeles, the manager of the campaign of the Los Angeles Bar Association to recall three Superior Court judges in 1932, and by this time was an ardent supporter of Governor Philip LaFollette's National Progressive party.

The Olson forces, mindful of the role played by Haight as the third man in the Merriam-Sinclair election fight, were determined to "remove Raymond Haight from contention in the finals, which will only serve to swing the election away from the Democrats to the Republicans."[22] They contacted friends of LaFollette in a successful endeavor to keep the Progressive leader from coming out to California to campaign for Haight,[23] and qualified Olson for participation in the Progressive primary against Haight. George T. Davis of San Francisco, attorney for the famous labor prisoner Tom Mooney and known as the LaFollette representative in California, supported Olson, but Olson was unable to win the Progressive nomination for governor at the August primary.

One minor candidate for the Democratic nomination for governor in 1938 worthy of notice was William H. Neblett ("That Fearless Flying Colonel"), former law partner of Senator McAdoo and McAdoo's unsuccessful candidate for state chairman against Olson in 1934. Long a stormy figure in Los Angeles legal and political circles, Neblett in a series of radio broadcasts that began even before his formal entry into the race assailed the other candidates and their supporters with unmitigated violence.[24] Although he caused his enemies, especially Senator Olson, much grief at the time (he accused Olson of participation in the Julian stock frauds[25] and of defrauding the federal government in a Utah mining promotion), Neblett's own very unsavory record came to light when the Sacramento County Grand Jury disclosed that he had used his partnership with Speaker of the Assembly Jones in order to extract "fees" from groups under investigation by an interim committee.[26] An example of Neblett's logic is in the following, from one of his speeches: "Olson is well fitted to be a Communist from his record in the Julian fraud and the Rocky Mountain Coal Company promotion. . . ."[27]

The primary election of August 1938 was complicated by the emergence of a new and dramatic cause, the so-called Ham and Eggs pension plan. Carey McWilliams has differentiated between it and its predecessors: "The early mass political movements in Southern California, characterized by marked social inventiveness, were a healthy manifestation of a people's impulses to do something for themselves. Continued frustration of this impulse, however, soon began to produce rank and unhealthy social growths. Of all these latter-day growths, the Ham and Eggs movement is, by all odds, the most fantastic, incredible, and dangerous."[28]

This exceedingly complex plan was an initiative measure sponsored by almost a million signatures.[29] It proposed to give thirty one-dollar pieces of scrip each Thursday to idle California residents over fifty, with spaces on the back of each piece of scrip for fifty-two stamps, one to be bought from the state and affixed each Thursday by whomever then held the scrip. The scrip was to circulate as money and at the end of the year the state was to redeem each piece at face value, retaining the four cents profit to cover the cost of administration. The scrip was to be accepted in payment of local and state taxes, and public employees were to be paid half in scrip and half in cash. The chief promoters of Ham and Eggs were Willis Allen, campaign director; his brother Lawrence Allen, an attorney; Sherman J. Bainbridge, "The Voice"; and Roy G. Owens, "engineer-economist" and author of the plan. Sheridan Downey, candidate for the Democratic nomination for the United States Senate in opposition to Senator McAdoo, also endorsed the measure.

The Ham and Eggs scheme gave Olson much grief during the primary campaign. One of his major opponents, Congressman Dockweiler, endorsed it enthusiastically a month before the primary and secured in turn the support of the pension leaders.[30] Olson was thus in great danger of losing the votes of thousands of southern Californians upon whom he had counted, unless he followed Dockweiler's lead, and in danger of losing many thousands of votes throughout the state if he did endorse the plan.

Some doubt as to Olson's stand (or lack of one) on the Ham and Eggs plan arose as the result of two telegrams, dated August 11 and August 15, sent over Olson's signature to Sherman J. Bainbridge.[31] Olson later denied that he had authorized them, for they put him on record as unequivocally in favor of the scheme, but for the time being he contented himself with trying to clarify his position with the adherents of the plan, and at the same time keep from repudiating the telegrams.

In his major speech on this subject, Olson told Ham and Eggs supporters of his record in behalf of all forms of social security, cited the contribution of the Townsend movement even though it failed of enactment, defended the right of the people to vote on the Ham and Eggs pension proposal and then took his own stand:

> I am fully aware that a great many people would like to have me say I believe this plan will work.

No honest and intelligent man can utter words of conviction that do not come from his heart and mind.

Let me say to you that there has never been any new legislation meeting any new problem that has ever been enacted that either its sponsors or its opponents were certain of its success or its failure, or that it would operate perfectly without change or modification.[32]

Without endorsing or opposing the plan, Olson went on to say that the movement had accomplished "the primarily important objective of informing and inflaming the people over the need for an economy of abundance and the old age retirement." In his election eve broadcast, Olson thanked the supporters of Ham and Eggs for "their support and faith in me."[33] His stand on this subject brought down upon Olson the wrath of those opposed to the scheme, but it could probably be assumed that few of them would have voted for him anyway. Even though it was a "straddle," its friendly tone tended to keep the Ham and Eggers from going all out for Dockweiler.

Senator Olson had been the first to enter the race for the Democratic nomination for governor, and he managed to retain the initiative throughout the primary campaign. "Stop Olson" maneuvers were a feature of the months preceding the primary, but the other candidates were never able to present a united front. State Chairman Argyll Campbell, a supporter of O'Connor, probably represented the views of old-line party leaders when he contended: "Olson would be the easiest man to nominate and the hardest to elect."[34]

Olson's campaign machinery was perfected early. The key figures in southern California were J. Frank Burke, radio station owner and commentator, who was chairman of the campaign committee; Superior Judge Robert W. Kenny, candidate for state senator from Los Angeles County, who was director of finance; and Kenneth I. Fulton, insurance man, who was treasurer.[35] In the north, the key persons were M. Mitchell Bourquin, San Francisco attorney, who was chairman of the campaign committee; E. W. Wilson, San Francisco banker, who was treasurer; Jesse W. Carter, Redding attorney, who was chairman of the planning committee; and Leo Cunningham, San Francisco attorney, who was San Francisco County chairman. These men were experienced campaigners and the campaign they conducted was a professional job, although some of them antagonized progressives, who might have been expected to support Olson but who feared the machinations of professional politicians.

The Olson campaign was well financed. After the primary election, Senator Olson filed a detailed statement of his campaign finances, reporting receipt of contributions totaling $90,824.02 and expenditures totaling $103,664.06.[36] Manchester Boddy, chief supporter of Herbert C. Legg, had reported before the election that Olson had "more money to spend than all of his democratic opponents combined," and claimed that the "reactionaries" were contributing it to Olson: "They decided months ago that Culbert Olson was the man they could beat. Hence, they have left no stone unturned either financially or through propaganda to insure his nomination."[37]

Olson was unable to get the endorsement of the AFL Political League, which supported Sheriff Murphy, but his friends were very active in AFL circles, and pointed to his position at the top of the list of labor's friends in the State Senate which had been published by the AFL.[38] Olson also failed to get the formal primary endorsement of Labor's Non-Partisan League, the political arm of the CIO, as well as of many AFL and Railroad Brotherhood units which made no endorsement for governor for strategic reasons. He did have the backing of the California Federation for Political Unity, a "united front" of liberals headed by Rube Borough, Los Angeles public works commissioner and former EPIC (president), and William J. Plunkert, former official in the State Relief Administration (executive secretary).[39] It was later charged that the CFPU was Communist-controlled, and that Communists had infiltrated into the campaigns of the candidates endorsed by the CFPU, especially in Los Angeles County.[40]

The Communists, evidently realizing that their formal endorsement would not advance the candidates they wanted to win, played a subtle role in the 1938 primary. Their organ, the *People's World*, concentrated upon attacking the Republicans and giving full publicity to the candidates supported by the CFPU. However, State Chairman William Schneiderman pointed out to his colleagues in the Communist national convention in May 1938 precisely what the California Communists were doing:

> We have become an important factor and a recognized force in the labor and progressive movement, and the progressive forces are beginning to appreciate and understand the role we are playing in the building of the democratic front.

During the past year, the first beginnings of a democratic front showed its outline, growing up around the progressive bloc in the State Legislature and the California progressives in Congress, in the struggle for social and labor legislation. This movement spread down below through the organization of hundreds of Democratic clubs throughout the state, developing a wide range of activity and initiative during the election campaign. Today this movement is gathering around the support of Senator Olson, the leading progressive candidate for the Democratic nomination for Governor in the August primaries.[41]

Olson's primary campaign featured attacks on the Merriam administration, appeals for the support of labor and small farmers, and a tendency to ignore the existence of his Democratic rivals. In the San Joaquin Valley he attacked the "corporation farmers" and processing interests, whom he identified as working through such agricultural writers as Ralph J. Taylor and such organizations as the Associated Farmers in order to exploit the dirt farmer.[42] He repeatedly called for the voters of the Central Valley to vote for the Garrison revenue bond bill at the November general election.

At Fresno he alluded to the intra-party Republican fight between Governor Merriam and Lieutenant Governor George J. Hatfield for the gubernatorial nomination, noting that the Sacramento County Grand Jury investigation into legislative corruption had "created a series of accusations between the Governor and the Lieutenant Governor, as to which has been the most subservient to the subtle and sinister lobbies maintained at Sacramento by the special interests. . . . In other words, Merriam accuses Hatfield, and Hatfield accuses Merriam—and they are both right."[43]

Olson spoke of the tidelands oil question at Modesto, telling of the Olson oil bill and the administration's failure to carry out its provisions while petitions were being circulated to hold it up to referendum, charging flatly that the "Merriam-Hatfield administration absolutely is under the domination and control of the Standard Oil Company and its affiliated interests."[44]

One of the handicaps political observers noted Olson seemed to possess was his close tie with Sinclair in 1934. In reply Olson stated that "I was a Democrat for more than 35 years before Mr. Sinclair came into the Democratic Party and I remain a Democrat since he left that Party," defended the majority of the EPIC Democrats in the Legislature and threw down the gauntlet: "I have no apologies to make for not bolting my party's nominee for governor in 1934, or for being chosen as chairman of the Democratic State Central Committee—no apologies for opposing the election of Governor Merriam."[45]

One of Senator Olson's major primary speeches was concerned with unemployment, which he reiterated was "a permanent problem which can no *longer* be *ignored*."[46] In this address he discussed ways in which the unemployed could be rehabilitated: the introduction of new industries and crops, public works, adult education, self-help and consumer coöperatives; and he pledged himself if elected to work along those lines. In it he also attacked the State Relief Administration's single men's camps, saying that Merriam's policy here "smacks of fascism." Olson pointed in other speeches to the resignations of Carl Sturzenacker, chief of the Division of State Lands, and his assistant, under fire for alleged corruption.[47] In one of his last major addresses, Olson defended his campaign personnel and the contributors to his cause, stating that he was bound by no commitments, that he had refused contributions offered by "underworld forces and by the agencies of special interests," and promised to give a full statement reporting his campaign finances within fifteen days of the primary election.[48]

The Democratic gubernatorial primary on August 30, 1938, resulted in an Olson triumph. The final figures were:

		PER CENT
Olson	483,483	42.09
Dockweiler	218,342	18.58
Murphy	137,740	11.90
Haight	125,012	10.88
Legg	80,586	7.01
O'Connor	71,999	6.23
Neblett	21,219	1.84
Tomasini	10,142	.88

Olson ran well in Los Angeles County, where he got 172,214 votes, compared with 118,421 for Dockweiler and 62,749 for Legg, his nearest competitors, but the percentage Olson received there was but 37.44, less than what he received in the state at large. In San Francisco County Olson ran a strong second to Sheriff Murphy, the figures for the top three being Murphy, 50,336; Olson, 46,534; and Dockweiler, 9,873.

Olson ran very well everywhere in the state, and especially well in the Central Valley. In all, he carried 53 of the state's 58 counties, losing two to Murphy (San Benito and San Francisco), two to Dockweiler (Colusa and Yolo), and one to Haight (Alpine).

The headlines the morning after the primary did not go to Olson's victory, however, for the really big news was the defeat of United States Senator William Gibbs McAdoo by Sheridan Downey. McAdoo, who was Democratic national committeeman, bore the personal endorsement of President Roosevelt, and had ridden through the state with the President in July. The defeat of McAdoo was accomplished by Downey in southern California, as the following final vote for the two chief contenders indicates:

STATE—TOTAL		LOS ANGELES COUNTY	
Downey	511,952	Downey	273,647
McAdoo	375,930	McAdoo	100,878

His friend George Creel said of McAdoo's 1938 campaign: "What he faced, in fact, was the same sort of popular madness that I had to buck in 1934."[49] For Downey was an outspoken advocate of the Ham and Eggs pension plan; in fact, he had delivered a funeral oration over the body of Archie Price, a sixty-four year old who had committed suicide in San Diego after declaring to reporters that he was too old to work and not old enough for a pension. As Carey McWilliams pointed out, "Poor lonely Archie Price became the Horst Wessel of the Ham and Eggs movement."[50] But Downey's support was not limited to the "senior citizens"; as the running mate of Upton Sinclair he had a claim to the remnants of EPIC; he was endorsed by Dr. Townsend; his campaign was financed in large measure by John B. Elliott, wealthy attorney and oil man who had broken with McAdoo; his campaign manager was Pierson M. Hall, former United States district attorney for southern California, and erstwhile associate of Senator McAdoo; and he had the support of Manchester Boddy, publisher of the state's chief Democratic newspapers.[51] McAdoo was outspoken in his opposition to the Ham and Eggs scheme, and in an obvious move to aid McAdoo, President Roosevelt himself warned against it a few days before the primary. McAdoo remained officially neutral in the governorship fight and Senator Olson, in spite of his past differences with McAdoo, was not anxious to have Downey as a running mate.[52]

The Democratic nomination for lieutenant governor went to Ellis E. Patterson, assemblyman from King City since 1933, who had campaigned vigorously for the office for over a year. Patterson had been a Republican member of the Assembly of pronounced liberal views, and in 1934 he had had the distinction of being the only Republican assemblyman endorsed by Upton Sinclair in the primaries. In 1936 Patterson supported President Roosevelt, and was himself defeated for renomination by a conservative Republican. Even though he had won the Democratic nomination, under the California election laws he was ineligible for a place on the ballot because he had lost his own party's nomination. Refusing to accept defeat, Patterson ran as a write-in candidate with Democratic support (the Democratic county central committees in his district had failed to fill the vacancy left by his disqualification), won over 12,000 write-in votes and defeated the Republican candidate, becoming the first disqualified candidate ever to win election in California.[53] He had thereupon become a Democrat. Patterson ran with the support of many labor organizations, including Labor's Non-Partisan League, although like Olson he failed to get the support of the AFL Political League. He won the Democratic nomination by a margin of about 75,000 votes over his nearest competitor, in a crowded field.

The Democratic ticket in the general election of 1938 was thus headed by three men of pronounced liberal views, representatives of the party's left wing. Democratic nominations for the other four partisan state offices were won by Republicans, following the California custom, so these offices were no longer open to contest. Olson, Downey and Patterson now had the task of uniting the party leaders behind themselves and of getting the registered Democrats to vote for their party's slate.

3 victory

FORTUNATELY FOR OLSON, HE FACED AN INCUMBENT GOVERNOR who was neither a popular figure nor an able leader, and who could scarcely rouse a flicker of enthusiasm for himself in any but the most devout of Republican party workers.

Frank F. Merriam became governor of California on June 2, 1934, upon the death of James Rolph, Jr.[1] A former state auditor of Iowa, Merriam had come to Long Beach by way of Oklahoma, and promptly reëntered Republican politics, winning an Assembly seat in 1916. After almost uninterrupted service as a conservative legislator and considerable experience at campaign managing, Merriam won the Republican nomination for lieutenant governor in 1930, at that time tantamount to election. In 1934 he won the Republican nomination for governor, after a sharp primary fight with former Governor C. C. Young, and at the general election defeated Upton Sinclair to win the governorship in his own right. In the summer of 1934 he had called out the militia in the San Francisco-waterfront general strike, incurring the hatred of many labor elements. Content to let others take the initiative, fond of pocket vetoes, Merriam was "an affable, rather ponderous old gentleman with few strong convictions."[2]

Again fortunately for Olson, Merriam had just emerged from a bitter primary fight of his own. His opponent was Lieutenant Governor George J. Hatfield of San Francisco, whose well-financed campaign was promoted by the astute Arthur H. Samish.[3] Samish, the chief lobbyist at Sacramento for the liquor industry, also represented such varied interests as billboards, horse racing, motor carriers and railroads with conspicuous success. The Sacramento County Grand Jury in 1937 began an investigation into charges of corruption in the Legislature, and its probings by 1938 had reached into the affairs of Samish.[4] When its funds were exhausted, the district attorney sought further financial support from Governor Merriam and received it. Samish's attorney, John Francis Neylan, bitterly assailed the Merriam administration and charged that the purpose of the investigation was "to put George Hatfield on the spot through information from my client's records."[5] Though he fought hard, Hatfield's candidacy failed to receive newspaper support and he lost decisively. However, the harsh words uttered by Hatfield and his supporters in the primary campaign remained to haunt Merriam, for the Democrats made wide use of them.

The Democratic state convention of 1938 was fully controlled by friends and supporters of the major candidates, Olson, Downey and Patterson. The platform adopted was in essence the Olson primary platform; indeed, in some parts the wording was identical, and Olson himself was chairman of the platform committee. The main differences from the Olson platform were a pledge to call a constitutional convention, a plank opposing cross-filing in elections, a clearer statement in favor of health insurance, and the final sentence: "We are determined to oppose equally the despotism of communism and the menace of fascism."[6] The chief problem foreseen was Ham and Eggs, for many delegates, especially from the north, were violently opposed to the measure and many others wanted to straddle. Willis Allen came to the aid of the Democratic politicians by requesting that no plank on Ham and Eggs be included in the platform, as the issue transcended party lines. "The convention's burst of applause was a vast sigh of relief."[7]

The selection of a new chairman of the Democratic state central committee showed that there were internal divisions within the Olson camp. Some of his supporters, including his son and law partner Richard, came out for Judge Robert W. Kenny, who had won both party nominations for the State Senate seat being vacated by Olson. Olson himself had been expected to support his primary campaign manager in the south, J. Frank Burke, but at the crucial time the major Democratic candidates agreed upon Assemblyman John Gee Clark of Long Beach, who was then chosen by acclamation.[8]

More sensational news came from the Republican state convention. Justus Craemer, retiring state chairman, charged that Olson's report of his campaign finances had failed to list a $5,000 contribution by Pete McDonough, San Francisco bail bond broker, whose license had been suspended after charges had been made that the McDonough establishment was the "Fountainhead of Corruption" in San Francisco.[9]

Olson at once denied that he knew of such a contribution, but promised to investigate. Ten days later—after the San Francisco *News* published a story giving full details[10]—Olson announced that he had found McDonough had contributed $7,200 and that the money would be returned.[11] After further prodding by the *News*, Chairman Clark removed the Olson campaign managers for northern California and San Francisco, M. Mitchell Bourquin and Leo Cunningham, and replaced them.[12]

The fact that Craemer had found a sizable contribution that Olson had not known about (or listed) tended to destroy the effectiveness of Olson's primary-campaign finance report, which had listed contributions of $91,000 and expenditures of $103,000,[13] much to the surprise of Californians, who were used to such reports as that filed by Governor Merriam after the primary, listing expenditures of $1,743.50.[14] The blow for honesty-in-campaign finance, which Olson had hoped to land, was thus made ineffective by quick Republican counterattack.

Fresh from a trip to Washington with his running mates Downey and Patterson, Olson began his general election campaign with a speech at Santa Ana.[15] He said that he, Downey, and Patterson had been "most warmly received" by President Roosevelt, and emphasized the unity of the Democrats in the campaign. He invited the support of Republicans "disheartened" by the Merriam administration. He failed to commit himself on the Ham and Eggs pension plan, but he did say that present old age pensions should be "materially increased," pending the establishment of a full federal system.

Olson's strategy was to gain the initiative against the Republicans, and to hold it throughout the campaign. In his first speech at Oakland after the primary, he assailed the Republican administration, charging it with favoritism to Standard Oil in the tidelands matter, with negligence and with weakness.[16] "I call attention," he challenged, "to the fact that outside of the presentation of the budget, and the revenue requirements to meet it, which the governor must present to the legislature in the first session of each regular session of the legislature, no recommendations of policy or purpose ever came to the legislature from Governor Merriam, except at a special session called this year for the principal purpose of passing an oil bill to circumvent the Olson oil bill before the people could vote on it."

At San Diego, the Democratic candidate identified "the real forces and influences" controlling Merriam's actions.[17] He said that the major ones were "Standard Oil and its affiliated corporate interests" and "privately owned public utilities." "Lesser private interests" controlling the administration Olson named as: usurers, "promoters of stockholding building and loan associations," "the cement trust," "favored contractors on public works," "favored contractors in the insurance field" and certain large processing and packing interests. "The personal manager of Governor Merriam, for all these special interests," charged Olson, "is Mr. Harry Chandler, of the Los Angeles Times."

Olson also castigated the Republican regime for its asserted milking of building and loan associations, when it should be regulating them to prevent fraud. He said that a solvent association had been placed in receivership and had had its assets drained off for the previous four years. "The office overhead expenses charged and paid from the assets of this one company to relatives and political friends of Governor Merriam and his immediate circle exceed a hundred thousand dollars a year, and the end is not yet in sight."[18]

The Ham and Eggs pension plan continued to cause Olson much discomfort, as it had in the primary. The San Francisco News tried to smoke him out, saying it was informed that Olson saw the fallacy of the scheme and therefore "it's his duty to say so to prove himself a sincere and conscientious guide to those who follow him."[19] When Olson still refused to commit himself against the plan, the News declined to endorse anyone for governor, saying, "Mr. Olson's compromise is tacit rather than active, which makes his departure from true liberalism all the more damning because it reflects moral cowardice."[20]

The Allen brothers, leaders of the pension movement, were not friendly to Olson, however, and apparently toyed with the idea of supporting Merriam in retaliation for Olson's refusal to endorse their plan.[21] This, in spite of Merriam's flat opposition to Ham and Eggs! The Allens did endorse Sheridan Downey, who supported the plan enthusiastically.

Several times Olson indicated his doubts about Ham and Eggs. On one occasion he told a radio interviewer, "I do not oppose the objective of this initiative, however doubtful I may be of its workability."[22] But he fought against making the scheme a party issue, charging: "Our enemy press would like to divert attention from our exposure of the indefensible record of the Merriam administration and from a discussion of the real issues between candidates, to a discussion of differences among Democratic voters on the workability of this proposition."[23]

This aspect of the 1938 campaign shows Olson at his most inglorious. Yet the extreme ticklishness of his situation should not be overlooked. Had Olson come out in opposition, the Ham and Eggs leaders would unquestionably have enjoyed denouncing him as a betrayer and throwing their support to Merriam. It seems probable that a definite stand on the pension scheme, one way or the other, would have cost Olson the election.

Olson and his colleagues, Downey and Patterson, were notably lacking in newspaper support, placing their chief reliance upon the radio for reaching the people. Downey was an accomplished and dramatic orator, something neither of the others was. Olson was slow-speaking and not very exciting himself, but a number of his supporters made up for his shortcomings. Notable were a number of programs presented by the Motion Picture Democratic Committee, featuring Hollywood celebrities.

Of the principal newspapers of the state, only Manchester Boddy's Los Angeles *Daily News* and *Evening News* endorsed Olson. The powerful McClatchy papers of Sacramento, Modesto, and Fresno remained benevolently neutral, considering Governor Merriam "the high priest of reaction" but unable to support Olson because of his lack of stand on Ham and Eggs and because of his frequent support of a pardon for the labor "martyr" Tom Mooney.[24] The Scripps-Howard San Francisco *News* was also neutral, though far less friendly to Olson than the McClatchy press. The rest of the metropolitan press was solidly for Merriam and Olson frequently took it to task as the "enemy press" and charged it with unfairness.

Olson received general-election support from most of his Democratic primary opponents. John F. Dockweiler, J. F. T. O'Connor and Herbert

C. Legg all broadcast for him during the campaign, and Dockweiler in addition headed the party speakers' bureau. Sheriff Murphy was conspicuously silent on the governor race, although he took an active part in the fight against Ham and Eggs and signed the argument against it in the voter's handbook. By the time of the general election campaign, William Neblett had been caught up in the Sacramento County Grand Jury graft investigation.

The few Democratic defections were more than made up for by the aid extended to the state ticket by the Roosevelt administration. The President endorsed Downey and Olson at a press conference on September 2, at the same time reaffirming his opposition to Ham and Eggs.[25] The President repeated this action in a letter to George Creel written on October 31.[26] Postmaster General James A. Farley endorsed the ticket in a transcribed radio broadcast, and Harry Hopkins did the same a day later.[27]

While the Democrats were fighting furiously against them, the Merriam managers—true conservatives to the bitter end—concentrated upon the "leftism" of Olson and his colleagues. The strategy was to repeat what had worked so successfully against Sinclair. The chief issue, according to the Republican platform, was again "sound Americanism in opposition to irresponsible radicalism and declared Socialism."[28] There is, however, a rather plaintive touch to it all, for they had to admit that their targets this time were a bit more difficult to hit, and they seemed to look back to the simpler days of 1934. "The opposition in large measure is the same," ran their platform, "but it no longer proclaims itself for what it is. In this contest we face less courageous and less sincere opposition; for, while some of them are identified as leaders in the rejected and repudiated radical Socialism cause of 1934, they are now less inclined to appear under their true colors. They seek public endorsement under guises which fail to reveal them in their true light."

The Republican platform was silent upon the question of the New Deal nationally, except where it claimed that Merriam administration coöperation with the federal government on unemployment relief "has put California at the head of the list of States having an efficient working understanding with Federal agencies." Indeed the platform proclaimed the progressiveness of the party: "Without a backward step since Hiram Johnson seized the banner of liberalism in 1910, the Republican Party of California has laid a foundation and built a structure of social justice, human rights, economic stability and governmental efficiency unsurpassed in the nation." The Republicans wooed the AFL by affirming their belief in collective bargaining and assailing "radical" CIO leaders. While condemning Ham and Eggs, they favored (rather vaguely) higher national old age pensions and recommended "careful study" of the Townsend Plan.

Governor Merriam made few formal speeches, confining his major efforts to brief, impromptu talks to meetings and the press. With nearly all the state's newspapers ardently advocating his reëlection and giving his campaign much news space, with substantial sums for billboards and other advertising, and with numerous orators in his camp, he sniped at the CIO, the Ham and Eggs plan, and the "radicalism" of the Democratic candidate. A characteristic Merriam advertisement, in red and black, was headed by the slogan "Californians—Watch Your Step! Keep California out of the 'Red,'" and invited citizens to "Vote *For* Governor Merriam and Your Own Interests" and "Vote *Against* Olson and CIO Domination in Our State Government."[29]

The Republican campaign against the "radicalism" of Olson, Downey and Patterson reached its peak on October 26. On that day the Dies committee in Washington released the testimony of two Californians, who had testified that Olson "fraternizes with and accepts the program of the strategy committee of the Communist party," that Downey was "the running mate of communist Upton Sinclair," and that Patterson and State Chairman Clark were members of the Communist party.[30] The procedure of the Dies committee on this occasion has been described by Father Ogden, its leading student:

> Harper L. Knowles and Ray E. Nimmo were the star witnesses at the hearings, Dies and Starnes apparently being the only members present. Knowles claimed that he represented the American Legion of California as chairman of its radical research department. Nimmo served as counsel for him. The procedure used was rather curious. At times Nimmo served as a questioner, and so relieved the Chairman of that duty; at other times he presented testimony or corroborated that of Knowles. The voluminous testimony touched on the Bridges case and denounced nearly all phases of union activity on the West Coast as Communistic. So numerous were the charges of Knowles and Nimmo that a hundred thousand dollars would not have been sufficient to investigate even a frac-

tion of them. . . . After this mass of testimony, which would take months merely to verify, Dies blandly announced that all would be given an opportunity to testify with reference to the facts adduced. But he dismissed Committee responsibility when he said that the accuracy of all the testimony could not be vouched for. All would be heard and in the end the Committee would predicate its finding upon facts. It might be mentioned that no public notice was ever taken in the hearings of the statement of Henry G. Wallis, Department Commander of the California Legion, in which he denied that Knowles spoke for the Legion. The Associated Farmers had also denied that Knowles was their spokesman, in face of repeated charges to this effect.[31]

The Knowles-Nimmo testimony on Californians offered only the oddest sort of "evidence" and was strikingly similar to that used before the committee to expose Governor Frank Murphy of Michigan, which had brought down upon Representative Dies the wrath of President Roosevelt.[32] Harper Knowles was an important officer of the Associated Farmers and "brought his 'testimony' with him—neatly typed and bound, with a copy for each member of the committee and one for the press."[33]

Unfortunately for the effect of these charges, an earlier Dies witness had listed among the Hollywood persons who had allowed their names to be used for Communist fronts the name of Shirley Temple, the child movie star! On the night the Knowles charges were making the headlines in the evening papers, Olson spoke to a mass meeting at the Los Angeles Philharmonic Auditorium, beginning: "I am sorry Comrade Shirley Temple is not here. She should be here to aid us in plotting to overthrow the government of the United States of America."[34] All the candidates denied Harper Knowles' charges, and Patterson and Clark filed libel suits against him.[35] Manchester Boddy called Representative Dies "unbelievably stupid" and said that he "has proved himself to be the best press agent communism ever had."[36]

The sort of response to the Knowles charges used by the Democratic campaigners is well illustrated by the following "Old Chinese Proverb":

> We're branded RED by Harper Knowles
> But we refuse to fuss.
> What's good for Shirley Temple
> Is good enough for us![37]

Knowles had obviously over-reached himself in his testimony, the Dies committee had obviously been used as a political weapon. But most importantly, the "red scare" was made ineffective because of the quick use made by the Democrats in California of that most deadly of political weapons, ridicule.

The campaign of Raymond Haight, the Progressive candidate for governor, failed to make any headway and on October 18 he withdrew.[38] The Democrats had been successful in their efforts to keep the La-Follettes away from the state and the McClatchy papers refused to support Haight, whom they had endorsed four years before. Haight refused to endorse either candidate, but he spent more time attacking Olson than Merriam and his withdrawal probably helped Merriam.

The role of organized labor in the 1938 general election was an important one, made more so by the presence on the ballot of an initiative measure, Proposition 1, which provided for severe restrictions on picketing, forbade hot cargo and secondary boycott, and made unions liable for damages caused by members.[39] The proposition was sponsored by the California Committee for Peace in Employment Relations, headed by State Senator Sanborn Young (Republican, Santa Clara County) and attorney Bartley C. Crum of San Francisco.[40] It was supported by the California Farm Bureau Federation, the Los Angeles *Times*, the Hearst press, and Philip Bancroft, the Republican candidate for United States senator.

While Governor Merriam took no stand on Proposition 1, the major Democratic candidates denounced the measure. The California Committee Against No. 1, which included Olson, Downey and Patterson, was headed by Professor H. Dewey Anderson of Stanford and William J. Plunkert, former State Relief Administration official.[41] Olson repeatedly denounced Proposition 1 during the course of his campaign for governor, saying on one occasion that it "contains provisions that strike at the principles of collective bargaining and will defeat legislation, labor organizations and honest labor activities."[42] The chief press opposition to Proposition 1 came from the San Francisco *News* and the McClatchy papers; the San Francisco *Chronicle* and the Boddy papers in Los Angeles remained neutral.

In view of the strenuous campaign waged by California's organized labor against this initiative, and the refusal of the governor to take a stand on it, William Green's endorsement of Merriam came as a surprise and created a furor. In a letter to J. M. Casey, organizer for the International Brotherhood of Teamsters in San Francisco, Green said that Merriam deserved reëlection and contended: "One of the main questions before the voters of California in the coming State election is whether or not a candidate shall be elected to the position of governor who has been espoused and backed by every enemy of the American Federation of Labor."[43] This referred to Labor's Non-Partisan League, which had endorsed the Democratic candidates, including Olson. Olson's response to Green was quick and vitriolic. In a telegram to the AFL president, Olson said:

> Your letter to the AFL organizer of the Teamsters Union published here today brands you as the chief labor faker in the United States. . . .
> In view of the fact that I have been endorsed by practically all AFL labor councils and locals in the State, I know that your action is not generally supported by the AFL membership, but represents only a selfish attempt on your part to maintain your unpopular position and control regardless of its cost to the labor movement.[44]

California AFL leaders at once asked Green to withdraw his endorsement of Merriam, pointing out that Merriam had called out troops in labor disputes, that Merriam's supporters were backing Proposition 1 and that Olson "has so far throughout this campaign lent his voice and his prestige, and the machinery of his organization on our side of the fight to prevent the adoption of initiative measure No. 1. . . ."[45] The San Francisco Labor Council voted 160 to 98 to write Green that the information given to him against Olson "is not the expression of the overwhelming majority of trade unionists of San Francisco."[46] In the council, the opponents of this resolution included Sheriff Daniel Murphy, Olson's opponent in the primary. The Green endorsement met with repudiation in almost every quarter of the AFL in California, and Olson and the other Democratic candidates had nearly universal organized labor support in California. The role of Proposition 1 in the campaign seems to have been decisive here.

In spite of such last minute troubles as those offered by the Dies committee and William Green, the Democratic candidates won the general election of November 8, 1938. With Downey winning over Bancroft and

Patterson defeating Dr. Walter Scott Franklin, Culbert L. Olson was elected the first Democratic governor of California in the twentieth century.

Olson won a decisive victory over Merriam, securing 1,391,734 votes (52.49 per cent) to the Governor's 1,171,019 (44.17 per cent). Of his margin of 220,715 votes, Olson secured 166,430 in Los Angeles County and 54,285 in the rest of the state, and carried 31 counties out of 58, including all the populous ones.

The percentage of the total vote cast for Olson by significant areas was:

Los Angeles County	55.76
Rest of state	50.17
San Diego County	52.84
Alameda County	49.48
San Francisco County	53.36
Sacramento County	54.07
San Joaquin Valley	
All eight counties	53.36
Kern County	58.66
Madera County	57.11
Fresno County	55.52

Of the major counties, Olson made his poorest showing in Alameda, which he carried by less than 2,500 votes. He showed his greatest strength, in percentage, in the lower San Joaquin Valley and in Los Angeles County.

The Ham and Eggs pension scheme lost by a vote of 1,143,670 yes to 1,398,999 no, and the labor initiative lost even more decisively; but Olson's two favorites, his own oil bill and the Garrison revenue bond bill, lost by margins of about three to one. The defeat of Ham and Eggs was of course no disappointment to Olson, and the defeat of the anti-labor initiative was in line with his stand, but the failure of the voters to approve the Olson oil bill and the Garrison bill indicated that the election did not go fully as Olson wanted, for he had campaigned ardently for both measures. The Sacramento *Bee* described their defeat as "victories for special interests against the welfare of the state as a whole": "Their failure can be traced directly to the lack of an effective and vigorous statewide campaign in their behalf. Both were grossly misinterpreted by the corporate interests against which they were directed."[47]

Ironically, the tide had already begun to go against the Democrats in California by 1938, the very year in which they finally won the governorship. Of the 13 contests for Congress (7 had been decided at the primary by one candidate winning both nominations), 3 were won by Republicans, as compared with a clean sweep for the Democrats in 1936. Two New Deal congressmen were defeated, and 2 seats vacated by Democratic congressmen who had run unsuccessfully for other offices were won by Republicans. In the 7 runoff contests for state senator, 4 Democrats and 3 Republicans were successful, as compared with 6 Democrats and 2 Republicans in 1936. In the 46 runoffs for assemblyman, 28 Democrats and 18 Republicans won, as compared with 31 Democrats, 11 Republicans, and 1 write-in candidate in 1936.

The election of Olson, Downey and Patterson in 1938 was not in line with the national trend of that year. The Republicans gained 7 seats in the Senate and 80 in the House of Representatives. Down to defeat went such liberal governors as Murphy of Michigan, LaFollette of Wisconsin, and Benson of Minnesota, with the number of Republican governors increasing from 7 to 18. One pro-New Deal writer described the election: "Some juicy morsels of comfort were tucked among the election returns, but it would be folly to deny that the net result was a sound shellacking for liberalism and labor."[48]

Why did not California go along with this almost nationwide pattern?

First of all, only one of the three successful Democratic candidates faced a Republican incumbent. And Governor Merriam was not a figure capable of inspiring much fervor, even among nominal Republican voters. Furthermore he had the handicap of an especially bitter primary fight, in which his lieutenant governor, backed by the powerful Artie Samish, had made serious charges against his administration. Also, the Republican candidate for United States senator was militantly anti-labor and the Republican candidate for lieutenant governor was a politically unknown doctor.

Furthermore, in California there had been no Democratic or third-party administration in power for the voters to react against in 1938. The "red scare" technique that had been used so effectively against Upton Sinclair in 1934 simply could not be used again in the same way. For one thing, Culbert L. Olson had not spent all his adult years as a controversial pamphleteer. And Olson early took and largely retained the initiative, sniping at the Merriam administration. The cries of "radicalism" were like the cries of "Wolf! Wolf!" repeated once too often. The Harper Knowles charges before the Dies committee miscarried, and Shirley Temple became a two-weeks heroine of the California Democrats.

Also, the Democrats gained from the great political turmoil in Los Angeles in 1938. A coalition of moral reformers and political liberals led by Clifford Clinton had persuaded the citizens of Los Angeles to recall Mayor Frank L. Shaw and replace him with Fletcher Bowron, at a special election on September 16.[49] The Shaw administration, corrupt and anti-labor, had been supported by the same interests—led by that oracle of conservative Republicanism, the Los Angeles *Times*—who had backed Governor Merriam. The Democrats took full advantage of the discomfiture of their Los Angeles enemies at this turn of events. Endorsed by Clinton, Olson appeared on the reformer's radio program on election eve and drew an analogy between the anti-Shaw campaign and his own fight.[50] "I am sure," he told his hearers, "that the majority of the citizens of this State will follow the good example you established in defeating corruption in Los Angeles City Government and shall further vindicate the cause of good, honest government by turning out Governor Merriam in the state election."

In any reckoning of the reasons for the Olson victory, account must be taken of the skillful, professional and enthusiastic campaign waged in his behalf. For once a Democratic campaign was well financed and for once a large body of party workers was effectively united and determined to win. All of this resulted in a very heavy vote (74.65 per cent of those registered), a record in modern California history for a gubernatorial election and an undoubted advantage for the Democratic cause.

The very enthusiasm of his supporters—many of them in the direst of circumstances as the long depression wore on—should have alarmed Olson, who well knew how very few jobs he could give to the faithful.

4 *beginning the regime*

IN HIS HOUR OF TRIUMPH AT MIDNIGHT OF ELECTION DAY,
Governor-elect Olson said that his victory meant "a new social, political
and industrial era throughout our great state," and "a state government
in sympathy with the principles and policies of the New Deal" as well as
"devoted to the services of human needs instead of a government controlled by forces interested only in human exploitation."[1] On the morning
after election, he met the press at his Wilshire home in Los Angeles and
discussed his plans.[2] On the burning issue of relief, he pledged his efforts
to secure a modification of the dole by establishing a self-help system.
He said that "adequate" old age pensions would be one of the first
problems tackled after inauguration, that he would try to promote
industrial peace, that he was still convinced of the innocence of labor
"martyr" Tom Mooney and intended to pardon him after a hearing, that
he would seek the rehabilitation of refugees from the "Dust Bowl," and
that his administration would conduct an investigation of possible graft
and corruption.

The Sacramento *Bee* noted that a change-over to the Democratic party
after forty years "presents the elements of novelty, surprise and speculation," and warned Olson not to rush his appointments, for his adminis-

36

tration would be judged initially by the calibre of his personnel.[3] But the *Bee* was candid enough to recognize Olson's predicament: "When one party has been out of power in California as long as has the Democratic, the starvation diet has created many sharp appetites." Upon the governor-elect's return from Palm Springs, the press reported that he would wait until he got back from a trip to Washington in December before acting on the 12,000 job applications he had received.[4] Late in December Olson noted that he was still receiving about 500 requests for jobs daily.[5]

The great patronage problem facing Olson was a very simple one: there were very few jobs within the power of the governor to fill, while the demand was enormous. The well-informed columnist Arthur Caylor estimated that Olson would have fewer than 1,000 positions to fill, not over half of which would pay anything at all, and only about 150 of which would pay well, and noted that while Olson himself had promised very few jobs, "persons who admit they call him Culbert must have promised 100,000 jobs in the process of raising maybe $1,500,000 in campaign funds and wangling all those votes."[6]

An initiative adopted by the voters of the state at the 1934 general election had provided the constitutional basis for an all-inclusive civil service system for California, replacing the rather haphazard personnel recruiting of the past.[7] And of course, the Republican Legislature blanketed into civil service the current office holders. One of the features of the California civil service system was its State Personnel Board of five members, serving ten-year staggered terms, with power to supervise the examinations and lists, and authority to provide for "temporary" appointments and to rule on cases. The administration was destined never to gain control of this board, as indeed had been the plan of the authors of the Civil Service Act. Thus there was no chance for the administration to secure a "friendly" relaxation of restrictions.

It was not until a month after his election that Governor-elect Olson made very clear to his supporters just how little he would be able to deliver. In a broadcast "victory speech," heard by assembled Olson workers in several cities, he said flatly that "there are only a few places to be filled by appointment" and noted, somewhat consolingly: "Our object in the recent contest resulting in our victory, was not for the benefit of office patronage and its emoluments."[8] But these words held little pleasure for the party workers who had worked so hard for the Democratic ticket, and many of whom were in financial straits. It is the opinion of some of the key figures in the Olson administration that the patronage problem was poorly handled at the outset, due to the failure of the new administration to make its position clear at once, and that the disillusionment which soon came over many Olson workers might have been avoided.[9]

Olson had less than two months in which to select the members of his administration and prepare his program—including the budget—before his inauguration. On November 10 he went to the Palm Springs home of the motion picture executive Joseph M. Schenck, where he could consult with his associates, free from the interruptions of reporters. From Palm Springs, where Olson stayed until November 15, came word of his first appointment: his son and law partner, Richard, would be his private secretary. Soon after his return to Los Angeles he announced the other key members of his office staff, Kenneth I. Fulton (assistant secretary) and former Assemblyman Ralph W. Evans (executive secretary), both of Los Angeles.[10] Each had played a vital role in the Olson campaign.

One of Olson's first important tasks was the new state budget. When he left for Sacramento on November 17, he announced that his chief aide in preparing it would be Professor H. Dewey Anderson, who would certainly be asked to serve in the new administration. A former Republican assemblyman active in the Democratic campaign of 1938, Anderson was a well known authority on California taxes, and it was widely assumed that he would become director of finance. It was soon learned that "liberal" Democrats were supporting Anderson for the post, while "conservatives" were for almost anyone else, shuddering at Anderson's view that the whole state tax structure should be reformed in accordance with the principle of ability to pay.[11]

When he returned from the capital with much of the budget work finished, Olson announced that he would inherit a deficit of $42,500,000, that he would need a special appropriation of $20,000,000 for relief until the end of the current biennium (June 30, 1939), and that in order to balance the budget it would be necessary to ask for new taxes.[12]

This grim news was followed shortly by the announcement that Anderson would be state relief administrator and that the post of director of finance had been offered to Phil S. Gibson, Los Angeles attorney and Olson campaign contributor. It was reported that Anderson would establish a new SRA based upon "self-help" for the unemployed, and after six months would replace Gibson, who wanted a judicial appointment.[13]

These two appointments were the most important Olson had to make, for under the California governmental system the director of finance is the number two position, and in the depression-ridden California of early 1939 the relief administrator was scarcely less important.

Meanwhile, Olson had announced other important appointments. On November 21, he said that his director of public works would be Frank W. Clark, Los Angeles engineer and president of a dredger manufacturing corporation. Clark's appointment came as a surprise, for although he was a close friend of Olson he had not been active in the campaign and had no political experience.[14] Herbert C. Legg, supposedly in line for the post, became instead WPA administrator for southern California, upon the recommendation of Senator Sheridan Downey.[15] On November 30, Olson announced that George G. Kidwell, San Francisco AFL official and Olson primary supporter, would become director of industrial relations. Kidwell was the secretary of the Bakery Wagon Drivers Union and had been active in Labor's Non-Partisan League and the Tom Mooney defense. At the same time the governor-elect said that his superintendent of banks would be E. W. Wilson, San Francisco banker, treasurer of the Democratic state central committee and Olson friend of forty years' standing.[16]

The appointment of Wilson was a disappointment to the veteran journalist Franklin Hichborn, who had proposed his old friend and "angel," financier Rudolph Spreckels, for the post. In a letter to Hichborn, Olson thanked him for his recommendation of Spreckels, asked Hichborn for further recommendations and said: "Regarding the office referred to, I had already chosen another person for that place and announcement will be made today. I am sure you will approve of my action. There may be some other place where Spreckels will fit."[17] But Spreckels was to receive no post in the Olson administration, Hichborn was to fail to secure positions for other old-line progressives, and the Administration was to lose its opportunity to forge a coalition of Democrats and progressives of the old California tradition.

Two other posts in the governor's cabinet were filled prior to the inauguration of Olson. On December 14, Olson announced that Dr. Aaron J. Rosanoff, Los Angeles psychiatrist, would become director of institutions. On January 2, the day of his inauguration, Olson announced that Democratic State Chairman John Gee Clark of Long Beach had been named chairman of the board of prison terms and paroles and director of penology. These early appointments, however unsatisfactory to organization Democrats and old-time progressives, met with a generally friendly reception in the Republican press. Typical newspaper comment was that of the conservative Berkeley *Gazette,* which in the course of a strongly anti-New Deal editorial said of Olson: "So far ... his early appointments to key positions have been of a decidedly gratifying character encouraging the hope that the new governor possesses a clear understanding of the basic needs of the State and a desire to meet these needs by tried and accepted governmental procedure."[18]

President Roosevelt had telephoned Olson on election night to congratulate him on his victory and invite him to come to Washington for a conference before his inauguration. In mid-December, after completing his preliminary budget study and making several major appointments, the governor-elect made the trip east in company with his son-secretary, Richard. He proposed to the President that the administration seek a national old age pension system, with full federal financing and administration. He also sought federal funds to help finance California's migrant labor relief, and to help set up self-help coöperatives to replace the dole system. In all of these matters Olson was unsuccessful, but he had renewed old acquaintances in the capital and was reportedly "a smashing social success."[19] Upon his return to Los Angeles he reported that he had been able to interest Jesse Jones, head of the Reconstruction Finance Corporation, in a plan to refinance the San Francisco–Oakland Bay Bridge, but found in general that the administration was wary about making commitments on public works or other projects that involved substantial sums of money.[20]

Olson's Inaugural Address

On January 2, 1939, Governor Culbert L. Olson delivered his inaugural address to a joint session of the Legislature.[21] It was a dignified, moderate, conciliatory statement of Olson's liberal political philosophy, obviously intended to sound the keynote of his administration. He began with a solemn pledge of devotion to the public service and a statement that he bore no grudge against his opponents of 1938. He said that he regarded the protection of civil liberties and of equality before the law as his "sacred duty," and especially important in view of the "destruction of democracy elsewhere in the world, accompanied by denial of civil liberties and inhuman persecutions, under the rule of despots and dictators, so extreme as to shock the moral sense of mankind. . . ."

Olson then sounded a familiar theme: the failure to solve the problem of distribution "that attends our newly-developed productive skills and capacities" and which led to the great depression. He then pointed out the direction in which he felt the people should go, and the basic reason for their failure so far to attain their goal:

> Until all the electorate shall have the benefit of a free education to aid them in the expression of their citizenship, it may be expected that in the future, as in the past, a large proportion may be confused and guided away from their purpose to go forward for their collective welfare, by deliberately false or selfish propaganda, superficial considerations or provincial circumstances. Such impediments may delay, but they must not be permitted to defeat the ultimate successful working of American democracy.

This recognition of "collective welfare" as the basic goal, and of the role of sinister "propaganda" used by "special interests" to distract the people from their task was the essence of the Olson political philosophy.

Olson recognized that the depression had promoted a new social consciousness in the United States, forcing each individual "to realize that he is a social being, not an independent self-sufficient entity." He contended that the policies of the New Deal saved the economy from collapse and "point the way forward—toward the achievement of the aspiration of the people for an economy that will afford general employment, abundant production, equitable distribution, social security and old age retirement, which our country with its ample resources, great facilities and the genius of its people is capable of providing." Olson said that the recent elections had not constituted a setback for the New Deal, that their results were locally motivated, "that the American people cannot go backward, if our democracy is to endure," and that instead there must be "further measures calculated to improve their general welfare and eliminate every form of special privilege or class control in our economic system."

Olson said that his election had been an indication of the desire of the people for a New Deal for California, as provided in the Democratic platform. "They have given a mandate to you and to me," he stated, "to translate those principles into law and sound government procedure as promptly and effectively as it is possible to do." He contended that his aims were essentially non-partisan:

> All of us, of all parties, employers, employees, the professions, the unemployed, the youth, the aged, and the helpless—are primarily concerned in the achievement of a common goal; a higher and more equitable standard of living, a higher and more cultured standard of thinking; the replacement of prejudice with reason; the eradication of the causes for class consciousness and group antagonisms, and a citizenship motivated by a sense of social and civic responsibility.

Noting that the state had been in the red during the past two administrations, Olson said that with the strictest economy "a heavy tax burden, during the next biennium, cannot be avoided." He noted the high costs of the dole system of state relief and its demoralizing effects on relief recipients.

> In order that we may discontinue, as soon as possible, the maintenance of employable people in idleness, I submit to the intelligence of the legislators, to the intelligence of the taxpayers, to the intelligence of the industrialists and businessmen of the State, to the intelligence of the unemployed themselves, that we should substitute for the present policy of paying niggardly cash doles for unemployment relief, a new policy of placing the unemployed at productive work to support themselves.

Olson contended that the current thirty-five dollars a month for needy persons of sixty-five and over was too little and that the age limit was too high, urged that the federal government finance the whole program, and said that until such a federal plan was adopted he favored state aid to the limit of the state's financial ability. But he said flatly: "That limit, however, because of the tax necessary for present unemployment relief, may for a time at least, be very nearly reached." He did hold out hope for a higher state pension if the self-help system were adopted.

Olson reaffirmed his fervent belief in public ownership of public utilities and pledged every effort to promote it. He drew an analogy between his victory and that of Hiram Johnson in 1910, saying that now it was the private utilities and oil and gas interests that had been set back, although he noted that they had been able to defeat the Garrison revenue bond and Olson oil bills at the recent election. "With the aid of a subsidized daily press, and cleverly designed and costly publicity methods, they have from time to time influenced the people to vote against their own interests, through false and misleading propaganda." Olson pledged that his administration would work for measures similar to the Garrison and Olson bills.

He then concluded his address on an optimistic note:

> Our hopes for progress are high; our desire for unity of action and accomplishment through a conscientious application of our respective talents and energies, as a grave concern of all alike. Surely, in each there is a full measure of loyalty and patriotism which will find expression during the months to come in advancing the welfare of the people of California.
>
> Preelection battles are behind us. Let them remain behind us. Let us now approach our duties and our problems without bias or selfish purpose.
>
> Memorable indeed should be this new year upon which we are embarking with courageous purpose to meet and solve our common problems.
>
> With solemn recognition of my sacred duty to the people of California, I enter upon the Governorship, deeply conscious of the great work which lies before us in the interests of social and economic progress through liberal government.

Olson's inaugural address, with its well-worn generalities, was a summary of his political and economic philosophy and placed him where he wanted to be, in the camp of Roosevelt's New Deal. It met with a moderately favorable press response. Most newspaper editors had warned their readers that the election of Olson would be a great calamity for the state. The moderate and conciliatory tone the new governor was taking must thus have been something of a surprise to most of them, assuming they had meant what they wrote in October and November.

The San Francisco *News* commented that the address "was pitched upon a high plane of idealism and had the ring of sincerity" and felt that a majority of the people shared Olson's goals and would follow his leadership toward them. But it pointed out that there were many generalities in the address and noted that Olson relied mainly for economy upon production-for-use, which "will seem tenuous until actually tried out."[22] The Stockton *Record* called the message "temperate, conciliatory and conservative."[23] The San Francisco *Chronicle* declared that Olson's "statement of his human objectives is surely what we all want" and asked that the new governor be accorded "an intelligent and sincere coöperation."[24] The San Francisco *Call-Bulletin,* a Hearst paper, noted that Olson showed "a deep sense of responsibility to the people as a whole."[25] Most enthusiastic about the inaugural was the Sacramento *Bee,* kingpin of the powerful McClatchy papers. Its editorial was entitled "A Liberal Leadership Is Promised by Governor Olson."[26] It noted that the address "did not embrace radical curealls," but that "rather a studious, honest and conscientious move will be made toward the goal of social justice which always has been a vital part of the political philosophy of Culbert L. Olson."

Other papers were not so friendly. The Sacramento *Union* said that the governor "made just about the kind of an inaugural address that might be expected from a new deal Democrat who recently returned from a trip to Washington."[27] Most hostile was the Los Angeles *Times,* but even it admitted that the address was generally "restrained, dignified, conciliatory and considerably less leftward than many had expected."[28] The *Times* pointed out that Olson was inconsistent when he reassured business: "At the same time he promises a system of State-subsidized production for use which will necessarily be in competition with private industry, higher taxes at least for this biennium, State-promoted competition by cities and districts with privately owned utility companies." The *Times* offered no coöperation of any sort to the Olson administration.

The 1939 Legislature

More significant for the future of his administration than his inaugural address or the press comment on it was the composition of the 1939 Legislature. And Olson could have had very little comfort as he looked over the roster of members. The 80-man Assembly included 44 Democrats and 36 Republicans and the 40-man Senate held 22 Republicans and 17 Democrats, with one vacancy. Most of the members of both houses were experienced legislators, as the lower house included 25 freshmen and the upper had 7.

The Republicans showed every indication of a determination to resist the new regime. Two weeks before the Legislature met, the Assembly

Republicans formed an informal steering committee headed by Assemblyman Charles W. Lyon of Los Angeles to fight Olson's New Deal with the slogan "No New State Taxes."[29] They were determined to elect the speaker pro tem, if not the speaker.

The election of an administration friend to the speakership of the Assembly was essential to Olson, for the speaker appointed the committees and by his action could determine the success or failure of the Olson program. The speaker of the 1937 session, William Moseley Jones, had been an unsuccessful candidate for attorney general at the 1938 primary, and was no longer in the Legislature.

At the Democratic state convention in September, Assemblyman Paul Peek of Long Beach was prominently mentioned for the speakership.[30] In mid-November the leading candidate was said to be Cecil King of Los Angeles, with twenty-five pledges, who "although not deemed too friendly by the leftists, the lobbyists or the conservatives, could win with some administration support."[31] Another possibility, Samuel William Yorty of Los Angeles, a strong administration supporter, was reported to be "among those considered unacceptable among many Democrats because of his leftist leanings." By the end of November, Yorty and Lieutenant-Governor-elect Ellis Patterson were putting forth Paul Peek as the administration candidate.[32] Just before the meeting of the Democratic caucus, Peek asked Assemblyman Alfred W. Robertson of Santa Barbara to nominate him in caucus, and Robertson did so. Robertson, a conservative, had been offered the support of other conservative Democrats if he would run for speaker himself, and when he nominated Peek the other candidates for speaker withdrew and Peek was chosen without a roll call and by acclamation.[33] On the next day the Legislature met and Peek was elected speaker by a strict party vote of 43 to 34 over Ray Williamson (Republican, San Francisco).[34] Although Olson had formally kept hands off the choice of the Democratic caucus for speaker, the press properly identified Peek as Olson's choice and interpreted his victory as the victory of the administration. Young, amiable, and an ardent liberal, Paul Peek had gotten well acquainted with Olson while handling oil legislation for him in the Assembly.

The Olson administration was not so fortunate in the organization of the State Senate. As early as September, the experienced journalist Franklin Hichborn pointed out in a letter that if Ellis E. Patterson were to be elected lieutenant governor and the Senate remained Republican, that body could take away from the lieutenant governor the power to appoint committees.[35] While Hichborn considered this course "improbable," he did note that a Democratic Senate had done it to a Republican lieutenant governor in 1887 and a Republican Senate had done it to a Democratic lieutenant governor in 1897.

Had the lieutenant governor-elect followed a conciliatory course he might have avoided the emasculation of his powers. But the ebullient and unpredictable Patterson had never learned to tread softly. Unconcerned by the effect his actions might have on the rural Senate, he moved his residence from King City to Los Angeles and spoke all over southern California to liberal and labor groups, often accompanied by such left-wingers as Assemblyman Jack B. Tenney and Samuel William Yorty.[36] In December 1938 he gained publicity when he picketed a Greek freighter loading scrap iron for Japan on the San Francisco waterfront.[37] On December 20, Patterson announced that he would run for the United States Senate in 1940 against Hiram Johnson, unless Governor Olson himself ran.[38]

When the Senate met on January 2, it promptly took from Patterson the power to appoint committees.[39] The authority was given to the rules committee, which was to be elected by the Senate as a whole. Only four Democratic senators stood by Patterson on this vote, which certainly boded no good for the Olson administration. Some newspapers enjoyed the irony of the situation: the governor had once supported such a measure aimed at a Republican lieutenant governor!

Jerrold L. Seawell (Republican, Roseville) became the new president pro tem of the Senate, securing 22 votes in caucus against 13 cast for a Republican backed by the administration.[40] This post was a crucial one, for its possessor was chairman of the rules committee. Of the other four members of this committee, only one (Robert W. Kenny) was friendly to the new regime.

On the first day of the session, the Senate voted 31 to 4 to confirm two Merriam interim appointments to the Board of Pilot Commissioners of San Francisco Harbor, and 27 to 8 to confirm Merriam's appointee, Rex B. Goodcell, for the post of insurance commissioner. Governor Olson wrote to the Senate withdrawing the three appointments, as well as those of three persons named by Merriam to the Pro-rate Commission. The Senate refused to back down on its confirmation of the first three, although it did permit Olson to withdraw the names of the pro-rate commissioners.[41] These confirmations by the Senate were properly described at the time as a "trouncing" of Olson and indicated that the new administration was heading for plenty of trouble.[42]

In the midst of these developing difficulties, Olson had to turn his attention to a bit of old business. Until it was cleared up, he felt, the new administration could not get under way.

5 *the end of the mooney case*

THE MOST DRAMATIC EVENT IN THE OLSON ADMINISTRATION—
and the deed that was to bring the governor his greatest fame—was his
pardon of Thomas J. Mooney, California's greatest labor "martyr." In the
midst of the feverish activity of his first week in office, Governor Olson
effectively ended the Mooney cause forever, just as his supporters had
expected he would. The pardon was headline news around the world
and made Olson (for a brief period) one of the most famous American
governors.

The Mooney case was intensely complex, packed with emotion and
long drawn out.[1] On July 22, 1916, an explosion at Market and Steuart
Streets in San Francisco killed ten persons and injured forty others,
during the course of a great Preparedness Day parade. An early suspect
was Thomas J. Mooney, labor agitator earlier acquitted of a charge of
complicity in a dynamite plot against Pacific Gas and Electric Company
property. Upon the testimony of John McDonald, a waiter, that he had
seen a person of Mooney's description emerge from a jitney with a suitcase which he left at the side of a building at Market and Steuart, officers
arrested Mooney and his wife Rena; Edward Nolan, a labor leader;

48

Israel Weinberg, a jitney driver; and Warren K. Billings, associate of Mooney with a previous conviction for possession of explosives. Billings, identified by McDonald as the man who came out of a saloon at the same corner and conferred with Mooney before going off in the opposite direction, was convicted of murder in September 1916 and sent to Folsom Penitentiary for life. Nolan was released after being held nine months in jail, and Weinberg was acquitted.

Tom Mooney went on trial for murder in January 1917 in the court of Superior Judge Franklin A. Griffin. An Oregon cattleman, Frank Oxman, testified that he had come to San Francisco from Woodland, where he was visiting friends, and had seen Mooney and Billings deposit a suitcase at the scene of the blast and then disappear. McDonald repeated his story, and identified Mooney and Billings. Two women placed Billings at 721 Market Street and Mooney at Market and Steuart Streets, both at noon, although just how the women could have observed both men in different places at the same time was a matter that caused the prosecution some difficulty. In his defense, Mooney offered photographs of himself and his wife, purportedly taken from atop the Eilers Building while they were watching the parade, each showing the same clock at different times. The "alibi photos" were attacked by the prosecution as of doubtful authenticity, and the time necessary for travel between the Eilers Building and the scene of the crime (a mile and a half away) was disputed. Mooney was convicted of murder and sentenced to hang. Rena Mooney, after a long incarceration, was tried and acquitted.

Soon after the conviction, Frank Rigall of Grayville, Illinois, signed an affidavit, supported by correspondence, asserting that Oxman had sought to induce him to come to San Francisco and testify falsely against Tom Mooney. Judge Griffin asked Attorney General U. S. Webb to petition the State Supreme Court for a new trial for Mooney, but the court ruled that it had no jurisdiction in the matter as it was unable to consider the affidavit of Rigall. A cry of protest went up, and President Wilson had the Federal Mediation Commission investigate the case. Its findings were that Mooney had been convicted upon questionable testimony and should be accorded a new trial. Governor William D. Stephens then could find no authority for ordering one. A second investigation by the federal authorities, this one by J. B. Densmore, head of the Federal Employment Service, resulted in the same finding, and on November 28, 1918, Governor Stephens commuted Mooney's sentence to life imprisonment. The interest of the Wilson administration in the Mooney matter was principally diplomatic, for Mooney was already a world famous labor "martyr" and his execution would have embarrassed the government abroad.

Frank Oxman was tried for subornation of perjury and acquitted, and the witness McDonald in 1921 repudiated his story at the Mooney trial. Mooney sought complete vindication, refusing to consider a parole, but he was refused either a new trial or a pardon by successive governors. Billings applied for a pardon to Governor C. C. Young, who agreed to consider the cases of Billings and Mooney as parallel. As Billings had a prior conviction of felony, the Governor could not pardon him without the recommendation of a majority of the State Supreme Court, and that was refused when the witness John McDonald once again contradicted himself in great confusion. After Mooney had been turned down by federal district and circuit courts in an attempt to secure a writ of habeas corpus, the United States Supreme Court ruled that he had not exhausted the avenues open to him in the state courts.

In June 1935 the California Supreme Court granted Mooney a hearing on a writ of habeas corpus. The hearing lasted over a year from its beginning in August 1935, and was presided over by Referee A. E. Shaw. Shaw took nearly six months to prepare his report, which recommended denial of the writ, and the California Supreme Court so ruled in October 1937. Although this exhausted the California court resources, the United States Supreme Court again refused to review the Mooney case in a ruling laid down on October 10, 1938, with two justices dissenting. Thus the fate of Tom Mooney seemed sealed, in the absence of a full pardon, for unlike Billings he steadfastly refused to consider the prospect of a parole, saying: "The acceptance of my freedom under such circumstances would place me in the position of a foul miscreant capable of committing this fiendish crime, which I would, at least by implication, be admitting, and promising reformation."[2]

In the absence of a pardon from successive Republican governors, friends of the Mooney cause hit upon the device of a legislative pardon. Assemblyman Paul A. Richie (Democrat, San Diego) led the fight in the lower house, and on March 10, 1937, by a vote of 45 to 28, succeeded in securing the passage of a resolution granting Mooney a full, immediate legislative pardon.[3] A breakdown of this roll call shows the extent of the division of opinion on the question. Voting aye were 33 Democrats and

12 Republicans, and opposed were 9 Democrats and 19 Republicans. Of the 12 Republicans voting for the pardon, 7 were from San Francisco, whose entire Assembly delegation of 9 voted for the legislative pardon for Mooney. Los Angeles County's 30-man delegation was split almost exactly along party lines: 18 for (17 Democrats and 1 Republican), 9 against (1 Democrat and 8 Republicans), and 3 absent (2 Democrats and 1 Republican). Alameda County's 5 Democratic assemblymen voted 4 to 1 for the pardon, and its 2 Republican assemblymen were opposed. Assemblymen from the remaining 34 districts of the state voted 16 to 14 against the resolution, with 4 absent. The Mooney pardon had become a party question in the metropolitan areas, except for San Francisco which was solid for Mooney. When this resolution reached the State Senate it went down to a defeat by a vote of 34 no to 5 aye (Republican senators from San Francisco and San Joaquin, Democratic senators from Los Angeles, Orange and Santa Barbara Counties).[4] In the Senate the principal speech for the Mooney legislative pardon was made by Senator Culbert L. Olson.[5]

Following the failure of this measure to pass the Senate, Richie tried a resolution asking Governor Merriam to grant Mooney a full, unconditional pardon. The new resolution passed the Assembly by a vote of 42 to 27, but was rejected in the Senate by a vote of 30 to 8.[6] The legislative fight to free Mooney reached a climax at the special session of the Legislature, meeting in March 1938. The Assembly voted 36 to 30 to subpoena Mooney,[7] and on March 10, 1938, Mooney presented his case in person to the Assembly, meeting in committee of the whole. On the next day, the Assembly passed a legislative pardon resolution by a vote of 41 to 29, but the Senate tabled it without a roll call vote.[8] It was clear that only a drastic change in the personnel of the rural and Republican Senate would provide Mooney with a chance for a legislative pardon or even a resolution urging the governor to pardon him.

The Republican San Francisco *Chronicle* advocated that the Mooney case be taken out of politics, describing the Assembly's 1937 vote for a legislative pardon as "a pure-political gesture."[9] The *Chronicle's* remedy was for the governor to commute Mooney's sentence to time served. This was a "solution" that pleased no one who really cared about the case, for it offered no satisfaction to those who saw the Mooney case as a struggle of good and evil. Anyhow, the plan needed the coöperation of the executive, and Governor Merriam refused to commute the Mooney sentence. An idea of the importance of the case to organized labor in California may be had from a description of the 1938 Labor Day parade in San Francisco: "a march of 80,000 organized workers, the AFL leading, the CIO closing, and a great float demanding freedom for Mooney and Billings rolling along in the space between."[10]

The Mooney case was injected into the 1938 elections, for it was evident that Mooney and Billings would have to depend upon the chief executive for their freedom. Two Democratic gubernatorial candidates were on record as favoring the pardon of Mooney, Senator Olson and Sheriff Murphy. Olson's plight has been well put by Franklin Hichborn:

> He is . . . desperately in need of the support of the McClatchy papers. The McClatchy papers are 100 per cent for him on his legislative record. But the word Mooney is a bad one with which to tempt McClatchy support. Olson knows it. But Olson takes the ground that prosecution under the guise of law enforcement, without regard to the question of guilt, is an un-American perversion of justice; that a conviction secured on perjured testimony in an atmosphere of prejudice obtained for the purpose of imprisoning any person because of his activities in the exercise of his civil right, is a treasonable prostitution of legal processes and is a disgrace to the administration of justice. Continued incarceration of a person so convicted purely on legalistic grounds, calls for immediate exercise of the pardoning power of the governor. Only by such a policy can confidence be maintained in the process of law. So says Olson to the Bee's fear that Olson will pardon Mooney.[11]

While his advocacy of a pardon for Mooney was well known, Olson avoided the subject in his election speeches and Mooney was scarcely an issue. The Republicans did not take up the Mooney case very actively in the campaign, for the leaders well knew that many of their own political supporters were convinced of Mooney's innocence and in favor of a pardon.

But if Olson had decided to be cautious in the campaign, Tom Mooney took his stand, reportedly over the objections of his chief attorney, George T. Davis, one of Olson's leading supporters in the Progressive party.[12] In a pamphlet published by his defense committee, Mooney endorsed Olson, Patterson, and Downey in the primary.[13] Mooney here stated that he was grateful to Sheriff Murphy for his early support, but that Murphy had no chance to win the nomination, and thus "Olson is the only candidate who will pardon me who can be nominated and elected. . . ." Mooney said that Olson had the best labor record of any state senator in California history, and condemned the AFL Political League for its failure to endorse him, charging that its convention was controlled by "misleaders" of labor. Mooney's pamphlet reprinted Olson's long speech in the Senate in 1937 in behalf of the legislative pardon for Mooney. Mooney offered it to his supporters as proof of Olson's attitude: "No one reading this speech can have any doubt what Senator Olson would do in my case if elected Governor."

Following Olson's nomination, Mooney wrote a letter of congratulation to the senator, and told of the work his defense committee had done for the Olson cause: a contribution of $500 to Olson's treasurer; payment of a $250 printing bill for Olson's program and platform; printing and circulating 300,000 copies of the pamphlet *Tom Mooney's Message*, with one copy going to each registered Progessive, at a total cost of $6,000; and payment of $395 for a radio broadcast to Progessives.[14] But Mooney was optimistic about his own future: "I seriously doubt that you will have a chance to act on my application for unconditional pardon . . . I think that before the end of the year I shall have been completely liberated and exonerated from all blame on the infamous crime on which I have been made to suffer so grossly and unjustly for the past 22-½ years." He even hoped to be out of San Quentin before election day, in order that he might take part in Olson's campaign.

But the United States Supreme Court in October 1938 refused to review the Mooney case, and once more Mooney's hopes were dashed. Two days later Mooney announced that his immediate hope for freedom rested upon the election: "I have every reason to believe that Olson will pardon me. He has not made any promises, and I have asked for none. I am going on his record in the legislature for the past four years. Every time my case has been considered he has supported it. I have no doubt in my mind that if he is elected, he will grant me an unconditional pardon."[15]

Mooney Pardoned

Mooney was not to be disappointed in Olson. On the day after his election Olson referred reporters to his 1937 speech on the Mooney case for his views: ". . . it must be clear to anyone that I will approach the consideration of Mooney's application for pardon with these convictions, giving opportunity for any and all entitled to a hearing to show cause why I, as Governor, should not pardon him."[16] Mooney's response to Olson's election was a gay one: "I'm facing the prospect of Culbert Olson's inauguration with a smile on my lips and a song in my heart."[17]

On the day of his inauguration as Governor, Olson received a delegation of labor and political leaders headed by George T. Davis, who formally presented to the new governor the application for pardon, and Olson that night announced that he would pardon Mooney the following Saturday, after a hearing.[18]

Olson was confronted with opposition to his projected action on Mooney. The new Republican attorney general, Earl Warren, former district attorney of Alameda County, presented the viewpoint of the professional law enforcement officer:

> I realize that an application for pardon is addressed to the conscience of the Governor and that there is no requirement in the law that he give consideration to any particular fact or to any legal decision involving the applicant. I trust, however, that in any action you may take on Mooney's application for a pardon you will bear in mind that today law enforcement is, at best, difficult of accomplishment and that you will neither cast any unwarranted reflection upon the agencies charged therewith, nor lend any encouragement to those forces that are opposed to the enforcement of our laws and to the maintenance of security of life and property.[19]

More hostile was the Sacramento *Bee*, which said that the hearing, if Olson wanted one, should be held in the governor's office, "not in keeping with a three ring circus."[20] The *Bee* thundered: "the law-abiding citizens of California will not join in these plaudits. They will not assist in that hand-clapping. Rather will they be thinking of the shame being perpetrated in the name of Justice to laurel and accolade a red handed murderer who richly deserved the gallows."

The Mooney pardon proceedings on January 7, 1939, were dramatic.[21] Governor Olson reviewed the case before the packed Assembly chamber, following along the lines of his 1937 speech to the Senate. Midway through his speech, which was broadcast coast-to-coast, he asked if there were any persons present who objected to the pardon, but none arose. Olson urged Mooney to prove by his future deeds that "you were incapable of committing the crime for which you have suffered imprisonment for so many years;" and urged him to disavow any philosophy of violent revolution in favor of a firm belief in orderly democratic processes. At the climax of the hearing, Olson asked Mooney to stand up, and gave him his full pardon, telling him that he was now a free man "at liberty to say something to the general public." Mooney then spoke for ten minutes, to the gathering and over the radio, pledging his aid to Warren Billings and to the labor movement, and denouncing fascism.

In his "Full and Unconditional Pardon for Thomas J. Mooney," Governor Olson refused to accept the advice of his Republican attorney general and repeated the thesis of his 1937 speech: Mooney was the innocent victim of a frame-up.[22] "I have made an extended study of the voluminous records of this case and am convinced that Thomas J. Mooney is wholly innocent of the crime of murder for which he was convicted and that his conviction was based wholly on perjured testimony presented by representatives of the State of California. In view of my convictions I deem it my duty to issue a pardon to Thomas J. Mooney." Governor Olson at his own expense had the state printer prepare 450 facsimile copies of the pardon, which were distributed to persons asking for them.[23]

Lavish praise, as well as violent hostility, was the lot of Governor Olson for his pardon of Mooney. An example of one type of praise is this anonymous letter postmarked Chicago, which read in full: "Dear sir you. Ar A Wonderful Man. You has plezed the harts of memey million workers in this country, by freen tom Mooney. Good luck to you. Governor Culbert L. Olson."[24] A telegram from Guy Emery Shipler, editor of the *Churchman*, praised Olson's "high courage and love of true justice and genuine Americanism," and termed the pardon a "noble restitution to an innocent man."[25] An Oklahoma legislator telegraphed: "Not since Altgeld has American executive equalled your courageous justice."[26] Hundreds of letters and telegrams from trade union locals and councils all over the United States poured in. John Haynes Holmes, the noted New York minister, wrote: "You have done more to vindicate and reestablish democracy in the confidence of mankind than any other public leader of our time."[27] Secretary of the Interior Harold L. Ickes sent his approval: "It was high time that California should elect as its Governor a man who not only hates injustice but who has the courage to right a wrong in the face of a very considerable public opinion."²⁸ In an editorial, the Scripps-Howard Washington *Daily News* concluded that Olson and those who had fought for Mooney through the years "have reasserted the essential decency of the human race."²⁹ The *Nation* said that the governor "has covered his name with glory by his historic act."³⁰ The *New Republic* thought that others had failed to give Governor Olson his full share of the praise:

> We wish we could share the belief of our radical friends that it was labor, rising in its might, that struck open the door of the jail, or alternatively, that we could second the opinion of the New York Times that the conscience of America at last began to itch to an intolerable degree. . . .
>
> The actual explanation is that California finally elected a Governor who was not terrorized by the state's conservatives, conservatives who knew Mooney was innocent but wanted him kept in jail anyhow.³¹

How widespread was the interest in the cause of Mooney is shown by the origin of some of the letters and cablegrams that Olson received. Congratulations came from the Australian Railways Union (Queensland Branch); the Amalgamated Printing Trades Union, Sydney; and from the Broken Hill Railway Town Labour Party, New South Wales. Others sending praise included Leon Jouhaux, secretary-general of the Confédération Générale du Travail; the South African Trades Council (Johannesburg); the Pretoria Trades Hall Committee; and W. E. Hurst, honorary secretary of a Middlesex borough branch of the Labour party.³²

Many hostile communications were received by Governor Olson following his pardon of Tom Mooney, and although the great majority of the messages were congratulatory, Olson received many that were violent in their hostility. One of the mildest was from a California businessman: "U. S. Supreme Court and five governors have said no stop you in your supreme judgment say yes stop California has four apprehensive years ahead."³³ A Michigan minister wrote, "You deserve the utmost contempt of every decent man on earth, for your cowardly action in pardoning Mooney."³⁴ More violent were such epistles as these: "Sir— You are a dirty crook— *Mooney* the irish murdered and you ought to be chained together and thrown into ocean—you are a crook." "You freed a notorious assassin whose infamy is world wide. *You have committed an enormous crime.* Your position was bought with the votes of collaborators of crime. You will surely pay the toll. Payment is already being exacted (*Let us hope the final one*). You and your family are accursed. You are held in abhorence by the whole non-shyster world. Poison gas for Sacramento."[35]

The pardon of Mooney was bitterly protested by the McClatchy newspapers of Sacramento, Modesto and Fresno, in an editorial entitled "Pardon Of Mooney Is Blot on Fair Name Of State."[36] The editorial was accompanied by a cartoon inscribed "Justice Is Outraged," which showed Justice holding her head down and carrying a broken sword. Superior Judge Frank H. Dunne of San Francisco, who had presided at the original Billings trial, was also bitter: "Hundreds of thousands of dollars have been used to create a misguided sympathy for Mooney and Billings. To my mind public sympathy might be more fitly directed to the families of the victims of the Preparedness Day outrage and to the witnesses, jurors and public officials who have been hounded and black-guarded for having done their duty in these cases."[37]

It was widely expected that Tom Mooney following his release would play an important role in the American labor movement, and his first actions indicated that such was his intention. After a lunch with labor and political leaders Mooney went to Folsom Penitentiary and visited Warren K. Billings, telling him that "the fight is on for you."[38] On the next day, Sunday, January 8, 1939, Mooney led a great parade from the Embarcadero to City Hall in San Francisco, in which an estimated 25,000 persons took part or watched along Market Street and another 25,000 listened at the end to speeches by Mooney and others. It was a great triumph for Mooney; as a newspaper caption put it, "He went off-stage the villain and came back the hero."[39] On the next day, Mooney took a brief turn on a picket line, gave some strikers half of the ten dollars given to him by the state and sent the rest to newspapermen striking against Hearst in Chicago.[40]

But Mooney's days of glory were very few. When his domestic diffi-culties came to light, he was bitterly assailed by many of his supporters who felt he had deserted the wife who had stood by him through all the years. Shortly after this he fell ill (gall bladder trouble complicated by stomach ulcers) and spent the rest of his life in hospital. He died three years after his pardon, and although 5,000 attended his funeral at the San Francisco Civic Auditorium, he had long since lost his importance.[41]

END OF THE MOONEY CASE   57

The Billings case was not ended so spectacularly or so decisively. Governor Olson said at the Mooney hearing that he considered Billings innocent and convicted on the same perjured evidence. But as Billings had previously been convicted of a felony, the governor could not pardon him without the recommendation of a majority of the State Supreme Court. The State Advisory Prison Board, to whom Olson referred Billings' case, voted three to two against recommending a pardon (with Attorney General Warren in the majority).[42] However, the governor wrote directly to the justices of the Supreme Court and they replied by recommending commutation to time served. Olson, on October 16, 1939, followed this recommendation, and the next day Billings was given the commutation papers at a brief ceremony in which the governor told him that he was sorry it was not a full pardon.[43] Billings after his release opened a watch repair shop in San Francisco, got married, and after a brief flurry in left-wing politics slipped into obscurity.

And thus ended the great Mooney case. Public interest fell off at once, for it soon became evident that neither the hopes of friends nor the fears of enemies were to be justified. In the eyes of the world (though not of all Californians) Olson had courageously righted a very great wrong. Certainly he began his administration with a great liberal act, even though this move deprived the American labor movement of one of its greatest symbols.

6 *the legislature disposes*

Saturday, January 7, 1939, after pardoning Mooney, he could look back
upon two months of solid accomplishment. His major appointments
had been generally well received, his inaugural address had met with
friendly comments even in some rather unexpected places, and his
leadership of his party was apparently undisputed. True, there were
some serious problems ahead. Most of his new administrators and aides
were lacking in experience and it would take some time until they could
be effective as a team. And, even more serious, the Legislature was not
going to be easy to handle. The Republicans—conservative almost to a
man—controlled the Senate. And while the Democrats had a small
majority in the Assembly, they were split into factions, as the record
of the 1937 session clearly indicated. But Olson was a fighter, and
confident of success.

At this point misfortune befell the new governor, with a mishap from
which his administration never fully recovered.

Olson was exhausted, having attended the inaugural ball the night
before and worked until six that morning preparing the pardon message.
He had next to attend a giant barbecue at the State Fairgrounds, given

in his honor by the California State Employees Association. There he spoke for about five minutes to a crowd of about 130,000. Suddenly his voice began to falter. Richard Olson had to take the microphone and tell the people that his father was unable to continue. At the end of his first week in office, the governor found himself in a hospital "suffering from nervous exhaustion as a result of overwork."[1] Olson remained in the hospital until January 19 while conjectures about his condition circulated widely. It was nearly a month later before he made his first public appearance, opening the Golden Gate International Exposition on Treasure Island in San Francisco Bay.

The illness of Governor Olson, necessitating his seclusion during the opening weeks of his administration, got his regime off to a bad start. The Legislature's initial session was declared to be "the least active and the least leadered of the long series." The political editor of the Sacramento *Bee* reported that legislators did not know what the Olson legislative program would be, and thus in the interim between the "split" sessions would have to concentrate on his budget and tax plans. An informal Assembly steering committee headed by Hugh M. Burns of Fresno was appointed to handle the administration's bills.[2]

During his own absence, the governor chose to act through an informal "Regency" with his son and private secretary, Richard, as spokesman. Soon dubbed the "Crown Prince," the thirty-one year old "Dickie" was handsome, convivial, brash—and always good copy for newspaper reporters. Lieutenant Governor Patterson, notably undiplomatic and an inveterate campaigner for office, was by-passed by the governor, but it is hard to see how even Patterson could have handled affairs less satisfactorily than "Dickie" did.

The climax of Richard Olson's troubles with the press came late in February, when he was quoted by B. W. Horne as telling the San Francisco Junior Chamber of Commerce: "We all know most of the Senators are bought and paid for, bound and delivered." When young Olson denied that he had made the remark, Horne said that three Republican assemblymen who had been present agreed that Horne's quotation was accurate.[3] Senator Jerrold L. Seawell (Republican, Roseville, president pro tem of the Senate) promptly wrote to Richard Olson that his charges were serious ones and that if they had been made in earnest "then I deem it your duty to come before the State and substantiate the charges made. . . ." Seawell asked for a reply by March 6, when the Legislature would be back in session. Richard Olson again denied he had made the statement Horne reported, saying he had merely charged that the Senate had been arbitrary in not confirming the governor's appointments to the Board of State Harbor Commissioners. Richard said he knew of no case of personal corruption in the Senate but concluded, with something less than tact, by saying: "I suppose it is possible that the Administration may think individual Senators are wrong in their votes and may sometime ask the people to retire some members to private life, but at no time, until evidence is presented to the contrary, will I let the debate between us sink to the level of personal attack."[4]

Richard Olson remained as private secretary to the governor until his resignation in April 1940 to reënter private law practice. Though he was much less in the limelight after his father's return to duty, he remained a delight to reporters of the generally hostile press, and there can be no doubt that he did the administration very little good during his tenure of office.

Trouble in the Legislature

The Legislature was slow in getting underway. Senate committee appointments were not announced by the rules committee until January 20, and Speaker of the Assembly Paul Peek did not present his rosters until January 23, two days before the Legislature began its constitutional recess. In the Senate, the Olson administration secured majorities in the finance and judiciary committees, but Republicans controlled the powerful governmental efficiency and revenue and taxation committees. Peek named Democratic chairmen and majorities for all committees and thus the administration appeared to be in full control of the lower house.

But even before the illness of Governor Olson, the administration had had a narrow escape with one of its important bills in the supposedly friendly Assembly. On January 5 the governor asked for a deficiency appropriation of $19,975,000 for relief until the end of the biennium on June 30. This request was embodied in a bill which passed the Assembly unanimously on January 6, but only after the administration had defeated an amendment by a Republican assemblyman to cut the appropriation to $11,750,000.[5] On this significant roll call, 4 Democrats joined with 32 Republicans to support the amendment, while 1 Republican voted with 38 Democrats in opposition. This was a close call, and it indicated that Olson would have trouble marshaling majorities even in the nominally Democratic Assembly.

Another bit of evidence of Democratic division came on January 13, when the Assembly voted down a memorial resolution by left-wing assemblymen Jack B. Tenney and Maurice Atkinson of Los Angeles County, petitioning the president to lift the arms embargo on the Spanish Republic. Only sixteen members, all southern California Democrats, voted in favor of the resolution, but they included Speaker Peek and Floor Leader Ben Rosenthal.[6] Assemblyman Tenney, speaking for his resolution, said that if the Spanish rebels were successful "the few remaining Democracies in Europe will be threatened and the same will be true of the United States because Spain is the gateway to South America." Chester Gannon (Sacramento Democrat) responded: "This resolution was sent out by the emissaries of Moscow." Charles Lyon of Los Angeles, Republican floor leader, said that the Legislature should not concern itself with international affairs.[7] One political editor noted that the Tenney-Atkinson resolution had split the Assembly into three groups: left-wingers for, "fascist-minded" against, and the majority who wanted to drop the matter as of no concern to the Assembly.[8]

Ominous for the future of the Administration's public ownership policies was a roll call in the Assembly in January. The lower house voted 49 to 28 against withdrawing from committee a resolution calling upon the Railroad Commission to make public data on private utilities' salaries above $5,000, attorney's fees, and contributions to organizations and political campaigns.[9] This roll call found the Democrats deeply divided and the Republicans almost solidly against withdrawal. As a motion to withdraw a similar resolution had carried 41 to 35 at the 1937 session, it was evident that the privately owned utilities had gained supporters rather than lost them. Cecil King (Democrat, Los Angeles), a defeated aspirant for the speakership, charged that the resolution was a "smear" device. Ralph Dills (Democrat, Compton) who had made the motion to withdraw, expressed surprise "that you Democrats have so soon forgotten the governor's remarks on public ownership in his inaugural address." The Sacramento *Bee*, apostle of public ownership, ran a cartoon showing Sacramento's two assemblymen (both Democrats who had opposed withdrawal) campaigning with a pledge "Never Shall We Fail in Our Duty to the People." In the lower part of the cartoon they were depicted lining up "For the Power Trust" instead of "For the People." The cartoon bore the inscription "Remember When?"[10]

Meanwhile the administration had run into hard sledding in the upper house. The governor had named to the Board of State Harbor Commissioners, the supervising body of the state-owned San Francisco harbor, three San Franciscans, J. F. Marias, an importer; Harry See, a Railroad Brotherhood official; and Germaine Bulcke, president of the International Longshoremen's and Warehousemen's Union, CIO. The Senate, holding the power of confirmation for the posts, was not friendly, partly because two of the appointees were trade unionists, but more especially because Bulcke was a close associate of Harry Bridges. The Senate adopted a resolution requesting the governor, in considering persons for the railroad commission and harbor board, to appoint those with agricultural knowledge and experience. Governor Olson attempted to rectify his error of judgment by withdrawing See's name and substituting George Sehlmeyer, master of the California State Grange. The Sacramento *Bee*, generally friendly to Olson, noted that "the people are justly suspicious of Bridges' influence," and said that Olson should have withdrawn the name of Bulcke instead of See, who was a "fair representative of Organized Labor."

The Senate rules committee, after hearing testimony from Richard Olson, Lieutenant Governor Patterson, and trade union officials, refused to send the appointments to the floor for immediate consideration. On the day it recessed, the Senate rejected a motion to withdraw the appointments from committee, by a vote of 26 to 9.[11] In March, the Senate followed its rules committee's advice by confirming Marias and Sehlmeyer and rejecting Bulcke.[12] The roll call on Bulcke showed 11 Democrats for confirmation and 7 opposed. Only one Republican voted to approve Bulcke. Governor Olson did not appear to be upset at the Senate's action, saying "I feel that if my batting average with a Republican Senate is two hits out of three times at bat, I shall get along very well indeed with the Senate, even as constituted."[13] As a consolation prize Bulcke was given a position on the Fish and Game Commission, where he was not subject to Senate confirmation.

The Budget and Tax Program

Two days before the Legislature recessed on January 25, Governor Olson submitted his budget.[14] Under the law the governor was responsible for recommending increased revenues if the budget estimates exceeded anticipated income. He was further required to accompany his budget with an explanatory message, and an appropriation bill was to be introduced to cover the budgetary expenditures not already covered by constitutional provisions. Governor Olson, while engaged in the preparation of the budget, had visited most of the state institutions and had concluded that they badly needed expansion. Furthermore, he disapproved of the deficit financing characteristic of the Merriam administration, which depended upon selling state warrants to the banks at a discount in order to meet demands on the general fund. Also, Governor Olson disapproved of deficiency appropriations, and determined that the budget should cover the full two years beginning June 30, 1939.[15]

As submitted, the Olson budget reached the record total of $557,163,355. He estimated that the general fund deficit would reach $44,746,925 by July 1, and that current taxes would raise only $525,193,764 during the biennium. The proposed taxes would not wipe out the deficit, but would reduce it to an estimated $12,428,553 by June 30, 1941. The proposed expenditure for unemployment relief was $73,660,000, almost exactly the amount that would have been spent during the last Merriam biennium, ending June 30, 1939. The major increases over the 1937 budget were for civil service salary adjustments, in conformity with the Civil Service Act of 1937; for the State Personnel Board and the Departments of Industrial Relations and Social Welfare (which opponents of the Merriam regime charged during the 1938 elections had been deliberately weakened); for the university and state colleges; for the state's institutions (including a new psychiatric hospital); for the state's regulatory and tax collecting agencies (including the Railroad Commission, the State Board of Equalization, and the Franchise Tax Commissioner); and for a new state office building in Sacramento.

The Olson tax program, designed to secure $63,900,000 in additional revenue, involved raising the rates and closing loopholes of the personal income, bank and corporation franchise taxes; increasing the taxes on liquor and beer; raising the rates of the inheritance tax; increasing the state's share of the income from horse racing pari-mutuels; diverting a portion of the income from oil royalties from the state park fund to the general fund; and establishing two new sources—a gift tax and a severance tax on petroleum, natural gas and natural gasoline. All of these taxes, with the exception of the liquor ones, were based upon the principle of ability to pay, as determined by one of Olson's chief fiscal advisers, Dewey Anderson.

Olson contended that substantial reductions in his budget could only be made by cutting appropriations for old age pensions, aid to needy blind and children, unemployment relief, schools, and institutions. "Only in these large items of expenditure," said the governor, "can material reductions be effected." He noted that the operating costs of general government totalled $23,692,000, an increase of $604,902 over total expenditures during the current biennium, even though his budget included new salary adjustments which alone cost $807,572.

The budget and tax program were important topics of discussion during the period of legislative recess (January 26–March 5). While the governor was still recuperating, his administration leaders praised the budget, and some Republicans launched an attack upon its size and its tax features. Senator Seawell said flatly that the budget was too large and that the Senate would not accept the Olson tax program. He opposed the severance tax in principle, and said that as the federal government and some individuals were operating with a deficit he could not see why California couldn't do so.[16] Franklin Hichborn reported that "Governor Olson's physical condition will have much to do with the outcome. Incidentally, the Senate Committee on Revenue and Taxation, which will have much to say about the action on the proposed tax increases, has been stacked against him."[17]

The troubles of a new administration whose leader had been forced to spend most of his time away from his subordinates were well illustrated by an incident which occurred soon after the Legislature reconvened in March. Frank W. Clark, director of public works and temporary director of motor vehicles, told a Senate committee that it should investigate the Department of Motor Vehicles before passing a deficiency appropriation which had been requested. There were hundreds of employees in the department, Clark said, who were not needed and there was no reason for the Legislature to grant the $1,500,000 increase for the department as requested by the budget. The Senate took Clark at his word and refused to pass the deficiency appropriation.[18] In spite of this example of the lack of coördination within his official family, Governor Olson expressed great confidence in the willingness of the Legislature to "go along" on the budget, noting that many "opposition party" members had assured him of their coöperation.[19]

The battle of the budget began in earnest late in March. On the 26th Olson made a broadcast, in which he summarized his budget message and challenged his opponents: "I invite any person of honest purpose to go through the budget with a fine comb to discover, if he can, any item of improper or unwise or uneconomical expenditure."[20] The Assembly ways and means committee reported out the budget bill, with a "do pass" recommendation *without a single cut.* One Republican member charged that ways and means had worked thirty-three hours during the interim and only three hours since March 6 on the budget bill. Three of the four Republicans on the twenty-man committee signed a minority report, assailing both the Olson budget and the total expenditures during the 1937–1939 biennium as excessive, and flatly opposing any new taxes or tax increases. The minority further opposed the creation of new jobs and the proposed salary adjustments. It advocated cutting the relief appropriation to $50,000,000 "pending further study and crystallization of policy." Observers noted that the Republicans in the Assembly had enough votes to block passage of the budget by the two-thirds vote necessary when proposed expenditures exceeded those of the previous biennium by more than 5 per cent.[21]

From March 29 until April 11 the Assembly was in committee of the whole, calling in state officials to testify. The Republican press assailed the budget as excessive and the tax increases as unwarranted.[22] Chief newspaper support for the administration came from the Sacramento *Bee,* which noted that through the years successive Republican budgets had been larger and larger, that most of the cases of alleged nepotism in the State Relief Administration (a favorite target of Olson's opponents) were hold-overs from the Republican regime, and that the administration had "inherited a large deficit from that same masterly management of state finances." Said the *Bee:* "There is such a thing as a man going into court with clean hands if he expects to get a fair hearing. But a number of the Republican legislators, who are very noisy, cannot qualify on this score as far as the budget and SRA attacks are concerned. In fact, their desire seems to be more to smear the Olson administration than to serve public interest."[23]

On April 10 Governor Olson sent to the Legislature copies of a "strictly confidential" inter-office memo issued by what the governor called "the inner council" of the California State Chamber of Commerce, and asked for an investigation. This memo contained suggestions to be passed along for putting pressure on the Legislature to cut the budget and defeat the tax program. The memo noted: "In order that the approach may be as subtle as possible, there should be no evidence of organized effort but the impression should be that of spontaneous personal appeal."[24] In a broadcast that same night, Olson told his hearers that they "should know that those groups who seek to avoid their just burden of taxes . . . are promoting this misleading propaganda and that they are not concerned in economy."[25]

The axe started to fall in the Assembly on April 11, in what one veteran reporter called "the wildest legislative scramble over a State budget bill seen in the capitol since 1923. . . ."[26] It began quietly when Floor Leader Rosenthal secured the elimination of $200,000 for preliminary work on health insurance, in order that it might be taken up in a separate bill. Seth Millington (Democrat, Gridley) then moved to strike out $351,662 from the appropriation for the alcoholic beverage control division of the State Board of Equalization, and his motion carried 43 to 27, with 13 Democrats voting in favor. Millington and other Democrats then won further cuts, which in effect restored the figures for the last biennium for such officials as the attorney general, state treasurer and secretary of state, and such agencies as the Board of Equalization. The climax was the vote of 42 to 34 to remove the entire relief appropriation from the budget and to handle it in a separate bill. On this significant roll call, the administration was supported by two Republicans, while nine Democrats supported the deletion. Protested one administration supporter: "This is the first Democratic Governor we have had in 42 years, and look how you are treating him."[27]

The reductions in the appropriation for the Board of Equalization brought a response from the Republican chairman of that body which must have surprised many. Fred E. Stewart told the Legislature that the cuts were severe but that the Board would "do the best we can with the money available," for it did not favor new or increased taxes. Olson's retort to Stewart was sharp, for by then it was obvious that the governor had been taken in by his opponents. Olson defended his own estimates: "I trimmed the budget request of the Board of Equalization by nearly $350,000, which I believed was not required, although asked for by Mr. Stewart, and allowed only those funds needed to collect taxes from sources heretofore escaping payment for lack of efficient enforcement."[28] The other members of the Board of Equalization repudiated the statement of their chairman and reaffirmed their budget request, pointedly refraining from taking an official stand on the tax program.[29]

It was at this critical moment, while the Republicans and "economy bloc" Democrats were slashing his budget, that Governor Olson suffered a great personal loss. On April 15 Mrs. Olson died. She had spent most of her time as California's first lady ill in bed. The governor himself had scarcely recovered from his own severe illness, and, grief-stricken, was ordered by his doctors to take a fortnight's rest. After spending the period in seclusion at Pebble Beach, the governor returned to Sacramento on April 30 to resume his duties. Once more Olson had been forced to absent himself from his desk at an exceedingly critical moment, leaving his forces for the moment leaderless.

In the interim the Assembly had continued its work on his budget. On April 18 the reduced budget bill failed to secure the required 54 votes for passage, even though all Democrats voting except one supported it.[30] The administration was unsuccessful in getting more votes, and the "economy bloc" had served notice that it would attempt to secure reconsideration, in order to effect further cuts. The key vote was on April 24, when the Assembly voted 41 to 32 to reconsider the final passage of the budget bill, with two Republicans opposing reconsideration and nine Democrats in favor.[31] These nine "economy bloc" Democrats, who constituted Olson's almost consistent intra-party opposition in the Assembly, were: Jeanette E. Daley, San Diego; Earl D. Desmond, Sacramento; Clinton J. Fulcher, Lookout; Chester F. Gannon, Sacramento; Gordon H. Garland, Woodlake; Joseph P. Gilmore, San Francisco; Seth Millington, Gridley; Rodney L. Turner, Delano; and Clyde A. Watson, Orange. The Assembly finally passed the budget on May 2, by a vote of 64 to 14, but not before it had slashed the funds for the Railroad Commission.[32]

Olson administration supporters fought back in a vain endeavor to restore the budget to something like its original figures. The Sacramento *Bee* called upon the Senate to consider the budget carefully, charging that the Assembly had passed a "butchered" bill. The *Bee* said that "most of the responsibility for this exhibition rests squarely on the shoulders of the Republican membership, whose shouted devotion to the principle of economy, applauded by a few recalcitrant Democrats, fooled no one, least of all themselves."[33] Olson assailed the "economy blockers," contending that they were serving great interests primarily concerned with dodging their proper share of taxation. He charged that "the whole period of legislative sessions up to this time has been a period of obstructions."[34]

The Senate finance committee, voting 5 to 4 along strict party lines, restored all cuts made by the Assembly. The full Senate, however, refused to approve the restorations by a vote of 22 to 14, with three Democratic senators joining the Republicans and no Republicans supporting the administration. Then the Senate voted to refer the bill to a special committee for consideration.[35] The majority report of this committee, signed by two of the four Democratic members and all five of the Republicans, proposed 170 amendments representing a general revision of the budget downward. After 18 of the majority's proposed amendments had been adopted individually, the other 152 were adopted by a single roll call by a vote of 30 to 9,[36] and on May 26 the Senate passed the amended budget bill, 27 to 8.[37] A free conference committee reconciled the positions of the two houses, recommending a budget totalling $468,071,624 (with relief to be handled separately), and the free conference report was adopted unanimously by the Senate and by a vote of 62 to 9 in the Assembly.[38] The California State Chamber of Commerce reported that the activities of the "economy bloc" had resulted in cuts totalling $15,431,734 (outside of relief).[39]

Governor Olson was scathing in his response to the work of the Legislature on his budget: "And now we have the odd spectacle of finding the so-called Economy Bloc, the so-called conservative elements of the Senate and Assembly, which is in fact a Republican bloc, lined up in favor of *crippling* the functions of government; lined up *against* paying off the State debt; lined up *against* a real balancing of the State's fiscal affairs."[40] While he was forced to sign the budget bill, Olson assailed the elimination of $4,500,000 for civil service pay adjustments; the reduction of a like amount for the construction of new buildings, principally a new office building in Sacramento and new facilities for mental patients; the reduction in funds for the Department of Agriculture; and a cut of almost two millions in funds for tax collecting and auditing agencies. The governor reminded his listeners of the secret memo of the State Chamber of Commerce and of his request for an investigation: "The Senate responded by investigating, not the Chamber of Commerce, but the Workers Alliance and other groups organized to ameliorate the condition of the unemployed and of the dirt farmers of California. Their investigation of the Chamber of Commerce was limited to inquiring with indignant concern how this secret document ever found its way into my hands."[41]

Of Olson's revenue proposals, only the gift tax passed the Legislature, and that was steered through by one of the governor's bitterest Democratic enemies, Assemblyman Millington.[42] A bill to increase the state's share of the receipts from horse racing at the major tracks passed the Assembly but was rejected by the Senate (where seven Democrats joined the opposition).[43] A bill to increase the inheritance tax failed by one vote to pass the lower house.[44] A bill to increase the income tax rates received 36 votes in the Assembly, 5 less than necessary, and a bill to increase the bank and corporation franchise tax failed by the same vote.[45] A bill to establish a severance tax on gas and oil secured 30 votes in the lower House, while 38 were cast against it.[46] The same familiar Democrats of the "economy bloc" generally held the balance of power and rejected the administration proposals. And few Republicans came to Olson's support. The result was that Olson's fiscal program was demolished.

The California business community rejoiced in the triumph of the "economy bloc." A trade journal observed: "The outcome of the budget battle affords a ray of hope to California industry as it means that those who would safeguard capital against confiscation are not without political strength."[47] However, the Sacramento *Bee,* representative of old-line California progressivism, said that the purposes of the economy bloc were "to keep California in the red for partisan purposes and to prevent the equalization of taxes for the benefit of favored special interests."[48] In an analysis of the budget fight the old journalist Franklin Hichborn pointed out:

> In my judgment, the conservative interests, including the Hearst properties, have made a serious mistake in their unreasonable attacks upon the Olson Administration and their misrepresentation of State fiscal condition and policies.
>
> The effect of all this has been to drive Olson, a well intentioned man but human, to the left. Saner treatment of the situation, an honest effort to meet the serious problems before the State fairly and squarely, would have found him receptive and sympathetic for reasonable solution. With Olson licked and more or less discredited out of the confusion we may look for all sorts of crack-pot schemes for raising needed revenues.[49]

The effect of the long and bitter struggle over the budget and tax program was to keep other legislative matters in the background. But when the Legislature did find time to deal with other bills, the Olson forces were given an almost uninterrupted series of defeats. While the administration was instrumental in securing the passage of legislation restricting "loan sharks" and providing for prorating of oil production (see chap. ix for a discussion of these measures), in both instances it had powerful allies in the Republican party and the business world. The administration suffered sharp defeats when the Legislature refused to appropriate funds to cover the costs of relief for the biennium (see chap. vii), to pass a measure paving the way for public distribution of power from the Central Valley Project (see chap. viii), to pass a compulsory health insurance bill (see chap. xiii), to approve an extension of the powers of the building and loan commissioner (see chap. xiii) or to approve a plan for reorganization of the state's revenue administration (see chap. xiii).

The Fight Against the Lobbies

One of the great fights of the 1939 session was over a bill by Assemblyman Hugh P. Donnelly (Democrat, Turlock), designed to restrict the activities of lobbyists. The state had been lobby-conscious ever since the Sacramento County Grand Jury investigation of 1938. A report submitted to Governor Merriam on December 28, 1938, by Howard R. Philbrick for the investigating firm of Edwin N. Atherton and Associates, covering lobbying and making certain suggestions for reform, was kept by the retiring governor. "He said he would not make public the original report because he did not want to 'smear' anyone and, anyway, in his opinion, the people were interested in eliminating the objectionable practices rather than in sordid details of past misdeeds."[50]

Governor Olson announced that he had telegraphed Merriam asking for the Philbrick report, saying that if and when he got a copy he would make it public.[51] The Senate passed a resolution requesting Merriam to give a copy to Attorney General Warren, "so that he may examine said report, and take such action as he may deem fit and proper...."[52] Merriam turned the report over to one of Warren's deputies on January 14, but Warren found many "libelous" statements in it and refused to release it to the press.[53]

Eventually Warren did turn the Philbrick report over to Governor Olson, who announced that as it had been paid for by state funds he considered that it was a public document. He had the State Printing Office run off copies for the press and for members of the 1935 and 1937 legislatures.[54] Governor Olson sent a copy of the report with a message to the Legislature, but on the next day Senator Seawell stated that the report had been "inadvertently entered" in the *Journal,* and moved that it be stricken out "on the ground that said report is not a public document, but only a prejudiced and unsupported confidential report of a private detective." The Senate, by voice vote, agreed and struck the Philbrick report from its journal.[55] However, the copies Olson had had printed served their purpose, and the report circulated widely, to the embarassment of some legislators and lobbyists (notably "Artie" Samish). Governor Olson made Howard Philbrick his director of motor vehicles and for a while Philbrick was prominent in state administration circles.

The Donnelly lobby bill provided for registration of all lobbyists, with full information from each regarding the interests he represented and the terms of his employment, and a public statement of receipts and expenditures by each. It forbade the practice of employment to promote or defeat bills on a contingency basis, and required that the report of each lobbyist should list all considerations paid to any legislator or attache for any purpose in the year preceding the legislative term (in order to throw light on campaign contributions). Mr. Donnelly's bill generally followed the recommendations of the Sacramento County Grand Jury and the Philbrick report.[56]

The reaction of Assemblyman Millington, leader of the "economy bloc," was probably typical: "If a lobbyist is sucker enough to buy me a steak or a scotch and soda or more, figuring he can get anything out of me, that's his lookout."[57] The Donnelly bill came to a vote in the lower house on May 11, and was defeated by a vote of 30 aye to 42 no.[58] Six Republicans joined 24 Democrats in voting for the measure, while 16 Democrats and 26 Republicans voted against it. The Democratic opponents included the "economy bloc" regulars plus a like number of normal administration supporters. Governor Olson in a radio speech suggested that his hearers study the roll call in order to see if their representatives were voting against the public interest.[59] Such papers as the San Francisco *News* and Sacramento *Bee* lambasted the legislators for this vote but it was all to no avail. A clean-up of the "Third House" was not to take place during the Olson administration, in spite of the governor's efforts.

Other Legislation

The labor legislation signed by Governor Olson in 1939 was not very impressive. One act authorized the director of industrial relations to act as voluntary mediator in labor disputes when requested to do so by both parties. Another set up an apprenticeship council, to supervise apprenticeship procedures in the state. While both of these measures had almost no opposition, a bill which outlawed certain types of industrial "homework" ran into more difficulty, though it eventually was passed.[60] Other labor measures went down to defeat. These included a bill forbidding anti-picketing ordinances, which secured 33 aye votes (6 Republicans) and 38 no votes (10 from Democrats) in the Assembly;[61] a bill providing for state agricultural wage boards to recommend wage rates, which mustered only 21 votes in the Assembly (including 3 Republican); and a bill providing for state-built farm labor camps. In addition, two measures, a "Little Wagner Act" and a bill authorizing the closed shop, passed the Assembly with a scant 41 votes each, only to die in the Senate committee on labor and capital. An anti-labor measure which prohibited the use of threats in labor disputes passed the Senate with only two dissenting votes, but was tabled in the Assembly by a vote of 43 to 19.[62] The effect of the 1939 session was to leave the state's labor laws essentially unchanged. Nor was the governor able to secure approval of one of his pet projects, exclusive state-fund operation of workmen's compensation insurance, even though he made a major effort in its behalf.[63]

Two attempts at primary-election law reform, closely associated by the administration with minimizing the influence of lobbyists and "special interests" in campaigns, were successful in the lower house but failed in the Senate. A bill to abolish cross-filing by requiring candidates to run only in their own party primaries passed the Assembly by a vote of 44 to 29, with nine northern California Democrats opposed.[64] Another measure which would have permitted cross-filing but required that the party affiliation of candidates be printed on the ballot was approved by the lower house by a vote of 46 to 27.[65] Both bills died in the Senate elections committee and the California cross-filing system remained in force. The Olson administration did not push either bill very vigorously, being preoccupied with other matters.

The 1939 Legislature finally adjourned on the night of June 22, two days after the clock had been stopped, to end the longest session in California history. Governor Olson's opinion of the activities of the Legislature was outspoken: "Its work was almost a total failure and its record on most vital issues of great consequence to the people is one of the worst ever made by any legislature." The governor said that a majority in both houses was "wholly reactionary," but he contended that Democrats representing districts containing a majority of the state's population had consistently supported his program. He said that "good votes here and there made by a few individual Republican members were offset by innumerable bad votes," and asserted that most Republicans followed the line laid down by the Chamber of Commerce, Associated Farmers and the "reactionary" daily newspapers. But Olson said he was not worried about the future, for the session had served the purpose of defining the "issues between the people as a whole and the mercenaries, the exploiters, the special interests, the lobbyists, and corrupt politics." He predicted "the replacement of the few Democratic members who betrayed their trust," as well as the defeat of "reactionary Republicans."[66]

This was not the first threat of a "purge" by the administration. On April 13, Richard Olson told reporters: "Purges must be made of certain Assemblymen who cry 'wolf' loudest and ballyhoo about radicalism as a smoke screen in the hope that their real motives may be concealed."[67] On May 7, the governor referred to the Democrats who were voting with the "economy bloc": "Why they should betray their party platform and the mandate of the majority of the people of the state will be for them to explain to their own constituents."[68]

On May 21, as the rout of his program became even more evident, Governor Olson drew an analogy between his situation and that of Governor Hiram Johnson at the close of the 1911 Legislature: Johnson had asked the people to study the voting records of the legislators and to elect members who would support the Johnson program, and the people had obliged.[69] A week later Olson concluded his regular broadcast by saying: "The whole scene sharpens the dire necessity for reform of our Legislative machinery and processes, and our elective processes. Incidentally, we need a new Legislature."[70] At the close of the session, Richard Olson reiterated his purge threat in a guest column written for the San Francisco *Call-Bulletin:* "The record has been made. With this record—and the bad votes against it registered by those who have defeated the governor's program—it is generally understood the governor will go before the people with his own candidates for the Senate and Assembly in 1940. The so-called 'purge' will be on."[71]

Olson, however, did not have to wait for the next election to strike back at his enemies. He had his power of veto. The most spectacular of his vetoes during the session was that of a bill which would have prohibited open grand jury sessions. The Sacramento County Grand Jury had had such sessions during its investigation of lobbying and corruption in the Legislature, to the discomfiture of many members, and this bill had passed both houses almost without opposition. Notwithstanding the fact that it had been introduced by an administration supporter, Olson returned it with a ringing veto message,[72] which the San Francisco *News* called "the strongest state paper he has issued to date."[73] The Assembly refused to override.

After the Legislature adjourned Olson disposed of other measures by pocket veto. One would have placed severe restrictions upon the use of dictographs and similar devices. Another would have given school boards the power to compel students to salute the flag under penalty of expulsion. Another (by anti-Olson Assemblywoman Daley) would have appropriated $6,700,000 to the counties to help pay the costs of old age relief. On this measure, which had passed both houses with little opposition, Olson issued a statement: "It seems to me hypocrisy under a pretense of State economy to defeat revenue measures advocated by my administration to enable the State to aid the over-burdened taxpayers by assuming a larger share of aid to the aged and then passing a bill making this appropriation for the payment of which the State has no funds."[74]

The most spectacular of Governor Olson's pocket vetoes was that of the "Bookie Bill," introduced by Assemblyman Fulcher, another "economy bloc" Democrat. This measure would have given to the State Board of Equalization the authority to issue bookmaking licenses on a basis of one for every 10,000 population, with the requirement that "bookies" located within fifty miles of a race track must close by 1:00 P.M. when racing was scheduled. The Fulcher bill was supposedly a tax measure, for it required license fees of $1,000 per "bookie" plus a tax of five per cent of the gross.[75] The California press almost unanimously opposed the bill; the Sacramento *Bee* published a cartoon showing the great seal of the state redrawn, with California downcast and the seal embellished with dollar signs and the slogan "Never Give a Sucker a Break."[76] The Fulcher bill had certain embarrassing features for the new Democratic administration, for it had passed the Assembly with the support of 29 Democrats and only 12 Republicans, while only 9 Democrats and 20 Republicans had opposed.[77] Furthermore it had been steered through the Senate by Senator A. L. Pierovich (Democrat, Jackson), an administration supporter. Nevertheless, Governor Olson pocket-vetoed the measure, after saying that it "would license gamblers to prey upon the cupidity of people who believe they can profit by gambling."[78]

Olson had little patronage to bestow on his legislative supporters, but he did what he could for them. At the close of the 1939 Legislature he appointed Senators A. L. Pierovich and Harry C. Westover to Superior Court judgeships in their respective counties, Amador and Orange. Jesse W. Carter of Redding, active in the Olson campaign and elected to fill a Senate vacancy on January 17, was appointed to the State Supreme Court on July 15. These appointments left the administration even weaker in the Senate than it had been, but they established the fact that Olson would reward the faithful when he could. On May 31 the governor appointed Assemblyman Rosenthal, administration floor leader, to the Los Angeles Municipal Court. In August Olson named Finance Director Phil S. Gibson to the State Supreme Court, to fill a second vacancy on that body. These appointments were among the first of the many that Governor Olson was able to make, affording Democratic lawyers judicial opportunities in a state whose courts were overwhelmingly Republican.

The close of the legislative session found the administration's program in shambles and Olson threatening to purge his enemies. The regime that had opened so auspiciously on January 2 was now anything but promising. Olson himself had proved to be inept in his handling of the Legislature. He had consolidated his opposition when he presented a tax program aimed at so many special interests. He had fallen into his opponents' trap by accepting at face value the budget estimates presented by Republican state officials. Most of the department heads under the governor were inexperienced and had difficulty in presenting their programs to suspicious legislators. Richard Olson's convivial heavy-handedness did his father's cause very little good. The administration made no serious attempt to secure the support of Republican legislators, attempting to act through Democratic party machinery even in the face of the fact that Republicans comprised a majority of the Senate. Most of the press was frankly hostile to Olson and his whole program and chose to picture him as a radical, an experimenter, and a would-be dictator.

But it was Olson's handling of the problem of unemployment relief that, more than anything else, brought his administration to grief in the first half of 1939. Here was clear evidence of his lack of administrative ability—and even clearer evidence of his political predicament.

7 *the nightmare of relief*

OLSON'S GREATEST PROBLEMS AS HE ASSUMED OFFICE WERE
relief for the unemployed and jobs for "deserving Democrats." For years
he had been outspokenly critical of the dole system and he had repeatedly announced himself in favor of "self-help" or "production-for-use."
It was his view that unemployment was "here to stay," and that the
state should assume the duty of helping those out of work to help themselves. It was his misfortune that the very agency which handled the
problem of relief, being the only sizeable part of the state government
not under civil service, was the only one open to his job-hungry supporters.

The State Relief Administration had been established as the successor
to the Federal Emergency Relief Administration, and under Governor
Merriam it grew to great size, spending almost $5,000,000 per month
during 1934–1938.[1] At the end of 1938 the SRA employed 4,661 persons
full time and had a case load of 70,063. Its "clients" comprised 38 per
cent of all relief cases handled by state and federal governments in
California at the time.[2] As its role was to care for those unable to secure
WPA assistance for any reason, its case load varied as the WPA funds or
policies varied, as well as with the changes in the seasons and in the

economy as a whole. Thus the size of the staff fluctuated, with a very rapid turnover—estimated at 100 per cent every eight or nine months.[3] It is no wonder that this "temporary" agency was the "weakest link in the entire state administrative organization, and consequently the object of both internal pressure and external politics."[4]

The State Relief Commission, composed of eight members serving at the pleasure of the governor, and the director of social welfare, determined the policies of the SRA. These policies were then carried out by the state relief administrator, also a gubernatorial appointee. Thus in the absence of specific legislative restrictions, the governor controlled the unemployment relief program of the state.

Harold Pomeroy, state relief administrator during most of the Merriam regime, resigned in December 1938 to become executive secretary of the Associated Farmers of California. This big grower-processor organization was obviously pleased with Pomeroy's work in the SRA, as well it might have been, for he removed persons from relief rolls whenever farm work was available, regardless of how far away it might be and regardless of whether or not a labor dispute was in progress. Liberal and labor groups attacked Pomeroy for this policy, as well as for the dole system he administered and for the single men's camps set up by the SRA.[5]

Dewey Anderson, selected by Governor Olson to be state relief administrator, announced that the SRA would be completely reorganized with "production-for-use" as its keystone. He said that experts would be put to work on the various phases, including the manufacture of clothes, canning of food, production of food and the distribution of commodities to the unemployed. He denied that this program had any connection with the ideas of Upton Sinclair or that it would have any harmful effect upon private industry. He promised to proceed slowly, noting that the program could not even be tried out before July 1.[6] The San Francisco Chronicle indicated its doubts about the plan, questioning whether it could fail to injure workers in private industry and pointing out that the program would require managers and skilled workers not available among the unemployed. But the Chronicle found it encouraging that Anderson recognized these problems: "The experiment clearly is one upon thin ice, but perhaps no thinner than other relief methods find themselves upon. It at least has the merit of not proposing to take rabbits out of hats."[7]

Unfortunately for the administration's plans, SRA funds were nearly exhausted, and the biennium still had six months to go. Olson sought and secured an emergency appropriation of $19,975,000 from the Legislature during his first week in office. A Republican effort to reduce this figure was defeated by a margin of only three votes in the Assembly. This vote was much too close to a defeat to give the administration much comfort, and was early evidence of legislative distrust of the administration's relief plans. And if the Legislature were to fail to make lump sum appropriations for relief and instead insist upon frequent small appropriations, the relief administrator would be unable to carry out any real planning for work relief or any other reforms.

Anderson's troubles did not end here. Even though he had boldly announced that there would be no "purge" of the SRA employees, he was the only official in the state government who had an appreciable number of non-civil service positions under his jurisdiction. With the governor ill and absent from his desk until the middle of February, Anderson had to face the hungry hordes of the faithful by himself.

Meanwhile the SRA case load was climbing. By January 31 there were 87,473 clients, representing 303,066 persons, the largest number on SRA rolls since the end of 1935, and an increase of 22 per cent over the corresponding date in 1938. Throughout 1939 the SRA case load was to be substantially higher than it had been the year before, chiefly because SRA had to take over more and more persons dropped from federal relief as WPA appropriations were reduced by Congress. This meant that Olson and Anderson would need to improvise and economize, or to ask for greater and greater appropriations.

At first, the administration seemed hesitant about what to ask of the Legislature. On January 16 Anderson estimated publicly that the cost of relief during the 1939–1941 biennium would be $100,000,000.[8] But the budget request submitted by Governor Olson on January 23 included only $73,660,000 for relief, almost exactly the sum that would have been spent by the end of the final Merriam biennium on June 30, 1939. On March 12, in his first policy broadcast after his illness, Governor Olson noted that the sum he requested for relief was "much less than will be required" if the dole system were to be retained, and said that perhaps he should have asked for more in view of the current WPA cuts.[9]

Governor Olson early in March appointed a commission on reëmployment, to study the problem of unemployment and make recommendations for production-for-use projects. In his charter to the commission, the governor outlined its tasks. "I ask you to survey all available production facilities which can contribute to normal human requirements. I ask you to explore the possibilities of bringing together unsalable surplus farm commodities and needy persons. I charge you with the responsibility of determining the best way for setting up projects out of which the essentials of life for those in need may be produced."[10] The commission was headed by John R. Richards, industrial engineer, investment

SRA Case Load, Showing Percentage of State and Federal
Relief Cases Carried by SRA

Month	1938		1939	
	Total	Per cent	Total	Per cent
January	71,904	46.3	87,473	44.2
February	79,683	46.2	97,438	45.4
March	80,611	42.9	95,045	45.8
April	68,440	38.5	91,403	46.3
May	60,454	35.0	81,884	44.8
June	55,115	32.8	74,621	42.7
July	55,609	33.7	78,306	47.4
August	53,232	32.5	79,139	53.3
September	48,412	29.9	82,796	53.6
October	47,364	28.2	84,188	52.5
November	50,782	29.8	94,153	53.2
December	70,063	38.0	104,101	53.5

banker and chairman of the finance committee of the Los Angeles Metropolitan Water District, and included seven other prominent Californians. Long-range plans for SRA were held in abeyance while the Richards Commission made its study.

Before the Richards Commission began its tasks, the first of a long series of legislative investigations of relief had been concluded, and the results gave the administration no pleasure.

The Assembly's interim committee on unemployment relief conducted a series of hearings throughout the state during February. Chairman Lee T. Bashore (Republican, Glendora) presided over one section of the committee and Assemblywoman Jeanette E. Daley (Democrat, San Diego) over the other. The testimony of industrial and political leaders of the state before the Bashore committee was chiefly concerned with problems of centralization or decentralization of administration, and with the means of instituting self-help and stimulating reëmployment of the jobless in private industry. Dewey Anderson told the committee flatly that "the state administration will not tolerate nor support any measure which turns the administration of aid back to the counties."[11] In this he reflected the liberal and labor viewpoint, for most of the county officials were conservative and close to the dominant economic interests in their areas. The case for county administration of relief was presented most eloquently by C. L. Preisker, chairman of the Santa Barbara County Board of Supervisors: "Take SRA out of Santa Barbara County and give us local control of relief and we can cut the present cost in half."[12] While Anderson was unprepared to give the committee specific plans on production-for-use, his opponents were quick to make known their objections. As Bashore put it: "Business leaders voiced general opposition to any scheme involving the establishment of competing economy, such as production-for-use. It is believed that an economic structure cannot exist within an economic structure without one or the other tumbling."[13]

Although his committee never made a formal report, Bashore on March 28 issued a set of "recommendations," which he said were concurred in by Mrs. Daley.[14] He proposed that the total relief appropriation be $48,000,000, the sum in Merriam's last budget, and that the amount expendable in any six months' period be limited. He favored a return of relief administration to the counties, as well as a ban on relief for aliens and an increase of the residence requirement to three years, instead of one. He also proposed to substitute grocery orders for the cash dole. While he said he wanted to put the employable to work, Bashore opposed any experiments with production-for-use. These recommendations were in large part accepted by the anti-administration forces in the Legislature.

"Radicals" in the SRA

Another source of trouble for Olson and Anderson was the repeated charge that the SRA was controlled by "radicals." Anderson announced early that the governor approved of collective bargaining for SRA employees.[15] This was an advantage for the militant left-wing State, County and Municipal Workers of America (CIO), then engaged in organizing the SRA staff. It could be inferred that if Olson felt the SRA employees were entitled to collective bargaining, then he must also favor collective bargaining for the relief recipients. Certainly this became the practice, to the consternation of conservatives.[16]

The Workers Alliance was the leading organization of the unemployed in this period. It fought vigorously in behalf of its membership, opposing the return of relief to the counties, the use of those on relief as strike-breakers and the sending of single men to camps. It sought the increase of relief budgets and handled its members' grievances with the SRA. Also militantly left-wing, its state organizer was Alexander Noral, twice a Communist candidate for United States Senator. Noral claimed that the Alliance had a network of 120 locals in the state by 1938, and that the organization grew rapidly during 1939, reaching by September of that year a total of 186 locals, 12,000 paid-up members, and 42,000 members in all.[17]

The furor over radicalism in the SRA came to a head shortly after the Legislature reconvened. On March 8 the Bakersfield chapter of the California State Employees Association demanded an immediate investigation of the activities of SRA officials in Kern County. On the previous day the county director had ordered the transfer of two staff members, who in turn had charged that a "new philosophy" was being instituted, with the CIO and Workers Alliance dictating appointments. On March 14 Dewey Anderson arrived in Kern County and held a staff meeting with SRA personnel, which turned into a public meeting with a large attendance. Charges and countercharges flew. Anderson readily identified the "new philosophy" as production-for-use. And, never noted for his tact, Anderson announced flatly, "We must have in the SRA only those people who are wholeheartedly with us in the new program we are undertaking."[18]

An examination of the background of the Kern County crisis shows clearly the implication for rural California of the coming of Olson into power. During a bitterly fought cotton-pickers' strike in the fall of 1938, the Bakersfield SRA officials carried out the "Pomeroy Strike Policy." They closed all SRA cases and refused new applicants on the grounds that work (i.e., strikebreaking in the cotton fields) was available. The Workers Alliance violently opposed this policy and was now out to "get" those in Kern County who had carried it out. Furthermore, the SCMWA was busily engaged in organizing the SRA staff in Bakersfield, and the older, established, conservative CSEA was resentful.

The Assembly on March 20 voted unanimously to direct its committee on social welfare to investigate the activities of SRA personnel.[19] The committee's hearings were dramatic and had far-reaching consequences. Loreta Adams, representing the Workers Alliance, read from letters written in January by Mitchell Saadi, administrative assistant to Dewey Anderson, which replied to the Workers Alliance request for removal of the Kern County SRA director and intake supervisor by saying that the SRA officials to be appointed in Kern County "will meet with your approval." Mrs. Adams admitted to the committee that she was a registered Communist. John E. Jeffrey, official of the SCMWA, testified that he knew of no intimidation of SRA workers in Kern County to force them to join his union, and said there was no tie between his group and the Workers Alliance. Sheldon Martin, the new Kern County SRA director, denied that workers had been ousted or transferred because they were Catholics or because they disagreed with the "new philosophy." But he admitted that he had discussed the transfer of one of the women case workers with William J. Plunkert, assistant state administrator, because he had had trouble with her before when they were co-workers in Santa Clara County. The SRA worker in question, Catherine Lanigan, testified that she had been told shortly after Martin took office that she did not fit in with the "new philosophy" and that her Catholicism had been in part responsible for her transfer. Director Martin admitted to the committee that he handled all Workers Alliance complaints personally and that as a consequence the members of that group were more successful in dealing with him than were non-members. Donald Dawalder, the transferred intake supervisor, testified that as a result of a speech by Director Martin, the Kern County employees felt that they "were on trial by the Workers' Alliance," and said that Plunkert had informed them that "if we did not see eye to eye with the present administration you had better get out."[20]

Following this hearing William J. Plunkert became a most controversial figure for a few days. He was a professional social worker, and had been ousted from his post in the SRA by Pomeroy in 1937 for lobbying against a bill which would have placed the control of relief funds in the hands of county boards of supervisors.[21] Later reinstated, Plunkert left the SRA and entered the 1938 campaign as executive secretary of the California Federation for Political Unity, a liberal-labor coalition supporting Olson, Patterson, and Downey in the primary. Plunkert became social service director of SRA under Dewey Anderson, then assistant administrator, and then social service director once more in March, following the Kern County episode.[22]

The charges mounted against Plunkert and his associate, Rosamund Timmons (Rose Segure), area field representative of SRA. David Price, newspaperman and ex-Communist, swore that Plunkert was a Communist party member under an assumed name, placed at the head of the CFPU by the party "for the purpose of engaging in the primary campaign of Governor Olson in order to have claims against him. . . ." Price said that Plunkert and Miss Segure attended meetings with William Schneiderman, state Communist party secretary, where they were instructed "as to how the Communist Party wanted the relief set-up conducted both with respect to personnel hired and fired, and the advancement of Communist Party doctrine."[23] In addition to the charges of asserted radicalism and "CIO domination," Plunkert was accused of nepotism (his wife was WPA research director in San Francisco).[24] Others were also charged with nepotism but Plunkert, because of the Kern County crisis, was especially vulnerable.

Demands for the ouster of Plunkert came from many quarters and Olson was confronted with a major crisis. Plunkert had become a symbol and those uneasy about SRA for any reason demanded his removal. Assemblyman Dan Gallagher (Democrat, San Francisco) said, "We are going to insist that Plunkert be dismissed and there be an end of Plunkertism in the SRA."[25] Democratic assemblymen reportedly demanded that "radicals" be purged from SRA, that relief recipients be forbidden to pay dues to organizations out of relief money, that SRA employees be forbidden to join any union, and that nepotism be eliminated.[26]

In the end the administration gave way. On April 4, Anderson fired Plunkert, in spite of the efforts of some liberals and labor leaders to save him. Anderson refused to discuss the details, but said: "Anytime I find anyone doing other than his duties in this organization, he's through."[27] Governor Olson, while refusing publicly to label Plunkert a leftist, told the press: "I am opposed to organizations of an oathbound kind, organized to acquire political power through secretive methods and with loyalty to a secret organization, whether it is in behalf of nazism, fascism or communism."[28] Plunkert charged Olson with "loss of nerve under fire," and said that the governor "hasn't begun to feel the full pressure, as yet."[29] Herb Caen, San Francisco *Chronicle* columnist, reported: "One faction of the pro-Plunkert forces is taking up a collection to buy Governor Olson an umbrella."[30] When a group of southern California liberals came up to Sacramento to protest the ouster of Plunkert, the governor "told them to leave the protection of the liberal cause to me."[31]

The Plunkert incident was highly important in the history of the Olson regime. Here was evidence of the breaking up of the broad "people's front" coalition which had elected Olson and Patterson, and which included Communists and their associates. While the *People's World* was displeased with Olson in this instance, it did not at once launch an attack on the administration. In another year, when Communist opposition to Olson was intense, a left-wing writer discussed the incident:

> Soon Olson was proving to the business interests his non-partisanship by "purging" from the State Relief Administration, as alleged Communists, many of his most energetic supporters, skilled social workers whom not even Merriam had dared fire. Olson hoped by this to induce his foes to support his relief budget. They never did. What is this craving deep in the bones of middle-class politicians to appease the "big Boys" for having challenged their arrogant power?[32]

Another critical problem facing State Relief Administrator Dewey Anderson was that of relief and labor disputes, especially those involving migratory farm workers. It has been estimated that by 1935 the state, with 4.7 per cent of the nation's population, had from 12 to 14 per cent of the dependent transients in the United States.[33] Labor relations had long been a difficult problem for growers, who depended upon the migrants for brief periods and then had no more work for them. Never organized more than briefly into unions, the workers had to accept what they were offered, which was generally very little indeed.

The policy of the SRA under Harold Pomeroy of forcing agricultural laborers to accept farm work regardless of the wage rate, and of supplementing the earnings of those workers when necessary with relief funds (in order to provide them with a subsistence) tended to depress prevailing agricultural wages.[34] Pomeroy in October 1938, at a time when striking cotton pickers demanded one dollar per hundred pounds, had declared that 75 cents per hundred for picking cotton was a fair wage and that all workers who refused to accept this rate would be cut off relief.[35] This policy was most unpopular in labor circles. Indeed, the State Relief Commission, which supposedly set the policies of the SRA, never formally approved the Pomeroy policy of "administrative determination" in labor disputes until September 24, 1938, although he had by then been carrying it out for two years. It marked a change-over from the "federal policy" of FERA, under which "the mere fact that the job being offered was under strike conditions, was sufficient to justify a client's declining to accept it."[36]

In May, 1939, cotton pickers in Madera County, led by the Workers Alliance, struck, demanding 27½ cents per hour in place of the 20 cents then prevailing. Governor Olson dispatched to the area an investigative commission headed by Carey McWilliams, chief of the Division of Immigration and Housing, Department of Industrial Relations. McWilliams reported back that 27½ cents per hour was a fair rate of pay for cotton picking. With the backing of the State Relief Commission, Anderson then announced a new policy: Workers were not to be denied relief if they declined to take work chopping cotton at less than 27½ cents per hour. This was the first time that an administrator had used his right, under the Unemployment Relief Act, to certify that a job might be declined.[37]

The reaction of California's agricultural interests, and their business and political allies, was quick to come and violently hostile. A proposal to provide for the appointment of state boards to recommend wage scales in agriculture, and thus formalize the procedure begun by Olson and McWilliams, was defeated in the nominally Democratic Assembly on May 31 by a vote of 21 aye to 44 no.[38] All of the proposal's supporters were from city districts. A more drastic measure, by Assemblyman Yorty and others, proposed the creation of wage boards to regulate wages, hours, and living conditions of agricultural workers employed in the production of commodities that were subject to a program of prorated marketing. These boards were to consist of representatives of employers and employees in the proration zone, as well as representatives of the public; and the measure further provided that "unless the recommendations of the wage board are approved, no program of prorated marketing shall be instituted."[39] The Yorty proposal never emerged from committee.

The Olson administration, in view of the numerous and quite controversial problems regarding relief, with the proposed work relief program under study by a commission, and with a very precarious Democratic majority in the lower house and a Republican majority in the upper, was in a most difficult situation. To make matters even worse, the governor announced on March 3 that Dewey Anderson had advised him that the emergency appropriation for relief secured from the Legislature in January would be exhausted by May 6.[40] Olson said that the January appropriation figure had been arrived at through consultation with relief officials of the Merriam administration, but that since that time cuts in the WPA rolls had forced the SRA to carry a larger share of the California relief load than had been anticipated.[41] The second deficiency relief appropriation bill was not passed until May 9, after its author voluntarily reduced its amount from $4,050,000 to $3,500,000, saying that there was enough relief money left to last "until almost the end of May."[42] The SRA advanced as reasons for this amelioration the securing of larger WPA quotas, the close coöperation of the State Employment Service in the placing of clients in jobs, and the discharge of some 800 employees.

The Relief Fight in the Legislature

Meanwhile the fight had been raging over the relief appropriation for the 1939–1941 biennium. On April 3, at the height of the Plunkert crisis, the San Francisco *News* asked that the relief appropriation be removed from the budget bill, and made the subject of a separate measure. The *News* said that the governor's request for approximately $73,000,000 was "not excessive," but suggested that the money be allocated by three-month periods, to make sure there would not be any deficit. The San Francicso *Chronicle* on April 11 had different advice. Pointing out that it was impossible to foresee how much money would be needed for the biennium, the *Chronicle* said: "It seems the part of wisdom to cut this appropriation now to about $50,000,000 with a clear understanding that a special session will provide whatever sums are later found to be needed."

On April 11 the Assembly voted to remove the relief appropriation from the budget bill. The roll call was 42 to 34, with 9 Democrats deserting the administration to vote with the Republicans in favor of the removal, while 2 Republicans sided with the administration.[43] This was a serious blow to Olson and Anderson, for uncertainty over the size and nature of the relief appropriation was now added to their already multitudinous relief woes. Pickets representing the Workers Alliance protested at the homes of southern California assemblymen who voted for the removal, thus making the administration's relations with the Legislature worse.[44] A committee entitled the Special Senate Committee to Investigate the State Chamber of Commerce, All Other Groups and Persons and Economic Conditions, and headed by D. Jack Metzger (Republican, Red Bluff) promptly announced that it would investigate the Workers Alliance. A month later this "Little Dies Committee" reported that the Workers Alliance had members in practically every relief project in the state, that it was controlled by Communists, and that relief clients used money paid to them by the state to pay their dues in the Alliance.[45]

The Olson administration was clearly in plenty of trouble with the SRA. Conservatives, unwilling to believe in the permanence of the unemployment problem, anxious to keep relief expenditures as low as possible and fearful that Olson and Anderson were building a political machine, lashed out at the "new philosophy." One of the ablest of them, Senator John Phillips (Republican, Banning) defined the "new philosophy" for the edification of the California Federation of Women's Clubs:

> ... first, one of liberality with the state's money; second, a policy which would completely wreck the morale of the people of the state beyond the point to which this damage has been already carried; and third, a policy of looking upon relief as some sort of a permanent institution like medicine or cosmetology to be professionalized and in which bureaus, departments and political organizations are to be built up as we see them building up in other functions of government.[46]

Senator Phillips said that the Legislature had the right to demand "a definite program" and chided the administration for not having any.

Olson fought hard for his relief appropriation, assailing "the economy blockers" in speech after speech. He told the California Conference of Social Workers that the administration was seeking "well considered plans" for work relief, contending that those who sought "a ready-made answer and a glib reply obviously do not understand the real magnitude of the job ahead." At the same time Olson reiterated his belief in the permanence of the problem of unemployment: "Hopes may be indulged and every possible encouragement given, but I do not believe that practices will be found whereby the unemployed portion of our citizens will ever be wholly absorbed by private industry."[47]

On July 11, just as both houses were about to vote finally on the relief appropriation for the new biennium, Olson said flatly that he would veto any plan to return relief administration to the counties, with the state paying part of the costs:

> It is obvious that such a measure would be going from bad to worse and in fact would spell chaos in the administration of unemployment relief of any kind. The problem of relief cannot be approached, much less solved, by leaving it to fifty-eight different boards of county supervisors, with fifty-eight different sets of rules, with fifty-eight different standards of relief. Some counties could not carry their share of relief.

The governor said that his general policy on relief was well known: to substitute works projects for the dole. "But our opponents pretend that this is not sufficient. No information is sufficient for them. They just naturally oppose *all* the plans and programs of this administration. They want the blue-prints of each individual project. They also want their own legislative committee to control the projects. In other words, they want to be relief administrators as well as legislators."[48] On the next day the Senate voted 23 to 14 to slash the relief appropriation to $21,320,000 for one year, with the requirement that the state was not to set minimum wages in agriculture. On this vote, the Olson administration had the support of 3 Republicans, while 6 Democrats voted for the cut.[49]

In the Assembly the situation was enormously confused. The relief bill as it came from committee appropriated $50,000,000. After the failure of two attempts to cut the amount, first to $24,000,000 and then to $30,000,000, administration opponents were able to block final passage. The vote was 48 aye (41 Democrats, 7 Republicans) to 27 no (all Republicans), with a two-thirds vote (54) required for passage.[50] As the Assembly clock had already been stopped—June 13 was the last day on which either house could consider its own bills—this action killed the Assembly bill. Administration leaders thus had to amend the Senate's relief bill, already passed by the upper house and thus eligible for consideration. Amid great chaos the Assembly voted to cut the amount appropriated from $50,750,000 (the figure to which it had been amended) to $42,500,000. On this roll call 29 Democrats and 6 Republicans voted to make the cut, while 26 Republicans and 8 Democrats voted against it!

But the bill was refused passage when the vote on the urgency clause fell eight short of the required 54.[51] On the next day (June 20), the Assembly voted first to expunge the vote whereby the urgency clause had lost, then to cut the appropriation to $35,525,000, and finally to pass the bill and send it to the Senate.[52]

The relief appropriation bill thus went into conference committee. It emerged as a piecemeal grant of $35,525,000, including $525,000 for an audit of relief funds by the state controller, with the condition that not over 40 per cent of the funds could be used during the three months beginning July 1, and not over 40 per cent during the succeeding three-month period.[53] Dewey Anderson was required to file a letter with the Legislature, pledging to agree to the appointment of impartial commissions representing all interests in farm wage disputes, and to abide by their decisions in deciding whether persons who refused to take jobs should be given relief, and stating that it was "not the desire nor the province of the SRA to set agricultural wages."[54] As a final part of the compromise, Governor Olson pledged to call a special session of the Legislature not later than February nor earlier than January. Both houses adopted the conference report, and the great relief battle in the 1939 Legislature was over.

The Olson administration had suffered a severe setback in its plans for work relief, at a time when the Richards Commission was still making its study. The administration's hands were effectively tied; not knowing what funds would be at its disposal during the biennium it could not plan effectively. The attitude of Olson's opponents was succinctly presented by the executive vice president of the California Savings and Building-Loan League: "This particular action is a combination of economy and political distrust. Between now and the time the $35,000,000 is exhausted, the Governor will be on trial and he may hesitate to wander off into a jungle of experimentation while the Legislature still holds the whip-hand. Moreover, with no new tax revenue, there will be no idle money to throw around and this should discourage waste."[55]

All of this was humiliating to Dewey Anderson, whose woes were truly monumental. As late as May 14 the governor had praised him as "a man of courage and imagination whose training and background make him particularly well qualified to understand this problem of unemployment."[56] But they had publicly disagreed on the question of nepotism in the SRA and Anderson had had to give way to Olson's disapproval of it.[57] Nevertheless, Anderson's own brother stayed on to complete a health survey for SRA, in spite of the fact that this bit of nepotism reportedly made some legislators "almost speechless with anger."[58] Although Anderson suffered somewhat from delusions of grandeur—understandable, inasmuch as he was the man who had the jobs to bestow in the administration—and was completely incapable of working harmoniously with the legislators, he ably represented the viewpoint of the professional social workers. Not having very deep roots in the Democratic party, he was not overly sympathetic to the clamor of "hungry" Democrats for jobs.

It was fairly obvious that Dewey Anderson's days in the SRA were numbered by the time the Legislature adjourned. In July Governor Olson precipitated a new crisis when he announced that the headquarters of the SRA would be moved from San Francisco to Los Angeles. The governor said that the reason for the move was the preponderance of the case load in the south, with 60 per cent of SRA clients living below the Tehachapis. Dewey Anderson seemed surprised by the announcement, saying that Olson had mentioned the matter to him "about a week ago," and that he was at present preparing a memo for the governor on the costs of the move. The move to Los Angeles was protested by San Francisco civic leaders and by northern California Democrats, and there was a general tendency in those quarters to term the move "a patronage matter." Governor Olson was adamant, however, and the move to Los Angeles was begun.[59]

Early in July the Los Angeles County Democratic central committee passed a resolution asking the governor to dismiss Dewey Anderson and appoint in his stead a "more practical" person.[60] The governor at first announced that he would hold a public hearing on the charges being levelled at Anderson, but then called it off.[61] On August 7 and 8 secret hearings were held in Los Angeles before Governor Olson, at which Anderson and his aides reportedly testified that all was going smoothly in the SRA, and at which charges of huge overhead expenses and administrative salaries were levelled at Anderson by southern California Democratic legislators and by Sam Houston Allen, the new Los Angeles County SRA director. The impending resignation of Anderson was rumored, and Governor Olson announced that Anderson was "unhappy." There were other rumors that Finance Director Phil S. Gibson wanted an appointment to fill a vacancy on the State Supreme Court, and that

Anderson would be offered the post of director of finance. Anderson said that he would be glad to accept it "if no political strings were attached to it."[62]

Anderson finally gave up on August 14. He sent the governor a remarkable eighteen-page open letter of resignation, taking that way to tell his tale of woe. And what a tale it was![63] He said that he had only accepted the post of state relief administrator after Olson had promised him that he would have full control of SRA operation, with "strict adherence to the non-partisan merit system in the appointment and retention of administrative personnel." Instead, Anderson charged, the governor had placed Walter T. Ballou on the administrative staff of SRA to take charge of political clearance. Anderson said that he had frequently found fault with Pomeroy's policies in the SRA. "However, I know positively," said Anderson, "that as bad as the Merriam-Pomeroy regime became, it never established a system of political clearance in the appointment of its staff. As a matter of fact, we now know that the vast majority of the staff even under the Republican administration, were registered as Democrats." He quoted a letter to him by Sam Houston Allen proposing to place fourteen politically prominent persons, untrained in social work, in the SRA. Anderson assailed the attitude typified by Allen: "It is vicious sophistry to presume that it is possible to staff the administration of SRA on a partisan basis and not have it reach down to the masses of reliefers, with most harmful results in discriminatory and wasteful practices." Anderson warned against any wholesale changes in SRA staff in the interest of politics, noting that SRA within a few months would have to defend its operations before a hostile Legislature. "It is a certainty that no Republican dominated Legislature will place in Democratic party hands a war chest in the guise of a State relief appropriation to build a political machine of State relief personnel."

While later he continued to profess a "warm attachment" for Olson and noted that he had not had the friendly coöperation of the Legislature during his days as head of SRA, Anderson caused the administration much grief. Olson at once announced that there was no reason for concern about the lowering of qualifications or standards in the SRA or about SRA succumbing to "any political pressure for jobs."[64] Two days later the governor said that he "preferred to treat the matter (of Anderson's resignation) with tolerance," although he did mention "the long statement Dewey Anderson saw fit to publicize clothing his disappointment in not being retained in the administration." On this occasion Olson reiterated that he would go through with the plan to move SRA headquarters to Los Angeles, saying that the action would cost no more than $32,000 and would result in administrative economy. He also admitted that "pressure is terrific" for jobs, but said that if all the SRA employees were removed and replaced with active political supporters of the administration there would be 20,000 others still pressing for jobs.[65] In spite of the governor's efforts to minimize the effect of Anderson's resignation, the administration had been placed in a quite unfavorable position. The Sacramento *Bee*, which had supported the Olson regime on most matters during the legislative session, published an editorial entitled "Dr. Anderson's Charges Demand A Thorough Probe," saying that the accusations "put the Democratic state regime very definitely on trial with the people of California." Said the *Bee:* "If these charges are disregarded and the conditions of which Dr. Anderson complains are not cleaned up, the Democratic Party in California is headed for plenty of grief."[66]

It had been rumored prior to the resignation of Anderson that the new SRA head would be Walter T. Ballou. However, Anderson's charges against Ballou had been serious ones, and Olson instead appointed Walter Chambers as acting administrator. Chambers, a professional social worker, was a member of the Los Angeles Council of Social Agencies, and had since July 1 been director of personnel in SRA. Chambers disclaimed any intention of making SRA a patronage vehicle: "I worked with Dr. Anderson ever since I came into the SRA July 1. He knows I didn't engage in any politics and he has no reason to assume I will." Chambers further announced that he was "thoroughly sold on a works program, to eliminate as far as possible the present direct dole."[67] Ballou at once resigned his SRA post, and it was announced that he had been "temporarily assigned to the Governor's office in San Francisco."[68]

It has been noted that the effect of the ouster of Plunkert in April and the resignation of Anderson in August "put Olson in bad with virtually all political groups."[69] But a more realistic view is that the elimination of Anderson and the move of SRA to Los Angeles strengthened the governor's position within his own party: "In yielding to the pressure of his supporters the Governor also strengthened his own political position. When he moved the SRA offices from San Francisco to Los Angeles

THE NIGHTMARE OF RELIEF

in the face of administrative reasons against the change, he gained enough patronage and power to dominate the Los Angeles Democratic machine and this gave him control of the state machine."[70]

But whatever temporary advantages there were from this move, Olson could look forward to more and more trouble with the SRA unless he could achieve an administration that could pass inspection by a hostile Legislature—and by the voters of California.

8 *the fight for public power*

NO PRINCIPLE WAS DEARER TO CULBERT L. OLSON THAN PUBLIC ownership of public utilities. As a state senator he had invariably supported measures to embarrass privately owned utilities (most notably the Pacific Gas and Electric Company) and bills to advance public ownership. As a candidate for governor he had repeatedly and clearly announced his views, pledging every effort to promote this favorite cause. In his inaugural address he said: "In this field of public utilities I see no justification for pyramiding private corporations owning or controlling the natural resources of the State and exacting tolls and profit, often exhorbitant, out of a business which should be no more than a nonprofit service to the general public for its health, comfort and welfare." Olson's chief interest was in the Central Valley Project, then under construction by the Federal Bureau of Reclamation. He especially wanted to see its electric power made readily available at lowest cost to consumers through the medium of publicly owned utility districts.

The Central Valley Project had begun on paper as a state project, with the passage by the 1933 Legislature of the Central Valley Project Act. The act provided that a state water project authority (consisting of the attorney general, treasurer, controller, director of finance, and di-

96

rector of public works) would administer the project, which was designed to transport excess water from the Sacramento Valley to the arid San Joaquin Valley. The project was to consist of dams and power plants at Kennett and Friant, a power transmission line between Kennett and Antioch—to provide power for pumping—and a series of canals to divert the water southward. Other purposes of the act were to control floods in the Sacramento Valley, to abate salt water in the delta area, and to improve navigation on the rivers. "In addition, construction of the Project would make a large amount of power available for the state's industries." To finance the project, the State Water Project Authority was authorized to issue $170,000,000 in revenue bonds, "provided, however, that the aggregate amount of such bonds hereby authorized shall be reduced by such an amount as the United States of America shall appropriate and make available as its contribution towards the constructing of said project or any unit thereof; . . ." A similar provision for a reduction in the amount of the revenue bonds was made for any contribution made toward the project from the state treasury.[1]

The Central Valley Project Act of 1933 was signed by Governor James Rolph, Jr., but held up to referendum by private utility interests. The governor called a special election for December 19, 1933, to decide the issue. Supporters of the measure included four of Rolph's Republican predecessors, including Senator Hiram W. Johnson, the California State Federation of Labor, the organized farmer groups, the Sacramento *Bee*, and chambers of commerce throughout the Central Valley. Opponents included the San Francisco and Los Angeles Chambers of Commerce. The act was approved by a close vote, 459,712 to 426,109.[2]

The State Water Project Authority, charged with the administration of the project, consisted of three elective officials and two appointees of the governor. This arrangement presumably was to keep the CVP "out of politics" through making it difficult for the governor to control its policies. The Authority differed from the familiar "special purpose district" only in name and in the absence of taxing powers. It was distinguished by its unique method of financing, for its revenue bonds were declared by law to be the obligations of the Authority alone.[3]

But supporters of the CVP from the beginning counted on federal aid. The state was in the depths of the depression and its financial situation was precarious. "An economically sound Central Valley Project was possible only with a federal grant, as large as possible, and provision for federally loaned, interest-free money."[4] The federal government entered the CVP in 1935 with the first of many appropriations for its construction, in response to the frantic lobbying of Californians and the activities of the California congressional delegation. In his letter appropriating funds to the CVP from the Emergency Relief Appropriation, President Roosevelt stated that "the funds hereby allocated shall be reimbursable in accordance with the reclamation laws." This meant that the construction of CVP would become a project of the Bureau of Reclamation, Department of the Interior. The dedication of Friant Dam, Shasta (formerly Kennett) Dam, and the Contra Costa Canal took place in 1937, the year Congress authorized the entire Central Valley Project as a Bureau of Reclamation activity.[5]

The chief opposition to the Central Valley Project was due to the plan to develop hydroelectric power. Shasta Dam was expected to generate 1,500,000,000 kilowatt hours of electricity annually, an amount equal to from 20 to 33 per cent of the northern California power market, 1942 demand.[6] As a federal reclamation project, the CVP's primary objective became cheap water, and the expected revenue from the sale of power was to pay for the project. "Where power revenues are not available to subsidize irrigation the effect is to increase the price which is charged for water."[7] The objections of the private utilities came from their fear of competition with cheap public power. This was quite understandable, for the California Central Valley Project Act of 1933 clearly defined the policy of the State Water Project Authority on sale of water and power: ". . . The authority shall grant preference to State agencies or other organizations not organized or doing business for profit but primarily for the purpose of supplying water or electric energy to their own citizens or members."

The advocates of public ownership of public utilities hoped at the 1935 and 1937 sessions of the Legislature to lay the groundwork for public distribution of CVP power. Senator J. C. Garrison (Democrat, Modesto) introduced bills at both sessions to authorize local units to issue revenue bonds to finance the acquisition of power distribution facilities and other projects (including fairs!) by a simple majority vote of the people. While revenue bonds "depend initially on the earnings of the Project for which they have paid for backing," it was not clear whether they had any general claim on the credit or taxing power of the issuing agency. California law required a two-thirds majority of the vote

cast for the authorization of revenue bonds and their issuance was restricted in other ways as well.[8]

Senator Garrison's revenue bond bills passed, but Governor Merriam
vetoed the 1935 measure, and the 1937 bill was held up to referendum
after Merriam had approved it. Senator Olson supported both Garrison
bills. At the 1937 session, as he had in 1935, Senator Roy J. Nielsen (Republican, Sacramento) introduced another revenue bond measure, considerably more restricted than the Garrison proposals. The Nielsen bill
was a simple amendment to the law permitting irrigation districts to
issue revenue bonds, and would have extended solely to districts organized to sell water and power the authority to sell revenue bonds to
the federal government or agencies created by the federal government.
The Nielsen revenue bond bill of 1937 passed the Senate with only four
dissenting votes (including those of Senators Olson and Garrison, who
were holding out for their more sweeping measure), but failed of passage
in the lower house when public ownership advocates split.[9] Senator
Nielsen charged that the "Power Trust" had encouraged legislators to
support the Garrison bill, knowing that it was vulnerable to adverse
court action or referendum, and to vote against the Nielsen measure.
Assemblyman Yorty supported Nielsen's charges, saying:

> The Garrison Bill is broad in scope. It allows the issue of revenue
> bonds for gas and other projects, and the power companies will
> be able to raise large slush funds from other utilities to contribute
> to fake taxpayer organizations on a referendum. If the Nielsen Bill
> were put up to a referendum, then the power companies would
> have to come out directly on whether the people should own their
> own power systems, and the voters would not be deceived.[10]

Evidence that public ownership advocates were out-maneuvered by the
representatives of the "power trust" was the fact that Seth Millington,
Democratic assemblyman from Gridley, who urged the passage of the
Garrison revenue bond bill, soon went on the P. G. and E. payroll as a
"lawyer" while holding his seat in the Legislature, and was conspicuously absent from the list of the Garrison bill's supporters at the 1938
election.[11]

The Garrison revenue bond bill was held up to referendum, and to
the delight of its enemies became Proposition 13 on the 1938 general
election ballot. The private utilities organized "front" organizations, to

THE FIGHT FOR PUBLIC POWER   99

fight the measure, such as the "California Tax Improvement Association," every cent of whose $23,430.99 expenditures was financed by power companies.[12] Senator Garrison was engaged in a fight for reëlection and Senator Olson was in the midst of his campaign for governor, but they lent support to the measure, which bore the endorsement of the California State Grange, the Sacramento *Bee,* and the San Francisco *News.* The campaign in behalf of Proposition 13 was poorly financed and lacked organization, while the opponents of the bill had the campaign management of the astute Clem Whitaker, plus a large campaign chest. The Garrison revenue bond bill was decisively rejected by the voters.

Governor Olson in his inaugural address deplored the "false propaganda" which had led the people to vote down the Garrison bill. But it was some time before it was clear just what direction Olson's advocacy of public ownership would lead him. At the outset of the 1939 session, Senator Garrison announced that he would introduce a new revenue bond measure "less far reaching in scope," confined to water, power and sewage disposal projects.[13] Speaker Peek called for the passage of a new revenue bond bill, during the period while the governor was still confined to bed by illness.

Governor Olson on February 15, 1939, sent a letter to Interior Secretary Harold L. Ickes in which he outlined a policy for the CVP. Olson proposed that the State Water Project Authority enter into a contract with the federal government whereby the authority would operate and maintain the project upon its completion. The governor said that the authority would repay the reimbursable costs of the project with revenues from the sale of water and power to public and private agencies. Olson further proposed that the state construct the steam plant, transmission, and distribution facilities with federal assistance, and that the state direct and assist in the organization of public districts to purchase water and power from the authority.[14]

Ickes replied to the Olson proposal with a letter dated April 15, 1939. He said that Olson had proposed to make the State Water Project Authority the agency to which the federal government would look "for repayment of its investment, both in water and power." But Ickes pointed out that there was an underlying requirement of the reclamation laws: "that repayment contracts shall be made only with agencies which have the power directly to assess and to create liens on the property of water users." As the state authority did not have such powers, Ickes said that it was doubtful whether it could be the contracting agency for the purchase of the principal part of the water.

Rebuffed in his efforts to secure state operation of the CVP, Olson turned to other methods of advancing the cause of public ownership. At first it appeared that he would push the sweeping new Garrison revenue bond bill.[15] However, in view of the hostility to any general revenue bond measure and of the disaster which befell its predecessor at the 1938 election, chances for the new Garrison bill were not bright.

It was late in May before it was clear just how the governor would seek to promote public ownership at the 1939 session. The measure he finally decided to push was drafted by the administration and handed to Senator A. L. Pierovich (Democrat, Jackson) for introduction. The Pierovich bill authorized the State Water Project Authority to use the proceeds from the sale of revenue bonds to assist in the financing of water and power distribution districts.[16] The amount of such bonds was to be $170,000,000, the figure set by the Central Valley Project Act of 1933. The authority had never issued revenue bonds, for the act provided that the amount would be decreased by any sums contributed by the federal or state governments, and the CVP in 1935 had become a federal project. Thus the proponents of the Pierovich bill spoke of "releasing" the bonds which had been authorized in 1933, even though this phrase caused some confusion. It was hoped that Pierovich's name might attract support by conservatives, for Pierovich was by no means a leading public ownership advocate. He had voted for a crippling amendment to the Central Valley Project Act of 1933 and had opposed the 1935 Garrison bill.[17]

The fight over the Pierovich bill was the most dramatic and hard-fought battle of the 1939 Legislature. On June 1, the Senate passed the measure by a vote of 24 (16 Democrats and 8 Republicans) to 15 (13 Republicans and 2 Democrats).[18] Olson intervened personally to secure the votes of doubtful Democratic senators. Republican Senator T. H. DeLap of Richmond charged that the bill was "circumventing the will of the people in their defeat of the State revenue bond law last fall."[19] Senator Peter P. Myhand (Democrat, Merced) gave notice of reconsideration, and on June 5 his motion was turned down by the slenderest of margins (19 to 18).[20] Following this action the Sacramento *Bee* published a cartoon entitled "The Main Event," portraying a tiny "Pierovich

Bill" wearing boxing gloves in one corner of a ring full of enormous, tough-looking fighters labelled "Power Trust Lobby."[21] Governor Olson, in his broadcast of June 11, urged his hearers to help him secure passage of the bill in the Assembly.[22] The administration secured a telegram of endorsement of the Pierovich bill from President Roosevelt. Secretary Ickes had already approved it.[23]

Following the passage of the Pierovich bill in the Senate, the Olson administration threw its full powers into the fight to get the measure through the Assembly. The first roll call came at 6:00 P.M. on June 20. When the measure failed to secure the required 41 votes, a "call of the house" was made and the clock was stopped, for this was officially the last day of the 1939 session.[24] Richard Olson and Director of Public Works Frank W. Clark set up a lobby headquarters in the office of Speaker Paul Peek. "Such lobbying and pressure methods as have seldom been seen were employed by the Governor and his men to get members to change their votes . . . Richard Olson, son and prime secretary to the Governor, was in and out of the administration 'high pressure' chamber. Some of the boys gave evidence of suffering from the 'bends' when they came out."[25] Don Allen (Democrat, Los Angeles) said that when the governor had asked him to support the bill he had told Olson that the people of his district had voted down revenue bond proposals, and that the governor had replied, "To hell with the people of your district, this affects the entire state." Allen said that he would continue to oppose the Pierovich bill, and challenged the Governor to come into his district and fight him.[26]

The opponents of the Pierovich bill used the argument that the CVP was primarily a water project, and that the issuance of revenue bonds for power facilities would endanger it. Assemblyman Millington asserted that the bill would permit the setting up of utility districts that might become insolvent, forcing the State Water Project Authority to take over their obligations. James H. Phillips (Republican, Oakland) read a letter from the Central Valley Project Association, an organization interested primarily in water, which opposed the bill because it prepared the way for making power the main product of CVP and water secondary.[27] Significantly, it was reported that opponents also said that the Pierovich bill "would have given the administration a fund of $170,000,000 to use in building a political machine to reward legislative friends and punish enemies."[28]

The final roll call on the Pierovich bill in the Assembly did not take place until 3:00 A.M. on June 22. After the Assembly had been deadlocked for twenty-four hours at 37 aye to 33 no, the call of the house was lifted and a new roll call taken. On this vote, Republican James E. Thorp of Lockford and Democrat Cecil King of Los Angeles, who had not voted before, pressed their "aye" buttons, and Democrat John W. Evans switched from no to aye and promptly collapsed. With the vote standing at 40 to 33 (one short), Republican Eleanor Miller of Pasadena switched from aye to no, and the vote stood at 39 to 34. The rear of the Assembly chamber was so packed with people, many of them lobbying, that it had to be roped off. Two Democrats, Jeanette E. Daley of San Diego and Rodney L. Turner of Delano, sat in their seats, steadfastly refusing to vote at all. One of the governor's secretaries had chartered a plane in Los Angeles to bring Assemblyman Godfrey A. Andreas (Democrat, Upland) up to Sacramento to vote, but the ailing Andreas was not able to leave his home.[29]

The Olson administration finally conceded the defeat of the Pierovich Bill at 4:00 A.M. on June 22. The vote then stood at 39 aye (34 Democrats and 5 Republicans) to 35 no (29 Republicans and 6 Democrats), two short of passage.[30] John H. O'Donnell (Democrat, Woodland), floor leader for the measure, apologized to his colleagues for "your great physical punishment which I've been responsible for," but said that the "progressivism" represented by the Pierovich bill would be the "established principles of tomorrow."[31]

Some observers felt that the Olson regime had injured the cause of public ownership by its high pressure lobbying for the Pierovich bill. However, the San Francisco *News* charged that the Legislature had "succumbed to the attacks of the power lobby." It said that the measure would be revived at the next meeting of the Legislature and its passage was "essential."[32] The Sacramento *Bee* said that "the vote revealed as nothing else could, the need for radical changes in the personnel of the legislature if the dominant lobby influence is to be curbed."[33] Governor Olson termed the vote "only a temporary defeat," and said that he was sure that the voters would elect a Legislature which would vote for "adequate outlets for water and power": "I expect to carry on the fight pledged in my party platform and in my inaugural address to bring to the people, at cost, through public agencies, water and power, which as natural resources, are their birthright."[34]

Although he never again came so close to success as he did with the Pierovich bill, Governor Olson never gave up the fight for public power. Throughout the remainder of his regime he sought means to advance his beloved cause and he relished the chances to slug it out with the Pacific Gas and Electric Company.

As early as June 29, 1939, one week after the defeat of the Pierovich bill, Olson announced that he would resubmit the measure at the special session of the Legislature scheduled for January or February, 1940.[35] As the time for the special session drew nearer, however, his determination appears to have wavered. The Sacramento *Bee* reported on December 28 that the governor was "not decided yet" on whether to include a revenue bond proposal for the CVP among the subjects for consideration by the Legislature. Speaker Peek asked the governor to leave the measure out of the call, considering it to be a "lost cause" that would only goad the administration's opponents into taking harsher measures against its proposals.[36] The governor was advised by Senator Garrison not to include "a single controversial issue unless it is a real emergency."[37] However, Secretary Ickes advised that the state should make itself "ready to act as a power distributor or ready to act in the interests of public power distributors."[38]

Under great pressure from California public ownership advocates, as well as from federal officials, Olson two days before the opening of the special session amended his call to include the request for a revenue bond measure.[39] He asked the Legislature to amend the Central Valley Project Act to authorize the issuance of up to $50,000,000 in revenue bonds. The governor said this "would place the State in a position to contract with the federal government for the distribution of the electric power developed by the project, instead of leaving the federal government and the people to be served at the mercy of a private power distribution monopoly which would be its only purchaser."[40] However, the State Water Project Authority refused to recommend this new bond bill and the public utilities committees of both houses kept it from emerging for a roll call vote.[41]

Olson's next major move was to announce himself in favor of a Central Valley Authority, to be modeled on the notably successful Tennessee Valley Authority. He said that he had the support of President Roosevelt in this and that enabling legislation would be introduced in the Congress.[42] Olson in his first biennial message, on January 6, 1941, supported the CVA idea, but asked the Legislature to pass a measure similar to the Pierovich bill as a "safeguard."[43] The legislators refused to do so, not unexpectedly, following the repeated failure of the State Water Project Authority to advocate such a bill. The attitude of Attorney General Earl Warren was interesting. As a member of the Water Project Authority he refused to support the Olson revenue bond proposals, yet at the same time he advocated federal construction of a steam plant as part of the Central Valley Project. At this time the Pacific Gas and Electric Company was conducting a successful campaign to block federal appropriations for the steam plant.[44]

The idea of a Central Valley Authority was short-lived. Director of Public Works Frank W. Clark soon found that a number of California congressmen would not support the proposal, largely due to the opposition of Interior Secretary Ickes.[45] Clark denied at a meeting of the State Water Project Authority on March 19 that he had ever recommended a TVA for the Central Valley, although on the previous November 26 he had advocated before the same body a "federal regional authority."[46] A hostile "grass roots convention," participated in by some Republican legislators demanded that Ickes "give California back to the people," thus throwing further confusion into the ranks of the advocates of a regional authority.[47] The most ardent supporter of the Central Valley Authority proposal was the California State Grange, which on October 24, 1941, endorsed the plan at its annual convention. The CVA idea was flatly rejected by resolutions of the California Farm Bureau Federation and the National Reclamation Association.[48]

Repeatedly rebuffed by the Legislature, and unable to make any progress with his plan for a Central Valley Authority, Governor Olson never let up his campaign for public power. In October 1941, Olson appeared with Secretary Ickes at a rally in the San Francisco Civic Auditorium in behalf of the latest proposal for municipal distribution of Hetch Hetchy power. Here Olson declared open war upon the Pacific Gas and Electric Company, saying that he wanted to see the company "taken over by the state" and urging "a fight to the finish."[49] But Olson once more suffered defeat. San Francisco not only rejected the Hetch Hetchy plan, but also elected new supervisors, who promptly asked Congress to amend the Raker Act to permit the city to continue to sell Hetch Hetchy power to the Pacific Gas and Electric Company. Governor Olson at once wired the House public lands committee in opposition to the amendment. The supervisors failed to secure the change in the Raker Act they sought and the Hetch Hetchy problem remained unsolved.[50]

The fight for public power had been long and bitter, and Governor Olson had been completely unsuccessful in his efforts to get new legislation. Undaunted, the governor campaigned for reëlection in 1942 as an advocate of public ownership of public utilities. Certainly no one could dispute his claim to the title!

9 *ham and eggs,*
loan sharks, and oil

ANY REJOICING THAT CONSERVATIVE CALIFORNIANS MAY HAVE indulged in following the defeat of the Ham and Eggs scheme at the 1938 general election was soon to prove premature. On the first Sunday after the election, 8,000 supporters of the pension scheme packed Shrine Auditorium in Los Angeles and the promoters were delighted by the most enthusiastic audience they had ever had.[1] Thus the second Ham and Eggs drive was launched, to the consternation of those who had just finished the fight against the first scheme.

By the end of January, however, there were signs of serious dissension within the high command of the pension movement. Sherman J. Bainbridge, "The Voice," resigned from the organization in a bristling letter to Willis Allen. Bainbridge pointed out that Lawrence and Willis Allen operated the Cinema Advertising Company, which handled the publicity for the pension plan. "If the Allens are to continue to receive salaries for services rendered to Life Payments, they cannot in all honor collect a commission in a dual capacity as agents." Bainbridge scored the leadership of the movement for its failure to coöperate with the Olson administration: Instead of backing the newly elected "progressive" governor, and thus earning the right to call for a special election on the

107

pension plan, they had tried to coerce Olson into giving them the election under threat of a recall and had thus associated with "reactionaries," who were unsympathetic with any old-age pension plan, no matter how it was drawn.[2]

But the second Ham and Eggs campaign went on, in spite of Bainbridge's defection. In April Lieutenant Governor Patterson told a pension rally in San Francisco that he "knew that the governor would call a special election."[3] In May Governor Olson was presented with petitions signed by some 737,000 persons asking that he call a special election on the pension plan, which had simultaneously qualified for a place on the next general election ballot through the presentation to the secretary of state of petitions with signatures of 366,180 electors. On May 18 the governor spoke briefly to a Ham and Eggs mass meeting at the Fair Grounds in Sacramento, promising that he would call a special election at a date that would be satisfactory to the Ham and Eggers. But at the same time the governor pointedly refrained from endorsing the scheme: "While I am in sympathy with its objectives, I do not want you to infer from my presence here, or the granting of your petition, that I believe in the feasibility of the plan proposed in this measure, or that it would accomplish its objectives, if adopted."[4] The usually friendly Sacramento *Bee* took Governor Olson to task for promising the election, saying that the governor knew that the plan was without merit, and implying that he had yielded to political pressure.[5]

On May 21 Governor Olson explained his reasons for agreeing to a special election. One was that so many people, a third or more of the voters, had come to believe in the Ham and Eggs scheme: "Their emotions will continue to be aroused; their sacrificing contributions made and their thoughts and activities centered upon securing the adoption of this measure until it is voted upon." He said that his other reason was that he did not want other issues on the 1940 general election ballot, including the election of the President, to be overshadowed or confused by the presence of the Ham and Eggs scheme.[6]

Meanwhile the pressure on the governor to fix the date of the election mounted. The Assembly gave an added impetus to the Ham and Eggs movement when it refused to approve an increase in old age pensions from forty to fifty dollars per month. The roll call on this was 24 aye (21 Democrats and 3 Republicans) to 44 no (28 Republicans and 16 Democrats).[7] The administration, at the time engaged in its fight for a relief appropriation and the adoption of the governor's tax program, was not friendly to the increased pension unless taxes to pay for it could be levied.

Early in June, Willis Allen told a mass meeting of his followers in Los Angeles:

> I think that in a few days now we will have the glad news about the date for a special election. And that date is going to be satisfactory to you.
> The newspapers would lead you to believe that this election is going to take place away next fall or next spring.
> Uh, huh. It's going to take place this summer.[8]

At another rally, Allen introduced Lieutenant Governor Ellis E. Patterson as "our next governor" and Patterson in turn endorsed the pension plan: "To all reactionaries in California, let me say—I don't know whether Ham and Eggs will work or not, but I'm anxious to see something done and I personally am going to vote for it."[9]

On July 1, Governor Olson issued a proclamation calling for a special election on November 7, 1939. The governor said that the secretary of state had advised him that ninety days were necessary for preparations, and he noted that some local elections were already scheduled for that date.[10] November was eminently unsatisfactory to the Ham and Eggs leaders, who wanted an early vote, while the enthusiasm of their followers was at its peak. Olson's proclamation calling for the election was unpleasant to the Ham and Eggs directors for another reason as well, as in it Olson denounced the pension plan: "I would be false to my own conscience and sense of duty if I failed to here express my belief that, if adopted, this measure would fail to achieve its objectives, would disappoint the hopes of its supporters, and would retard instead of aiding our progress to a better economic order."

The second Ham and Eggs plan differed substantially from the 1938 measure.[11] While it included provision for thirty dollars per week in stamp warrants for those fifty years of age and over, it also wrote the current three per cent sales tax into the state constitution and added a three per cent gross receipts tax. It provided that the warrants should not be subject to the gross receipts tax, presumably in order to make them more desirable than money as a medium of exchange. It also required the governor to appoint as the first administrator of the pension system either Roy G. Owens or Will H. Kindig, both Ham and Eggs leaders. The administrator would have wide powers of appointment, control over the new state banks to be set up, and authority to call special elections to decide amendments to the initiative constitutional amendment setting up the system. The people would choose the "State Retirement Life Payments Administrator" at general elections beginning in 1944, for a four year term, with the first administrator (Owens or Kindig) serving at least until January 1945.[12]

Governor Olson got into the fight against the second Ham and Eggs measure in August, but in a rather left-handed way. The San Francisco *News* published a special eight-page supplement on "Objectives and Accomplishments of California's Democratic Administration," featuring a center two-page advertisement against Ham and Eggs that included large pictures and statements of President Roosevelt and Governor Olson.[13] An official publication of the Democratic state central committee protested bitterly, charging that copy for the supplement had been written by George Killion and David L. Foutz of the governor's staff, and quoting the telegram sent by Governor Olson to the publisher of the *News* in protest against unauthorized use of the pictures of the president and himself. The party paper asked editorially, "Is Big Business Trying to Kidnap Gov. Olson?," and spoke disparagingly of the number of "new" Democrats in the Olson administration (including Finance Director Gibson, Killion, and Foutz).[14] Governor Olson then sent a second telegram to the publisher of the San Francisco *News*, apologizing for his earlier criticisms, saying that he had learned that copy for the supplement "had the approval of a publicity man connected with my administration without my knowledge." Killion was punished by being removed from his $5,000 post as assistant secretary to the governor and appointed a deputy director of finance at $7,500 per year![15]

The fight against the Ham and Eggs plan of 1939 once again found the state's newspapers united. Much of the criticism of the scheme was like that expressed by Eugene Lyons: "It is the quintessence of demagogy: economic perpetual motion in one-syllable words for those who think with their intestines."[16] Other opposition centered about what the *Nation* termed "the fascist blueprint" in the amendment.[17] In a radio broadcast to farmers, conservative Republican Senator John Phillips of Banning said: "I think Mr. Hitler must look with envious eyes on the powers given the Administrator under California's Ham 'n' Eggs proposal."[18] The opposing argument in the voter's handbook assailed the method of designating the administrator and the latter's lack of responsibility to either governor or legislature; the inflationary aspect of the warrants; and the effect upon governmental units of the requirement that they accept the warrants in payment for taxes and other charges. "Inevitably the senior citizen would be without any pension, the needy without relief, the public employee without salary, the worker without wage, government without funds." Upton Sinclair, who had considerable claim to the title of founder of the old age pension movement in California, added his name to the long list of the plan's opponents.[19]

As late as November 5 the Republican papers were twitting Governor Olson about "his refusal to take a definite stand on the Ham and Eggs pension issue."[20] This was in spite of the governor's remarks in his July 1 proclamation, which had earned him the animosity of the Ham and Eggs leaders. The governor's rather equivocating attitude toward the first plan caused him embarrassment, and he took to the air on November 5 to explain his position. Said Governor Olson: "It cannot be truthfully claimed by anyone that I ever in the primaries, in the election or since, have stated that I believe the plan proposed in Proposition No. 1 or in the Ham and Eggs proposal of 1938 is workable, or that it would do other than tragically disappoint its supporters."[21]

Lieutenant Governor Ellis E. Patterson, almost alone of the state's important political figures, lent his support to the Ham and Eggs scheme of 1939. The official argument in favor of Proposition 1 was signed by Roy G. Owens, "Engineer-Economist" and first choice of his fellow promoters for the plan's administrator. Owens' emphasis is shown by the conclusion of his argument:

> CALIFORNIANS, show the way to security!
> CREATE more jobs for workers.
> CREATE more business for merchants and manufacturers.
> REDUCE your taxes by
> VOTING *YES* ON "RETIREMENT WARRANTS"

The Ham and Eggs promoters emphasized in their campaign literature the soundness of their proposed "Credit Clearings Bank" and the convertibility into money of the proposed warrants thirty days after date of issue.

Interest in the 1939 special election was extraordinary, largely because of the Ham and Eggs pension plan, and 82.48 per cent of the registered voters of the state cast ballots. This was a substantially larger turn-out than that for the 1938 general election, when almost the same number were registered and only 74.65 per cent bothered to vote. The Ham and Eggs plan was decisively defeated, failing to carry a single county. The vote was: yes, 993,204; no, 1,933,557. Willis Allen and Roy G. Owens, speaking for the Ham and Eggers, were vitriolic in their denunciation of Governor Olson, announcing that their group would at once begin the circulation of petitions for his recall.

Olson did not relish being on the conservative side in any battle. Nor did he want to lose the "senior citizen" vote. He announced that he was prepared to ask the Legislature to memorialize the federal government to assume full responsibility for old age pensions of sixty dollars per month at sixty years of age, or at least lower the age limit to sixty years and increase the federal contribution so that the state could do so. He said also that, pending federal action, he was prepared to ask the Legislature to lower age requirements for the current pension to sixty years and to waive the rights of the state and counties to property left by pensioners.[22]

Meanwhile the Ham and Egg leaders were going ahead with their plan to recall the governor, whom they looked upon as a turncoat. Conservatives, who had opposed Olson in 1938 and throughout the legislative session, rallied to the defense of the governor. Said Hearst's San Francisco *Examiner:* "The attempt to recall Governor Culbert Olson of California for his wise and patriotic opposition to the foolish and fanatical Ham and Eggs proposal should be vigorously denounced and resisted." The *Examiner* said that "a vote of confidence and congratulation" ought to be given the governor, even by those who disagreed with the other parts of his program.[23] Others coming to the aid of Olson on this occasion included former Governor C. C. Young and James Rolph III, son of the late former governor.[24]

Although he tried to explain away the now famous telegrams of endorsement of the first Ham and Eggs plan, Olson was embarrassed by his own somewhat devious role in 1938. While his opposition to the second scheme was of great importance, conservatives and many liberals blamed him for calling the special election in the first place. And he had acquired the undying animosity of the Ham and Eggs leaders, who were exceptionally able haters.

The "Loan Shark" Acts

When the Legislature convened in 1939, California and Nevada were the only states which had failed to place some limit on the interest or charges personal property brokers could require the borrowers of small sums to pay. Small loans were defined as those in amounts of $300 or less, and were extended usually to persons of moderate circumstances, in emergencies, by personal property brokers or unsecured money lenders, often at high rates of interest and high carrying charges.

The basic California legal restriction on usury was a constitutional amendment adopted in 1934, which set the maximum contract rate of interest at 10 per cent per year but excepted certain types of lenders (including personal property brokers), the regulation of whom was left to the Legislature. A measure setting the maximum rate of interest at 2 per cent per month on unpaid balances up to $500, and 12 per cent per year on amounts over $500, passed the Legislature at the 1937 session only to be pocket-vetoed by Governor Merriam.[25]

Newspapers strongly supported regulatory measures aimed at the "loan sharks." Numerous bills were introduced in the 1939 Legislature to regulate the practices of personal property brokers and unsecured money lenders. These measures fell roughly into three groups: the "legal aid" bills, the "lenders" bills and the "1 per cent"–"2 per cent" bills.[26]

The "legal aid" bills, introduced by Democratic Senator John F. Shelley of San Francisco and Republican Assemblymen Albert J. Wollenberg of San Francisco and James Phillips of Oakland, were sponsored by the San Francisco Legal Aid Society and Attorney General Warren. They prescribed that the maximum charge by personal property brokers and unsecured money lenders for small loans should be 3½ per cent per month on the first hundred dollars, and 2½ per cent per month on the balance between $100 and $300.

The "lenders" bills, introduced by Republican Senator Ed Fletcher of San Diego and others and by Democratic Assemblyman Gordon Garland of Woodlake and others, were much more generous to the "loan sharks." They prescribed a maximum interest rate of 10 per cent *per year*, but added that the lender could make an initial charge of seven cents on the dollar, a monthly charge of two cents on the dollar on the unpaid balance if the loan were unsecured, and a monthly charge of 1 per cent on the dollar (up to a maximum of two dollars per month) if the lender were a personal property broker. In addition, the borrower was required to pay any necessary statutory fee, and the legal maximum on small loans was raised to $500. Because the assembly bills drew the most attention, these measures were also known as the "Garland bills."

Bills of the "1 per cent" or "2 per cent" type were numerous, but attracted little support until Governor Olson entered the fight. On April 2, he announced that he would recommend to the Legislature a constitutional amendment and bill "fixing reasonable rates of interest and service charges to cover *all* lenders; and with special regulatory provisions for special classes of lenders as the facts appear to warrant."[27] Four days later Olson summoned the authors of the various "loan shark" bills, and told them that while he had not yet determined what the proper rate of interest on small loans should be, he was prepared to support legislation to eliminate excessive rates. On April 18 he sent to the Legislature a special message urging the adoption of effective regulatory measures to deal with the problem.[28] The governor accompanied his message with a bill prescribing a 2 per cent per month maximum charge on small loans plus a specified service charge, "a rather loosely worded 'catch-all'" in the opinion of the chief student of this subject. Olson's recommendations were incorporated by amendment into a bill which passed the Assembly on May 25 only to die in Senate committee.[29]

The effect of the Olson recommendation, however, was to convince the authors of the "legal aid" bills that they must lower the rates prescribed in their own bills if they were to get the governor's signature, or even secure passage in the Legislature. Shelley's bills had passed the Senate unanimously on April 10, but as the budget had not yet cleared that house and as they implied an appropriation, there was some doubt as to their legality. Late in May Shelley and Wollenberg got their bills amended to provide a maximum charge on small loans of 2½ per cent per month on the unpaid balance up to $100, and 2 per cent on that between $100 and $200.

Following this action the situation in the Legislature got quite confused. On May 30 the Assembly passed the Wollenberg-Phillips bills by a wide margin, but on June 1 it also passed Garland's "lenders" bills. On June 16 the Senate passed both the Garland and the Wollenberg-Phillips measures.[30]

Governor Olson had reason to be pleased with the result of his actions on "loan sharks." While he did not secure the inclusive restrictions on all small loan rates he had sought, he had helped force the supporters of the "legal aid" bills to lower their maximum rates. The governor signed the Shelley bills, and the Wollenberg-Phillips bills, for in spite of their being almost parallel the measures had some differences, and the governor decided to play safe.[31] However, he pocket-vetoed the Garland bills, and issued an explanation: "These bills permit of the charging of much higher rates of interest per month than the bills signed—so high in fact as to permit borrowers to repay their loans only with the utmost difficulty if at all."[32]

The interests opposed to "loan shark" regulation did not give up easily, however. Unsecured lenders simply became personal property brokers, thus evading the restrictions aimed at themselves, and joined with the personal property brokers in securing a referendum on the Shelley and Wollenberg-Phillips property brokers acts.[33] On September 13, petitions to hold the acts up for referendum, bearing more than the needed 132,573 signatures, were filed with the secretary of state, and the measures went on the ballot for the special election of November 7.[34]

Governor Olson asked the voters to approve Propositions 3 and 4, saying that they "embody a part of the anti-usury, anti-loan shark program of my administration."[35] He made a one-minute transcribed broadcast which was used in the campaign in behalf of the bills.[36] The press of California was almost unanimous in support of the "loan shark" measures, and the voters approved both overwhelmingly. The Shelley Act carried all but five small counties, and the Wollenberg-Phillips Act all but four. The vote was:

SHELLEY ACT (PROPOSITION 3)
yes   1,853,663
no   753,480

WOLLENBERG-PHILLIPS ACT (PROPOSITION 4)
yes   1,850,811
no   732,873

Although these measures were essentially nonpartisan, having the support of Republican Attorney General Warren and the Republican press, they represented the achievement of a portion of the Olson platform, and the governor had played an important role in securing the approval of the voters.

HAM AND EGGS, LOAN SHARKS, OIL   115

The Atkinson Oil Bill

When Governor Olson took office there were no restrictions upon the production of oil and gas in California. The state had been represented in the drafting of the Interstate Compact on Oil Conservation, which had set up machinery for production quotas for each member state, but California had never ratified it.[37] Governor Olson in his private law practice had come to know a number of "independent" oil operators, and had been impressed with the idea that they were "exploiters," interested in getting all they could out of their wells "here and now."[38] The governor had also played an important role in the fight over state-owned oil in the tidelands at Huntington Beach, where he had fought the battle of the small producers against Standard Oil. Olson had pledged himself to conservation of natural resources in his platform and speeches of the 1938 elections, and his inaugural address contained this paragraph: "It shall be the policy of this administration to conserve and protect our great natural resources and control their exploitation in the common interest. The use of these resources and their products is essential to the lives of all of the people of the State, and must be obtained at the lowest possible cost to the people."

Maurice E. Atkinson, freshman Democratic assemblyman from Long Beach, introduced at the 1939 session a bill which had been handed to him by CIO leaders representing oil workers.[39] The measure, designated as the "California Oil and Gas Control Act of 1939," set up an "Oil Conservation Commission," consisting of the director of natural resources (chairman and administrative officer), the director of public works, and the director of finance, all members of the governor's cabinet and appointees of the governor. Section 10 of the Atkinson oil bill included among the powers of this commission the authority to investigate the petroleum industry in all its aspects and the power "to limit and prorate production of crude petroleum and natural gas."[40] The interest of representatives of the oil workers in such legislation is easily explained, for the regularization of production would presumably have resulted in stabilization of employment.

The Atkinson oil bill lay buried in committee until early in the morning of June 15, when it was withdrawn to the floor by an Assembly vote of 44 to 31.[41] Speaker Paul Peek had at first tried to hold the measure back, knowing that it had the support of some major oil companies and might bring the administration to grief, but following the exertion of pressure on Governor Olson by the national administration (principally by Interior Secretary Harold L. Ickes, the watchdog of conservation), the governor had secured approval of the measure by a Democratic caucus.[42]

The pressure in the Assembly was terrific. June 13 had been the last day on which that body could consider bills originating on its side of the Legislature. Administration leaders stopped the clock and held the house in continuous session for over thirty-four hours, until the Atkinson bill finally passed.[43] After the measure was approved by a party caucus, Speaker Peek himself took a leading role in securing passage, having the state printer set up a third-reading calendar containing the Atkinson bill prior to its passage on second reading, in order to forestall the anticipated objection of the veteran Republican floor leader, Charles Lyon of Los Angeles.[44] The vote on final passage by the Assembly was 44 aye (31 Democrats and 13 Republicans) to 28 no (21 Republicans and 7 Democrats). Three Republicans protested that consideration was illegal, being within seven days of adjournment, and secured the printing in the journal of a postcard addressed to one of them, bearing the postmark "San Francisco, June 14, 1939, 7:30 P.M." Three Democrats inserted in the journal the following explanation of their vote: "Our vote for the Atkinson oil control bill was not cast on the basis of our own knowledge, and we regret the precipitate manner in which, necessarily, the subject was considered on the last day for the disposal of the Assembly bills. We voted our confidence in the judgment and wishes of the Governor."[45] The Atkinson bill passed the Senate on June 19, by a vote of 27 aye (16 Democrats and 11 Republicans) to 11 no (9 Republicans and 2 Democrats).[46] Notable on this roll call was the opposition of Democratic Senator Robert W. Kenny of Los Angeles. Governor Olson signed the bill.

The Olson administration was greatly embarrassed by charges that it had "sold out" to the Standard Oil Company. The Governor said the Atkinson oil bill was "the most important bill passed by this legislature; a bill which would not have passed, but for the fact that large interests in the oil industry, as well as small interests, found themselves compelled to admit the falsity of the idea that government must not interfere with or control private business." He said also that "it opens the way to public control and regulation of the production, transportation, marketing, and the prices to the consumers of the oil and natural gas resources of this State and their products."[47]

The Atkinson oil bill, bitterly opposed by the "independent" oil interests, was held up for referendum and appeared on the ballot at the special election of November 7, 1939. In addition to the governor, supporters of the measure included President Roosevelt, former President Hoover, Secretary of the Interior Ickes and all the metropolitan press of northern California (including papers normally as far apart as the Sacramento *Bee* and the Oakland *Tribune*). Olson emphasized the regulatory aspects of the measure, while conservatives emphasized the conservation features.[48]

The opponents of Proposition 5 used the slogans "Stop Standard Oil Political Dictatorship" and "Keep Gasoline Prices Down."[49] The political complexion of the opponents, like that of the proponents, was badly mixed. The Los Angeles *Times* was flatly opposed to the measure, saying that its passage would bring "State control" of the oil industry "which, by the admission of its backers, would be extended as soon as possible to similar government control of other natural resources."[50] Democrats opposing the Atkinson Bill included Senator Kenny, erstwhile administration floor leader; Lieutenant Governor Patterson; Assemblyman Millington, leader of the "economy bloc"; and J. Frank Burke, Olson's southern California campaign leader in the 1938 primary.

The Atkinson Bill was decisively defeated by the electors. The state vote was: yes, 1,110,316; no, 1,755,625. The measure lost in southern California, where the vote in the eight counties below the Tehachapis was: yes, 443,405; no, 1,123,565. The Atkinson oil control bill actually carried twenty-five counties of the state, including San Francisco and Alameda, and was accorded a majority of approximately 15,000 north of Tehachapi Mountains. For once Governor Olson found that his support came from northern California and his opposition from southern California.

The fight over the Atkinson bill was a curious one from start to finish, illustrating well the chaos that so frequently characterizes California politics. The effect was to injure the administration, for it added to the growing list of militantly anti-Olson forces the wealthy and formidable "independent" oil interests, without gaining the permanent support of the "major" oil companies.

10 *the revolt of the assembly*

AS 1940 OPENED, GOVERNOR OLSON LOOKED FORWARD TO MORE
trouble with the Legislature. He had committed himself to call it into
special session in January or February to provide more funds for unemployment relief. The problems of the State Relief Administration
were mounting all the time, as relief rolls climbed. With charges and
countercharges flying, the Olson administration could trace most of its
woes directly to the SRA. The governor hoped for the defeat of his chief
foes at the 1940 elections, but meanwhile he had to try to implement his
program as best he could, in spite of the strength of his enemies and his
own very limited supply of weapons.

However, under the law the governor had the authority to limit the
subjects upon which a special session could legislate. On December 17,
he announced that he would ask for relief funds for the remainder of
the biennium, new taxes, liberalized old age pensions, a state housing
authority and approval of constitutional amendments reorganizing certain state departments.[1] But before he issued his formal call, he circu-
larized his friends, asking for their advice. One of these, Senator Garrison, replied that he would stand by the governor "on any program you
feel is necessary," and went on to analyze the situation with considerable
foresight.

119

First we just as well realize that we are weaker, especially in the Senate, than we were at the last session, and that the wolves are after us stronger if that could be possible. Second, more good can be accomplished by keeping Olson as Governor than by anything this Legislature will do in its best behaved moments. Third, the enemy will quite adequately finance their members while the real sacrafice [sic] will fall upon and be a penalty to your friends who must pay this extra expense out of their own pockets, if there is any there to get. Fourth, the enemy is in control of far the greater part of our means of communication, and will twist every happening at the special session to your own disadvantage if at all possible. Fifth, a long drawn out chaotic session would play right into their hands and be a useless strain upon you and your friends that you do not deserve. You will be blamed with everything that comes out of this special session as they are now trying to convince the People that you are responsible for everything that is included in the call. For these and many other reasons I feel very strongly that you should make it as short and snappy as possible. I would not include a single controversial issue unless it is a real emergency. It is not your fault that these matters were either not taken care of at the last regular session or have to wait until the next.[2]

Olson nevertheless went ahead with his plan to give the Legislature wide scope by asking approval of the proposals noted above, plus a new revenue bond bill to promote public power.

That anti-administration assemblymen would attempt to oust Speaker Paul Peek at the special session had long been rumored. Wesley E. Robbins, political writer for the Oakland *Tribune*, reported late in October that a number of anti-Olson legislators had attended a banquet given by Fred E. Stewart of the State Board of Equalization for his employees. Robbins said that they had discussed plans to remove Peek and replace him with a conservative Democrat. He reported that the favorite candidate was Gordon Garland of Woodlake, and that "probably" ten Democratic assemblymen were in favor of the move.[3] On December 6, Garland formally announced his candidacy for speaker, and said that it was likely he would try to unseat Peek at the special session.[4] On January 28, ten anti-administration Democrats met together, agreed upon Garland as their candidate, and then joined the Republican caucus to work out plans for the *coup*.[5]

When the Assembly met on January 29 the members voted down, 43 to 33, a resolution to retain the officers from the regular session. After hearing Alfred W. Robertson (Democrat, Santa Barbara) re-nominate Peek, they listened to the enormous voice of Seth Millington (Democrat, Gridley) proposing Garland:

> The man I nominate will not hold us here hour after hour so that men can be brought in here from their sick beds to vote. He will not delay announcing the votes whether it meets with his approval or not, in an effort to change the result.
> Nor will our candidate have any pipe line to the corner office. He will bring back constitutional government to California, restore the time honored separation of the legislative from the executive branch.[6]

Then, by the same 43 to 33 vote, the Assembly elected Garland.[7] One Republican, Michael J. Burns, of Eureka, who had supported much of Olson's program during the 1939 session, voted for Peek, but all the other Republicans present supported Garland. Nine Democrats voted for Garland—neither Peek nor Garland voted for himself—and 32 for Peek. The nine Democratic rebels were: Don A. Allen, Los Angeles; Jeanette E. Daley, San Diego; Earl D. Desmond, Sacramento; Clinton J. Fulcher, Lookout; Chester F. Gannon, Sacramento; Seth Millington, Gridley; Rodney L. Turner, Delano; Ernest O. Voigt, Los Angeles; Clyde A. Watson, Orange. Garland and his nine Democratic supporters (with the exception of Voigt, whose defection came to many as a surprise) had been consistent opponents of the Olson program at the 1939 session.

Upon his election, Gordon Garland mounted to the rostrum and, with photographers' bulbs flashing, pulled out by its wires a telephone which the newspapers reported "was connected directly with the office of Governor Olson."[8] This gesture was supposed to signify the breaking of the "pipe line to the corner office." Peek denied that the telephone was on a direct line to the governor's office, contending that it was an ordinary telephone which had long been situated at the clerk's desk, but which he had taken up to the rostrum so that he could telephone frequently to the hospital, where his little daughter was ill.[9] Whatever the facts about the telephone may have been, Garland's action symbolized the declaration of independence which the anti-Olson majority in the Assembly had made.

In his speech of acceptance, Garland told the Assembly he wanted to keep "any State agency from embarking on improper activity," and to reverse "the increasing trend toward collectivism." He expressed his opposition to higher taxation and his hope that the Legislature would enact unemployment relief legislation which would "reduce the possibility of abuses to the minimum. . . ."[10] The post of speaker pro tem of the Assembly was given by unanimous vote to a Republican, Gardiner Johnson of Berkeley, after incumbent Democrat Hugh P. Donnelly of Turlock refused to stand for reëlection. Donnelly assailed the ten bolting Democrats, declaring: "I don't want my name considered for speaker pro tem or any other office until this house is controlled by democrats."[11]

The election of Garland as speaker was a great blow to the Olson administration. Garland, white-haired at 42 and distinguished looking, had been a member of the lower house since 1937. He operated a general ranch at Woodlake, Tulare County, where he raised oranges, lemons, grapes, walnuts, hogs and cattle.[12] He had voted against almost the whole of the Olson program at the 1939 session, and was conservative to the core. Governor Olson had announced on October 7, 1939, in Fresno that he would enter Garland's district in 1940 and "ask for his defeat as an obstructionist." Said Olson of Garland: "He has not been faithful to the party platform and spent his time getting through the loan shark bill the loan sharks wanted and then offered to vote for the Pierovich Central Valleys bill if I would sign his loan bill." Garland had defiantly replied to the governor's charge, saying that the situation had been reversed: word had come to Garland from the governor's office that Olson would sign the Garland loan bills if Garland would vote for the Pierovich bill.[13]

On the day following the Assembly's ouster of its speaker, Governor Olson called into his office the 33 members who had voted for Peek and announced that he had chosen Peek to replace the late Secretary of State Frank C. Jordan. As the position did not require confirmation, the governor had gotten revenge of a sort.[14]

Speaker Garland announced his committee appointments on February 1.[15] His Democratic supporters were given the most important chairmanships: public utilities, social service and welfare, rules, judiciary codes, ways and means and revenue and taxation. Of the 55 chairmanships, 35 went to Republicans, 9 to Garland Democrats, and 11—mostly unimportant—to Olson Democrats. All important committees were packed with enemies of the administration. The rules committee included only one member who had supported Peek. Six of the nine members of the oil industries committee had voted against the Atkinson oil bill at the

1939 session. Eight of the eleven members of the public utilities committee had voted against the Pierovich bill. Nearly every member of the revenue and taxation committee had opposed the whole of Olson's 1939 tax program. A clear majority of the social service and welfare committee had opposed the governor's relief program. Ways and means was packed as heavily with opponents of Olson as Peek had packed it with friends in 1939. The Assembly was now completely in the hands of the "economy bloc."

Tempers were frayed by the Assembly revolt. Governor Olson lashed out at the ten "economy bloc" Democrats: "These 10 men should resign from the Democratic party and join the Republican party, because they talk, act and vote Republican."[16] The Sacramento *Bee* assailed the Assembly majority: "Hopes that the special session of the legislature would accomplish something of a constructive nature in the public interest were blasted yesterday when a combination of reactionary Republicans and equally reactionary Democrats seized control of the assembly."[17] The Sacramento County Democratic central committee repudiated Gannon and Desmond, and similar actions were reported under way in the home counties of the other Garland Democrats, at the urging of the Olson administration. But the conservatives fought right back. Mrs. Daley said, "I feel I'm a better Democrat than before." Millington said, "I'm supporting the state of California, not the looting politicians."[18]

The Olson administration now had to watch the whole of its program bottled up in unfriendly committees and most of the activities of the Legislature concentrated upon investigations of the SRA. However, the February special session was to bring it one more bit of grief.

The "Dictograph Case"

On February 21, Speaker Garland took the floor on a point of personal privilege, to announce that he had discovered a microphone in his room in the Hotel Senator.[19] The Assembly then voted, 58 to 12, to create the "Assembly Investigating Committee on Interference with the Legislature" and provide it with $5,000.[20] Garland named Harrison W. Call (Republican, Redwood City) as chairman, and the other four members included only one administration supporter.

The facts of the "dictograph case" were complicated.[21] Police traced the microphone wires to a room occupied by Robert E. Voshell, a private investigator formerly associated with Howard R. Philbrick in the legislative graft investigation of 1938 and later in the employ of SRA upon Philbrick's recommendation. In Voshell's closet the police discovered a sound recording device, which they removed on February 21. Shortly after this removal, Voshell apparently discovered his loss and fled the state after borrowing money from Philbrick. When summoned back to California by Philbrick, Voshell stated that he was in the employ of Paul H. Rowe, Philbrick associate and operator of a recording concern. Rowe in turn said that he had been engaged in an investigation of legislative graft and had planned to look to Philbrick for payment of Voshell and himself, depending upon their results. Voshell admitted that he had listened over his equipment to conversations in Garland's room since February 2, but said he had heard nothing incriminating.

Howard Philbrick was a leading figure in the administration, having been Olson's Director of Motor Vehicles since September, so this disclosure did the governor little good. Nor was Philbrick the only member of the Olson regime implicated. George F. Cake, agent for Federal Laboratories, Incorporated, testified that Lieutenant Colonel Charles Henderson, Governor Olson's military aide, had in October secured from his organization a device for recording conversations. Cake told investigators that on February 14 Henderson told him that the equipment was not working properly and directed him to go to Voshell's room on the eighth floor of the Hotel Senator, bring the equipment down the stairs to the fifth floor and see what was wrong with it. Cake said he had done so, and found that it had been hooked up to an improper microphone. Police had found another recording device in Voshell's room, but had not removed it. Henderson denied that it had been his, and produced his own, which he said was used to record the governor's extemporaneous speeches. Henderson denied the whole of Cake's testimony about the activities of February 14.

Another twist to the complicated story of the "dictograph case" provided further circumstantial evidence involving the governor's office. It was soon revealed that Voshell had been given a check drawn on the governor's secret fund for "extraneous" investigation while employed by the SRA as an auditor, and that Rowe, who was then in the employ of Voshell, had been given an even larger amount from the fund. The checks had been signed by M. Stanley Mosk, Executive Secretary to Governor Olson.

After weeks of headlines, Philbrick resigned. He denied that he had ordered the installation of the dictograph or that he had known of its installation until February 21, but admitted that he had hired Rowe to continue the graft investigation after he himself had become Director of Motor Vehicles. Governor Olson denied that he or his office staff knew anything about the dictograph. He said that the only criticism that might be leveled at Philbrick was that, after hiring Rowe, Philbrick "did not supervise or control his activities so as to prevent the use by him, or anyone employed by him, of improper methods."[22] It was announced on April 16 that Philbrick had been hired to run the Central Casting Corporation by the Association of Motion Picture Producers, at a handsome salary.[23]

The majority report of the Call committee (signed by all members except F. Ray Bennett, Democrat, Los Angeles) was a severe indictment of the administration.[24] It began with a statement that "rumors" of spying on members of the Legislature had circulated during the 1939 session. "The rumors were rendered capable of belief by administration announcement of a 'purge list' composed of members of the Assembly obnoxious to the administration because of their independence in voting for or against pending legislation in a matter [sic] contrary to administration desires." The report complained that administration officials had hampered the efforts of the committee and had deliberately withheld information, but said that the committee "is satisfied it has established guilt for the dictograph incident." After implicating Philbrick, Voshell, Rowe, Mosk and Henderson, the report censured the governor:

> The Governor of the State of California, Culbert L. Olson, must also share a burden of responsibility for tolerating his direct appointees, secretaries and aides, or persons being subsidized from funds appropriated for the support of his office to engage in such activities. If the Governor is ignorant of the activities of these employees, it constitutes extreme negligence upon his part to suffer them to use State moneys appropriated to him without knowledge for what purpose it is being used and to permit his appointees such extreme latitude in their pursuits.

The Call committee majority put no credence in the testimony of Colonel Henderson, who had by this time resigned his position, and they accepted Cake's story fully. Their report described Philbrick as "the spear of this investigation," and accused him of being a confirmed snooper, careless of the rights of others. The report excoriated Mosk for his issuance of a statement to the press on March 6 charging that the whole incident was a "frame-up" instigated by the enemies of the administration. The report said that the committee believed Mosk had been "truthful" when he denied that he had any knowledge of the dictograph in Garland's room, but charged him with "gross negligence" regarding the funds under his jurisdiction and with "indiscretion." The majority recommended that the Legislature either place restrictions on the governor's secret fund or eliminate it entirely from the budget, that the attorney general be requested to give an opinion on the use of money from the secret fund for investigative purposes, that the attorney general be requested to investigate any irregularity in the payment of SRA funds to Voshell, and that the Legislature place severe restrictions upon the use of dictographs and sound equipment.

Assemblyman Bennett's minority report was a defense of the Olson administration.[25] It charged that "politics played a major role throughout the entire incident." It said that the planting of the dictograph was due to the "over-zealous work" of investigators engaged in an inquiry into corrupt lobbying. Bennett charged that "a small clique" on the Call committee had run its hearings with an aim of "getting" Philbrick. It pointed out that the committee had uncovered no evidence that Philbrick had known of the dictograph before February 21. It noted that Rowe had admitted he had not been paid for his spying on Garland, and that Mosk had merely paid Voshell and Rowe for other work, prior to the installation of the dictograph. Bennett said that, while the committee had been charged with investigating "interference with the legislature," it had done nothing about checking the activities of the lobbyists. The report disagreed with the recommendation for restricting the use of the governor's secret fund, but supported, with some qualification, the recommendation that the use of dictographs and similar equipment be restricted.

The Struggle Over SRA

While the revolt of the Assembly and the "dictograph case" were the most dramatic events of the Capitol in the early months of 1940, the real struggle was over the State Relief Administration. The nightmare of relief remained the most difficult of Olson's problems, and the chief source of friction with the Legislature.

The administration's long-range relief plans were at last clearly stated, when the governor accepted in full the recommendations of his Commission on Reemployment, embodied in its report of September 30, 1939. The Commission proposed that a new state planning board, responsible to the governor, be set up as a coördinating agency among the departments of the state government and as a liaison body with federal agencies "in attacking the problem of unemployment." It advocated that a works program for the unemployed be established and controlled by the SRA. It said that "direct production projects" should be set up by the SRA to create consumer goods, which would in turn be distributed to members of the coöperatives. The Commission proposed that the SRA buy California farm surpluses and distribute them to the unemployed. It advocated the establishment of a state housing authority, to coöperate with the federal government in a rural housing program. Among the specific administrative reforms it recommended for SRA was the introduction of the civil service system for all employees, through examination and not "blanketing in."[26]

So pleased was the governor with these proposals that he chose the Commission chairman, John R. Richards, to be director of finance, following the resignation of Director Phil S. Gibson to take an appointment on the State Supreme Court. Under the severe restrictions imposed by the Legislature upon the expenditure of relief money, the director of finance was necessarily an integral part of relief administration.

The winter of 1939–1940 was the most critical in the history of the SRA. Rolls climbed to unprecedented heights, while the percentage of total relief cases carried by SRA mounted. The case load at the end of December was 104,101 (compared with 70,063 at the end of December 1938) and at the end of January reached 114,693 (compared with 87,473 at the end of January 1939).[27] These totals represented heads of families as well as individual single persons, so that the total number being supported by SRA was about 400,000 on January 30, 1940. The percentage of total federal and state relief cases being carried by SRA was 53.5 on December 31 (as compared with 38.0 a year before) and reached 56.0 on January 31, 1940 (as compared with 44.2 for the same date in 1939).

Criticisms of the SRA had persisted, growing more vocal as the date of the special session neared, and Olson was forced to take cognizance of them. In his January 7 broadcast he asserted that "in 1939 we discharged fewer persons from the State Relief Administration and hired fewer new persons than did the preceding Administration during 1938," and denied that SRA was ridden with job politics.[28] On January 14 the governor announced that he was appointing a five-man SRA Board of Personnel Standards and Appeals headed by Finance Director John R. Richards, to act in a manner similar to the State Personnel Board.[29]

When the Legislature met, the Senate interim committee on relief, headed by John Phillips (Republican, Banning), made its report.[30] This

SRA CASE LOAD, SHOWING PERCENTAGE OF STATE AND FEDERAL RELIEF CASES CARRIED BY SRA

Month	1939		1940	
	Total	Per cent	Total	Per cent
January..............	87,473	44.2	114,693	56.0
February.............	97,438	45.4	112,354	54.6
March................	95,045	45.8	96,230	49.9
April.................	91,403	46.3	82,472	47.3
May..................	81,884	44.8	72,731	45.7
June.................	74,621	42.7	70,060	49.4
July..................	78,306	47.4	66,243	45.4
August...............	79,139	53.3	53,691	41.3
September............	82,796	53.6	47,315	38.0
October..............	84,188	52.5	39,264	33.6
November............	94,153	53.2	39,263	32.9
December............	104,101	53.5	45,027	35.7

committee, like all interim committees created in 1939, was hampered by two decisions of the California Supreme Court, which declared that the Legislature had no authority to create committees with power to sit after adjournment. The report consisted of State Relief Administrator Dewey Anderson's letter of resignation and a private investigator's findings on SRA. The latter report, privately financed, was prepared by the firm of Edwin N. Atherton and Associates of San Francisco. This Atherton report charged that the State, County and Municipal Workers of America (CIO) exerted an "unwarranted influence" in establishing SRA policy and that the Workers Alliance worked closely with SRA employees who belonged to the CIO union. By these means, the report said, relief clients were encouraged to join the Workers Alliance in order to get preferred attention. The report further charged that numerous shifts in policy and personnel had resulted in a breakdown of morale within the SRA itself. The point of view of the Atherton report is indicated by this excerpt: "A dangerous condition indicated is the increasing number of people who think in terms of guaranteed support by the State; people who have lost pride and independence and demand they be permitted to live in idleness." The Atherton investigators relied principally upon the testimony of "disgruntled" SRA workers. Many of these aimed their criticisms especially at Los Angeles County SRA Director Sam Houston Allen, whom they charged with inefficiency, political-mindedness, and closeness to the Workers Alliance.

In view of these charges—and of the Assembly's action in ousting Peek—it was a grim Olson who came before the Legislature to request more relief funds on January 29. He told the legislators that money for SRA would be exhausted by February 5, and that if they could not make their appropriation for the rest of the biennium by then, he would have to ask for an emergency grant.[31] He asked $95,500,000 for relief for the period ending June 30, 1941, noting that if the Legislature were to set a ceiling on monthly family budgets, establish a three-year residence requirement, and adopt more rigid eligibility rules, some $30,000,000 could be saved. However, the governor contended that "no such reduction is possible without causing untold misery and hardship." Admitting that his budget request for relief for the whole biennium had been only $73,300,000, Olson noted that the SRA case load was currently almost double what it had been the year before, largely due to the curtailment of WPA activities in California. He further recommended a provision in the appropriation bill limiting administration costs in SRA to not over 15 per cent of the amount expended.

Instead of taking up at once the governor's request for SRA funds for the remainder of the biennium, the Legislature passed an emergency appropriation of $1,600,000 to carry the SRA until the end of February. Olson, forced to sign the bill, noted that its "Little Hatch Act" provisions forbade SRA employees to be politically "active" while at the same time it made it unlawful to deprive any person of employment in the SRA because of his political activity![32]

But the main concern of the February session was the investigation of the SRA. Assemblyman Samuel William Yorty (Democrat, Los Angeles) secured approval of a resolution setting up a five-man Assembly relief investigating committee, with an appropriation of $500.[33] Speaker Garland, in accordance with custom, appointed Yorty chairman. The other members were Jack B. Tenney, Los Angeles Democrat and close

REVOLT OF THE ASSEMBLY   129

friend of Yorty, with a similar left-wing background; Seth Millington, Gridley Democrat, leader of the "economy bloc"; and two Republicans, Harrison W. Call of Redwood City and Lee T. Bashore of Glendora.

Ever since December Yorty had been charging that Communists occupied key positions in the Los Angeles County SRA headquarters. Yorty's outburst had come as a great surprise, for, as Earl C. Behrens noted, Yorty had been "recognized as one of the principal left-wingers of the Legislature."[34] In 1937 and 1939 Yorty had supported measures to repeal the California Criminal Syndicalism Act, and he had been one of those advocating the 1939 resolution asking the president to lift the arms embargo on the Spanish Republic. Very early in the Olson administration, Franklin Hichborn had written: "Yorty of Los Angeles, is a bit to the left of the administration, but counts himself decidedly of the administration."[35] His former associates lost little time in denouncing Yorty when he began his attacks upon the SRA. Labor's Non-Partisan League, his staunch supporter in the past, resolved that it would oppose him for "any office which he may seek in the future."[36] Sam Houston Allen told reporters that if Yorty came to his office on official business, he would be respectfully welcomed, but added: "Such a visit will be interesting because it will be the first time Mr. Yorty has come to see me without seeking political favors."[37]

By the time the Yorty committee began its hearings in Los Angeles on February 5, the SRA was in great confusion. On January 26 Governor Olson had announced that on the advice of his new SRA Board of Personnel Standards and Appeals, and in view of the recent move of state SRA headquarters to Los Angeles, he had ordered the abolition of the Los Angeles County headquarters as an economy move. At the time, Sam Houston Allen said that the action of the governor had been "carefully considered" and in line with policies of economy in SRA.[38] A few days later, however, Allen went to Sacramento in the company of a delegation representing Los Angeles liberals and left-wing labor, and Governor Olson, following a conference with Allen et al., announced the temporary withdrawal of the order closing the county headquarters. Phillip M. Connelly, state CIO president and member of the delegation calling on the governor, charged that the closure had been made not for purposes of economy but in order to get rid of Allen: "Because Assemblymen couldn't dictate to Allen and his assistants the men who were to work for the SRA they have sought his job."[39] Yorty assailed Olson for suspending his closure order, charging that the governor "is yielding to pressure of communistic groups, and those who have been fooled by them." Tenney said that Don Healey, Los Angeles County secretary of LNPL and one of the delegation which persuaded Olson to suspend his closure order, had participated in secret meetings with Communists when plans were made to gain control of Local 47 of the American Federation of Musicians in Los Angeles, of which Tenney (the composer of "Mexicali Rose") had formerly been president.[40]

The Yorty committee hearing on February 5 in Los Angeles was a spectacular affair. Sam Houston Allen flatly denied that there were any Communists in the county SRA headquarters, and made no secret of his contempt for the hostile committee, especially Messrs. Yorty and Tenney. Paul Cline, executive secretary of the Communist Party of Los Angeles County, told reporters that he wanted to testify before the committee: "Ironically enough, the last time I had the pleasure of talking to Mr. Yorty and Mr. Tenney together was right in Mr. Yorty's own apartment in Sacramento, whither he had invited William Schneiderman, state secretary of the Communist party, and myself to discuss certain 'problems' the nature of which I am not at all adverse to divulging." Cline further said that Yorty had a "personal grudge" against the Communist party because it had refused to support him for mayor in the 1938 recall election.[41]

On February 12 the Yorty committee submitted a report charging that the Communists for the past two years had been successfully engaged in infiltrating into the SRA "with a view toward domination of the same."[42] It discussed the Communist technique of the "united front," by means of which they were able to secure key positions in such organizations as the American League for Peace and Democracy, the Workers Alliance, the SCMWA, and the Los Angeles LNPL. The Yorty report said that Sam Houston Allen had given the Communists "a free reign" in the Los Angeles county headquarters, and that as a consequence SRA personnel was "completely demoralized."

In view of these charges—and of the general suspicion with which the administration's plans for relief were by now regarded—Olson never got his desired SRA appropriation. The Senate early in February passed three bills, the effect of which would have been to provide funds for SRA until June 30, after which relief administration would be returned to the counties, though it would still be paid for—in part at least—with state funds. While the rural Senate voted 26 to 10 for the main county administration bill,[43] it never emerged from Assembly committee.

The governor had long charged that the county administration proposal was being fostered by "certain large business interests intent on avoiding taxes on their profits" and anxious to shift the relief burden onto local property taxpayers.[44] Senator Shelley of San Francisco contended that more political pressure could be exerted upon fifty-eight scattered relief administrations than upon one centralized state one.[45] After the Senate had passed the county relief bills on February 3, Olson charged that the plan would force counties to raise property taxes, permit only dole relief, force the abandonment of the school lunch and food stamp program, and eliminate state sponsorship of WPA and NYA projects. He said that he would veto the bills if they reached his desk.[46]

However, county administration of relief was the great goal of the members of the "economy bloc." An indication of the reason for this attitude is found in remarks made by Senator Peter P. Myhand (conservative Democrat of Merced): "Sending relief back to the counties means that relief will be policed by neighbors and chiseling kept to a minimum. Administration will be under constant scrutiny of those who pay the bills, and they will make sure that the local units are not dictated to by subversive groups who now sit on both sides of the conference table in the SRA."[47] A new county relief bill by Assemblywoman Daley passed the lower house on February 23 by a vote of 41 to 35.[48] On this roll call 10 Democrats and 31 Republicans voted for the Daley bill, and 32 Democrats and 3 Republicans voted against it. On the same day the Senate passed the measure, by a vote of 27 to 7, all of the opponents being Democrats.[49] The governor at once vetoed it and no attempt to override was made in the Assembly, where it would have been impossible for proponents to secure the required 54 votes.

Rebuffed in their efforts to eliminate the SRA, Olson's enemies then worked out a bill to appropriate $12,200,000 for unemployment relief until June 1, with severe restrictions upon both expenditures by SRA and qualfications for relief. This measure established a three-year residence requirement for relief, and provided a five-year residence requirement for those entering the state after February 1, 1940. Reducing dole budgets substantially, it placed a 15 per cent limit upon expenditures for administration, and prohibited relief clients from paying dues to "subversive" organizations. Governor Olson promptly vetoed this measure, too. He said that the appropriation was 19 per cent less than the actual expenditures for the same period in 1939, while SRA rolls had to carry far more people. He further noted that the bill would eliminate any serious effort to change over to a program of work relief and would inflict severe hardship upon persons on relief.[50] Notwithstanding the objections of the governor, both houses on February 23 passed it over Olson's veto, the Senate by a vote of 30 to 5, and the Assembly by a vote of 56 to 22.[51]

Another feature of the "economy bloc" relief program was further investigation of SRA. On February 24 the Assembly voted $3,000 more to its relief investigating committee.[52] A much more elaborate unit, the "Joint Fact Finding Committee on Employment," was set up by joint resolution on the same day. This 17-man committee, headed by Senator Phillips (Republican, Banning) was given $30,000 and: "authorized and directed to gather, assemble, study and analyze all facts relating to any and every phase of employment, with a view to formulating such a plan and preparing and submitting such legislative measures as will enable the State to bring about and assure the gainful employment in private enterprise of all its able-bodied citizens...."[53]

On February 25 the Legislature declared a recess until May 13, or earlier at the call of its officers. This device was employed instead of adjournment, to permit legislative investigating committees to work in the interval. The funds appropriated for unemployment relief were to be exhausted by June 1, and the "economy bloc" expected to work out a relief program for the rest of the biennium in the interval. Olson, stubbornly defiant, proclaimed:

> I shall continue to fight for the progressive policies and measures no matter how powerful the opposition or how rough the going may be. I will rely on the people's support in this fight. I believe it can and will be won as the other fights for the common good have been won when their leaders have remained true and steadfast to the trust and confidence imposed in them by the people. I have experienced legislative defeats before only to find victory ahead by faithfully keeping up the fight.[54]

Between February and May, newspapers were full of charges and countercharges emerging from the hearings of the Yorty and Phillips committees. Olson deplored the emphasis of the committees investigating relief "upon charges of waste, inefficiency and chiseling," saying that these things had been going on in relief from its inception and that his administration had been long engaged in locating and removing such things. The governor contended that consideration of these matters so exhaustively had precluded consideration of real problems, such as means for putting the unemployed to work producing things for themselves! "*We* say that when a man works for his living there can be no such *thing* as chiseling. . . ."[55]

Three important committee reports, in addition to that of the Call committee investigating "interference with the legislature" already noted, were delivered to the first special session after it reconvened on May 13. The Assembly revenue and taxation fact-finding committee recommended against any new revenue measures, contending that the "present tax system is capable of taking care of the State's immediate needs if economy is practiced in the spending of State money."[56] The joint fact-finding committee on employment (Phillips) majority report, signed by all but two members, urged the consolidation of the Department of Social Welfare, SRA and the Department of Employment; county administration of relief with state supervision and financial support; and a five-year residence requirement. It assailed the governor's program for work relief and production-for-use, and the continued presence of "subversives" in the SRA.[57] However, Olson refused to agree to a legislative request that he call a new special session and thus permit the Legislature to enact the wide-ranging recommendations of the Phillips committee. The assembly relief investigating (Yorty) committee reported further on "Communist infiltration" into the SRA.[58] It reiterated its former contention that the chief source of Communist strength had been the presence of Communists in various "united front" organizations, especially in the 1938 campaign of Olson. The Yorty committee charged that the administration had not seriously attempted to oust "subversives" from the SRA. The Assembly authorized an additional $2,500 for the Yorty committee on May 24, by a vote of 44 to 12.[59]

The fight over the appropriation for relief at the May session was once more bitter and involved. After complex maneuverings, in which Olson supporters fought a losing battle, a bill emerged from conference committee bearing an appropriation of $24,347,091 for the period from June 1, 1940, to March 31, 1941. As the measure had passed both houses by a two-thirds majority, Governor Olson made no attempt to fight back with another veto, and as funds were rapidly running out, he signed the bill on May 29. But in a radio broadcast shortly after the recess of the Legislature, the governor protested that the appropriation was inadequate and the eligibility rules were so severe "that thousands of persons, honestly and desperately in need, will go hungry, because they cannot qualify for any relief from their destitution." At the same time Olson warned that the anticipated expansion of economic activities due to the national defense program would not take care of the unemployment problem.[60]

The State Relief Administration, as a result of the restrictions of the February and May appropriation bills and the charges of the various investigating committees, went through a very chaotic period during the first half of 1940. The number of persons employed by SRA dropped precipitately, and as the administrator and the Board of Personnel Standards and Appeals had to choose which employees should be discharged, the whole atmosphere of SRA was permeated with charges and countercharges. Assailed from both right and left, Administrator Walter Chambers spent a very unhappy several months. As early as January, the Los Angeles County Democratic central committee had asked for the ouster of Chambers, and as the months went by the demand had become more insistent.[61] At least three groups were interested in the removal of Chambers: left-wingers who resented the purges of SCMWA members from the SRA; patronage-minded Democratic politicians who blamed Chambers for firings of the faithful; and conservatives who believed that Chambers was not drastic enough in his measures of reform (and who distrusted anyone close to Olson). Finally, Chambers quietly resigned, effective June 30.

Governor Olson appointed Sidney G. Rubinow as his third state relief administrator. The appointment was made upon the recommendation of the SRA Board of Personnel Standards and Appeals, headed by Director of Finance John R. Richards.[62] Rubinow at the time of his appointment held the post of assistant director of agriculture, and formerly had been engaged in public relations work for the California Farm Bureau Federation.

A man of great energy, Rubinow began at once to speed up firing of employees of SRA. On August 9, he told the Phillips committee that he had made only one appointment since he took office, and had discharged from 1,300 to 1,400 employees. Rubinow told the committee of what he had found in SRA: "In my 30 years of experience in public life I've never seen as chaotic a condition as I found in SRA, both as to personnel and operation. Its only purpose seems to have been lost sight of. I've reduced its mechanism to the purpose for which it exists." He asked the legislators to provide enough money for the SRA until the Legislature met again (the Phillips group was then assessing the request of the administration for additional funds for the remainder of the third quarter of 1940), and requested an opportunity to operate on a "decent basis" until then. Mrs. Daley replied to Rubinow: "We've heard that before. First from Dr. Anderson, then from Mr. Chambers and now from you. They're out on their ears and now we hear that pretty soon you'll be out on your ear. What can we do?"[63]

The September session of the Legislature, called by Olson partly to provide for additional SRA funds for the remainder of the quarter, was "something of a personal triumph for Rubinow."[64] A bill appropriating $1,450,000 for relief for the remainder of September and $650,000 for the extension of the food stamp program sailed through both houses with only one dissent, that of Assemblyman Bashore, who objected to the Assembly's devoting but twenty minutes to a discussion of the measure.[65] Rubinow won great praise from Assemblyman Yorty and Senator Phillips, the chief thorns in the side of the Olson administration in matters of relief, and Republican Assemblyman Frederick F. Houser, member of the Phillips committee, said: "The legislative committee has confidence in Rubinow but the majority hasn't any confidence in the governor. I don't see how long Rubinow will remain on the job. I doubt if he will be there much after November 6th." Mrs. Daley regretted that the Phillips committee had not approved a proposal that would have tied up all relief money in the event the governor fired Rubinow and kept it tied up until the Senate had approved its successor.[66]

While Rubinow was winning friends and influencing people, his time was running out, as the "economy bloc" legislators soon recognized. He had lost his great friend and sponsor when Finance Director John R. Richards resigned in September, after a long series of disputes with Governor Olson. Among other things, Richards had been quoted as saying that "some of the SRA employees run the gamut from near-morons to morons and crooks." The governor charged that Richards had not adequately backed up his own financial estimates before the Legislature, thus giving aid and comfort to the enemy.[67] In his letter of resignation, Richards told the governor he had indeed made the remark on SRA employees, but that he had "great confidence in the correction of the abuses" in SRA through the activities of Rubinow.[68]

Governor Olson, in his review of his administration's activities before the Democratic state convention at Sacramento on September 19, praised by name most of his department heads, but Rubinow was conspicuously absent from his list. Before the assembled Democrats, the governor discussed at length the problems of relief, and the failure of the Legislature to approve his plans to get rid of the dole. He contended that it had been equally impossible to predict the great rise in the relief load during the past winter (due to WPA cuts) and the "spectacular drops" of the past few months (due to defense work).[69]

Early in December Rubinow, in testimony before the Phillips committee, challenged the accuracy of statements by Finance Director George Killion and Director of Professional and Vocational Standards Dwight W. Stephenson. Rubinow told the committee that the SRA Board of Personnel Standards and Appeals, of which Killion and Stephenson were members, was assuming powers belonging to the state relief administrator in the rehiring of personnel, and that he was abolishing the board.[70] Finally Governor Olson, on the eve of his departure for a trip to Washington, dispatched a special delivery letter to Rubinow dated December 8, which began: "I feel sure you will be pleased to be relieved of the office of State Relief Administrator and will welcome this notice that upon receipt of this letter you are so relieved." The governor's letter announced that he had appointed Ralph J. Wakefield, chief of the SRA Camp Bureau, as acting administrator.[71]

The ouster of Rubinow and appointment of Wakefield brought on another great crisis in the hectic history of the SRA. Senator Phillips at once announced that by the ouster of "the best relief administrator the state has had," Governor Olson had restored "the influence in SRA of the Walter Ballou group, that has desired all the way through to use the State Relief Administration for political purposes."[72] The San Francisco *Chronicle* said that the ouster of Rubinow was "as cheap a piece of politics as has ever been pulled off in this State," and thundered: "The time has come for the Legislature and the people of California to make clear and expressive their contempt for the sort of politics the Governor persists in practicing."[73] Dewey Anderson wrote to the governor from Washington, where he now occupied the post of executive secretary to the Temporary National Economic Commission, saying that "surely" Wakefield's appointment was "only very temporary":

> Even so, it is alarming and will further demoralize a badly con-
> fused administrative staff who must know, as you and I do, that
> he is wholly incapable of discharging the duties of Administrator.
> I would not defend Rubinow's administration but I am greatly
> concerned as to the fate of the SRA and its program before the
> January Legislative session. There the fight will be made to return
> relief to the counties. Wakefield will be utterly helpless before
> these men.[74]

Anderson urged Governor Olson to find a man of recognized ability and integrity at once.

Fortunately for everyone concerned, increasing economic activity in the state due to the national defense program in the summer and fall of 1940 resulted in a marked increase in employment. When the SRA case load began its "normal" seasonal drop in the spring of 1940 it kept on dropping, failing to pick up at all until December. Thus the members of the "economy bloc" in the Legislature could point to the constantly decreasing case load and SRA payroll as evidence of their foresight and of the effectiveness of their tightening up of relief qualifications. Rubinow received their accolades for his discharge of increasing numbers of SRA workers, many of them ardent Olson Democrats. Governor Olson, with his frequent warnings against the assumption that defense spending would automatically solve the unemployment problem, had been proved to be a poor prophet (he admitted nearly as much before the Democratic state convention). The administration's luck once more had been bad, and leaders of the opposition did not fail to take advantage of it.

On December 14 the newspapers announced that the members of the Phillips committee had been summoned to Los Angeles to hold hearings on the ouster of Rubinow and appointment of Wakefield. This marked the beginning of the end of SRA, and properly belongs in a discussion of Olson's second Legislature.

11 *elections —
and threats of elections*

MUCH OF CALIFORNIA'S ATTENTION DURING 1940 WAS TAKEN UP by elections, and in these Olson and his administration played important roles. Though 1940 brought the governor his greatest glory—when he headed the delegation to the Democratic national convention and returned as Democratic national committeeman—it also brought him bitter disappointment when his attempt to "purge" his opponents in the Legislature failed. And, through most of the year, hanging over the governor's head was the constant threat of a recall election.

On December 7, 1939, Olson told the Los Angeles Democratic Luncheon Club that "conditions seem to demand the drafting of Franklin D. Roosevelt for a third term." Olson reiterated this in his speeches to the Los Angeles Jackson Day Dinner on January 8 and to the Oregon Commonwealth Federation at Portland on February 17. The governor was outspoken in his praise of the national administration, telling his hearers that the fight must go ahead to extend the reforms so far achieved under the New Deal.[1]

Olson, however, was faced with the problem of Democratic party factionalism in every attempt to work out a slate of delegates for presentation at the presidential preference primary. At least four significant

139

groups of Democratic politicians were, with varying degrees of strength, endeavoring to win control of the Democratic party in California. These were:

1. The McAdoo-Creel group, consisting principally of federal office holders and their satellites, strongest in the San Francisco Bay area, but badly crippled by the defeat of Senator McAdoo in the 1938 primary and the passage of the Hatch Act.

2. The right-wing group, consisting of anti-Olson Democratic legislators and other conservatives, numerically weak but well-financed.

3. The left-wing group, consisting of CIO and Labor's Non-Partisan League leaders as well as such mavericks as Lieutenant Governor Patterson and Senator Kenny.

4. The Olson group, consisting of members of the administration, AFL and Railroad Brotherhood leaders, and most Democratic members of the Legislature.

Governor Olson began preparations for the selection of a convention delegation with a series of meetings designed to work out a slate consisting chiefly of persons from his group, plus such people as Patterson and Kenny. Olson did not want McAdoo, his old enemy and now the head of American President Lines, and he did not consider the right-wingers as Democrats.[2] Lieutenant Governor Patterson, backed by CIO and LNPL leaders, was dissatisfied with the way the selecting was being done, and on March 7 dispatched a telegram to Democratic State Chairman Paul Peek saying that he hoped "no group will act too hastily in filing with the Secretary of State a delegation that is not representative of all the ranks of our party." Patterson asked that Democratic leaders issue a call for a conference.[3]

Administration leaders in Washington were worried about California. President Roosevelt asked Secretary of the Interior Harold L. Ickes to go to the coast and try to straighten things out among the factions.[4] According to Ickes, the President "realized that the situation was delicate and doubted whether anyone could solve it," but he dispatched Ickes to California with a penciled scrap of paper reading: "*Coalition* ticket to include *some* from all administration groups including Governor Olson, McAdoo. F. D. R." Ickes then phoned Olson and McAdoo and informed them that he was coming out and asked them to withhold action until he arrived. "McAdoo readily agreed," Ickes wrote later, "but it required some persuasion to convince Olson. I was not encouraged by the fact that each of these men talked bitterly about the other over the telephone."

Ickes arrived in San Francisco on the morning of March 13. At first he conferred with the "neutrals," and then with the leaders of the Patterson group. He found that while the latter were in favor of a coalition Roosevelt slate, they most strenuously opposed having it headed by Governor Olson. The Patterson group suggested to Ickes that Olson go as a delegate-at-large, but that the delegates-at-large should be arranged in alphabetical order, thus dropping Olson from the top spot. Ickes found that this arrangement was satisfactory to George Creel and McAdoo, who came in to see him, and—much to his relief—Governor Olson agreed. That afternoon a "harmony slate" was worked out, including some from each New Deal faction but with most from the Olson group. According to Ickes, the chief difficulty was with Patterson, who upon their first meeting "made a bad impression on me, which he later justified." Finally, according to Ickes' version, Patterson and his followers agreed to the slate. Patterson denied that he had accepted the slate, contending that he had neither agreed to it nor opposed it at the meeting with Ickes.[5] Ickes left San Francisco with the assurance that all (excepting possibly Patterson) were in line.

Ickes' visit was far from successful, although it is doubtful if it could have been, under the circumstances. At once E. E. Ward, executive vice president of Labor's Non-Partisan League of California, issued a statement in which he said that he regretted that Patterson and Senators Kenny and Shelley had accepted positions on the "harmony" slate, for it was not a "liberal" but rather a "McAdoo" slate.[6] Manchester Boddy wired Olson that he could not accept a place on the delegation.[7] Lieutenant Governor Patterson quit the ticket on March 20.[8] After questions about the legality of his presence on a party convention ticket had been raised (under the Hatch Act),[9] McAdoo retired from the ticket.

The break between Olson and his lieutenant governor seemed complete when a left-wing ticket pledged to Patterson for president was entered in the Democratic presidential preference primary. The Patterson slate included leaders of the CIO and LNPL, Carey McWilliams, Sam Houston Allen, Assemblymen Ralph C. Dills (Compton) and Paul A. Richie (San Diego), and other southern California liberals. The viewpoint of some members of this slate is indicated in a letter written by

Carey McWilliams, an important official in the Olson administration, to the governor. McWilliams said that he had "serious doubts" as to whether President Roosevelt was the "most logical leader" to carry on the battle for the New Deal reforms. He felt that the Democratic party nationally was neglecting the "paramount issue of unemployment" and thought that the Roosevelt administration was concerning itself too much with foreign affairs. McWilliams offered to resign from his post as chief of the division of immigration and housing if Olson wanted him to go.[10] Upon the advice of McWilliams' superior, Director of Industrial Relations George G. Kidwell, the governor decided to leave McWilliams in his post at least until after the election.[11] Indeed, McWilliams, a man of great energy and ability, and author of *Factories in the Field,* was retained in his position by Olson throughout the whole of the administration.

Two other tickets were entered in the Democratic presidential preference primary. One was pledged to Vice President John Nance Garner, and consisted of conservative Democrats opposed to a third term for Roosevelt. Garner had carried the state over Roosevelt in 1932, and his followers were still so active in 1940 that they led Raymond Moley to write in all seriousness that Garner "has a surprisingly good chance of getting a solid delegation" from California.[12] Members of the Garner ticket included four "economy bloc" legislators and the slate was endorsed by Assemblyman Seth Millington of Gridley, chairman of the ways and means committee of the reorganized Assembly. Typical of the Garner campaign literature was a throw-away newspaper bearing the headline "ROOSEVELT NOT TO BE A CANDIDATE" and carrying the slogan "NOW IS THE TIME TO END 'OLSONISM' IN CALIF.!"[13] The fourth ticket in the preference primary was pledged to Willis Allen for president, and included the names of other leaders of the Ham and Eggs pension movement. It was rather transparently a vengeance vehicle, an attempt to repay the governor for his opposition to the 1939 pension initiative.

The Roosevelt ticket contained the most illustrious names in the Democratic party leadership of California. It was headed by Isidore B. Dockweiler, a leader of the party for decades, and included, in addition to Governor Olson, San Francisco County Chairman William M. Malone, J. Frank Burke, Los Angeles County Supervisor John Anson Ford, Secretary of State (and State Chairman) Paul Peek, seven congressmen, four state senators (including Kenny and Shelley), and four members of the Assembly. A rather ludicrous note was added when Representative Lee E. Geyer of Gardena tried to withdraw from the Roosevelt slate, found that he couldn't do so without jeopardizing the legality of the whole ticket, and ended by throwing his support to the Patterson slate (while his own name was on the Roosevelt ticket).[14]

The chief excitement in the Democratic presidential preference primary was provided by the bitter words between the governor and the lieutenant governor. In a speech at Fresno, Olson said, "No laboring man can oppose Roosevelt without betraying labor," and added that it didn't matter whether it was "John L. Lewis, Ellis E. Patterson or Labor's Non-Partisan League." The governor said he feared that the Patterson slate had been organized by "direction from without the state and possibly from without America." Patterson in reply said that Olson was "stooping to the lowest red-baiting tactics." Patterson, never a very placid individual, said also that "both Olson and Roosevelt think they are dictators and bosses rather than servants of the people," and defied the governor: "I don't intend to let Olson sell out the Democratic party. He is a liberal before election but forgets liberalism after election."[15]

The result of the Democratic presidential preference primary on May 7, 1940, was a resounding victory for the Roosevelt-Olson slate. The vote cast for the leaders on each ticket was: Roosevelt, 723,782; Garner, 114,594; Allen, 90,718; and Patterson, 48,337. Following this ignominious defeat, Lieutenant Governor Patterson lost little time in climbing on the third-term bandwagon, in what Earl C. Behrens said was "a political flipflop . . . that makes the man on the flying trapeze look like a rank amateur."[16] The members of the "economy bloc" were handed one of their few defeats during 1940, and the Olson administration was given a badly needed bit of success.

As chairman of the California delegation to the Democratic national convention in Chicago, Governor Olson played a leading role in the proceedings. A member of the resolutions committee, he urged his colleagues to insert a plank in the 1940 platform pledging the party to complete government ownership and distribution of electric power.[17] Olson was chosen by the delegation to succeed William Gibbs McAdoo as national committeeman. Helen Gahagan Douglas, wife of motion picture actor Melvyn Douglas, himself a delegate and former member of the State Relief Commission, was named national committeewoman.

A number of the governor's friends had for some time been urging him for the vice presidential nomination. Some claimed that Olson could count on 206 votes after the first ballot, from California, Utah, Nebraska, Colorado, Tennessee, Kansas, Ohio, Wisconsin, Washington, Minnesota, Oregon, Nevada, Hawaii, and Texas.[18] Harry Hopkins informed Olson that President Roosevelt would run for a third time, but Hopkins said that he did not know the president's choice for running-mate and said that Olson might be the one. Shortly after that, however, he received word from Hopkins that Secretary of Agriculture Henry A. Wallace had been chosen by the president, and Olson at once announced to the press that he would support Wallace.[19] He made one of the seconding speeches for the nomination of Wallace, praising his record with glowing words.

The friends of Olson who had been attempting to push his candidacy for vice president told the governor that the chief stumbling block to his advancement was the fact that Ellis Patterson would inherit the governorship. According to Olson, some of these friends put through a telephone call to Patterson in California, and handed the telephone to Governor Olson, urging that he talk Patterson into resigning. Exactly what was said in the conversation is a matter of dispute. But convention reporters immediately published accounts of the episode, and when Sacramento reporters found Patterson, the lieutenant governor was furious. Patterson said that Olson had called him and tried to get him to resign, but said that he had told the governor, "You go to hell!" "... From now on I'm going to be the governor while I'm on the job. I'm going to take care of every blank blank thing which comes to the governor's desk. If Olson doesn't like it he can come back and be the governor himself."[20] Governor Olson, in announcing his withdrawal from the race for the vice presidential nomination, said that he would carry on as the governor of California because the people "did not elect anybody else for that position."[21]

The sequel to this episode took place when Lieutenant Governor Patterson announced that he had appointed James K. Moffitt to the Board of Regents of the University of California, and said that he was considering persons for the vacancies on the State Board of Education. Olson's executive secretary, M. Stanley Mosk, the only important administration official in Sacramento at the time, announced that the appointment of Moffitt had not been made at the request of the governor. On the next day Mosk got to the secretary of state's office ahead of Patterson, and filed the commission of appointment of M. Stanley Mosk as a regent of the University of California! Mosk denied that the governor had left behind a number of blank commissions for use in case Patterson decided to "be governor," but few people believed him. Mosk told reporters, in all seriousness, that the governor had signed his commission before he left for the convention, though the appointment would be temporary. Governor Olson rushed back to California, cancelling a proposed trip to Washington and New York.[22] Moffitt, a long-time member of the Board of Regents, was eventually appointed by Olson to fill another vacancy. Mosk remained on the Board until May 1941, when he resigned and was replaced by Brodie E. Ahlport.

Following his hasty return from Chicago, Olson had almost at once to plunge into the great "purge" campaign against the "economy bloc" Democrats. His particular targets were Speaker Garland and his nine Democratic supporters; Assemblymen Yorty and Tenney, key figures in the relief investigating committee; and the conservative Democratic senators.

Administration candidates for the Legislature were encouraged by the governor's office to file only for the Democratic ticket and to emphasize their devotion to party principles. Olson contended that cross-filing resulted only in confusion and denied that the Legislature was a nonpartisan body. He had earlier hoped to lead the fight for an initiative constitutional amendment to abolish the State Senate, and even yet had not abandoned hope for such a reform, but he decided to make a strong bid in 1940 for the nomination and election throughout the state of Democrats friendly to his administration, for seats in both houses of the Legislature.[23]

Plans for the great "purge" got under way rapidly. As early as February, one of the governor's appointees to the State Board of Education wrote to Olson to tell of her participation in the selection of a candidate to run against Assemblyman Don A. Allen ("economy bloc" Democrat, Los Angeles).[24] The governor's chief agent in the selection of administration candidates for the Legislature was his assistant secretary Walter T. Ballou, former secretary of the Democratic state central committee and frequent object of attack by legislative investigating committees for assertedly "playing politics" in SRA. State Chairman Paul Peek and others argued against the formal presentation of a long list of administration candidates, and urged a more subtle strategy, but the governor felt very strongly that he should have supporters running in every district and that the voters should know who they were.[25]

Governor Olson on August 19 made a radio speech in which he named 76 Democratic candidates for the Legislature and asked the Democrats to nominate them in the primary.[26] He said that he spoke to Democrats as both governor and national committeeman, feeling it to be his duty to let them know which candidates were devoted to the Democratic platform. "I have a right to assume," said Olson, "that the vast majority of the people throughout the State are registered as Democrats because they approve the achievements of the Party and because they favor the principles and measures proposed in our party's platform. . . ." The governor said that he had left out of his list districts in which there existed no contest for the Democratic nomination or in which there were a number of "liberal Democrats" in the running, any one of whom would support the platform. The governor took cognizance of the fact that his opponents and their newspaper supporters had made much of the word "purge" in the campaign. Said the governor of this: "In the same sense, of course, it might be said that the Republicans are trying to purge President Roosevelt out of the White House with Mr. Willkie, and that the Republican candidates for the legislature are atttempting to purge Democrats therefrom."

Paying no heed to the lack of success that President Roosevelt had met with when trying the same thing two years before, Governor Olson stumped the state in behalf of his candidates for the Democratic nominations. And his opponents used the same strategy as had Roosevelt's opponents.

Typical of the defense measures employed by incumbents against Olson candidates was a newspaper advertisement run by "Sacramento Citizens Non-Partisan Committee," in behalf of the three Sacramento County legislators opposed by the administration. This advertisement carried the banner head, "A Declaration of Independence," and said that the Sacramento legislators had been placed on the "purge list" because they had not been "robots," "rubber stamps" or "yes men."[27] The administration received a blow when the state's chief Democratic newspaper, the Los Angeles *Daily News,* endorsed all three of the Democratic assemblymen the administration was trying to defeat in Los Angeles County, as well as such Republican stalwarts as Assemblymen C. Don Field, Lee T. Bashore, Gerald C. Kepple and Jesse Randolph Kellems.[28]

The result of the August 27 Democratic primary was a severe setback for the Olson administration. Eleven Republicans (mostly incumbents) won both nominations for state senator, thus assuring continued Republican domination of the upper house. Twenty-eight Republicans plus eight of the Democrats whom Governor Olson was attempting to "purge" won both nominations, which assured that the anti-Olson bloc in the Assembly would be numerous no matter how the November run-offs turned out. Only five Democrats were elected to the State Senate at the primary, and of these only two had Olson's pre-primary endorsement. Only 23 Democrats were elected to the Assembly at the primary, and of them eight were on the "purge" list and five others did not bear Olson's endorsement.

The only casualties among "economy bloc" Democrats at the 1940 primary were Chester F. Gannon of Sacramento and Clinton J. Fulcher of Lookout, who were defeated for renomination by administration candidates. Both Gannon and Fulcher, like their colleagues of the "economy bloc," won Republican nominations, but as these two had not won the nomination of their own party they were disqualified, and the Republican nomination vacancies were filled by committee-designated candidates. Of the 14 candidates for state senator endorsed by Governor Olson, only 6 won Democratic nominations. Of the 62 candidates for Assembly endorsed by Olson, 30 won Democratic nominations. Nor did the unpleasant aspects of the 1940 primary end here for the Olson administration. Three strong administration supporters in the Legislature went down to defeat in attempts to win seats in Congress. Furthermore, three of the eleven persons whom Olson had elevated to Superior Court benches were defeated at the 1940 primary, and one other was forced into a November run-off. For all his "purge" efforts, Governor Olson had only knocked out Gannon and Fulcher, and he could now look forward to two more years of legislative opposition to his program. Without substantial newspaper support and large sums of money for radio broadcasts, Olson in August 1940 could finally realize just how precarious his own political situation really was.

Nor could Governor Olson get much satisfaction out of the outcome of the contest for the Democratic nomination for United States senator. Lieutenant Governor Ellis E. Patterson had long been in the race, but whatever chance he may have had to obtain Olson administration support was lost when Patterson headed a separate slate in the Democratic presidential preference primary. Another candidate was Assemblyman Samuel William Yorty, recently converted left-winger, who had gained fame as the head of the Assembly's relief investigating committee. Yorty had become a violent critic of the administration, as is evidenced by this excerpt from a letter to Speaker Garland, published in the journal of the lower house: "The Governor would do well to postpone his 'Purge' of legislators who refused to let him establish a 'Dictatorship of Reds' in California until he has cleaned up his blundering administration. There is a reason why no legislator is on the 'Purge' list who voted against investigating subversive activities in this State."[29] Whatever strength the administration was able to exert in this race was used in behalf of John Anson Ford, Los Angeles County supervisor and ardent New Dealer. Ford's northern California campaign was directed by State Chairman Paul Peek and San Francisco County Chairman William Malone. Governor Olson called for the defeat of Senator Hiram W. Johnson, saying that Johnson "hasn't a progressive hair on his head."[30] But the effort in behalf of Ford was too little, and Hiram Johnson won reëlection at the primaries. The vote for the major contenders for the Democratic nomination was: Johnson, 507,389; Patterson, 206,479; Ford, 175,110; and Yorty, 74,332.

Governor Olson took an active role in the 1940 presidential campaign in California. He introduced Henry A. Wallace to mass meetings, at Hollywood Bowl on September 28 and at Sacramento Memorial Auditorium on September 30.[31] Olson took great delight in fighting against Wendell Willkie, for the latter seemed to him to symbolize the "power trust" which Olson had so long opposed. Typical of the Olson pronouncements in the general election campaign was his contention, *"There are no Willkie Democrats."*[32] Thus Olson was able to share in the great Roosevelt-Wallace victory in California, where the ticket won by a majority of over a half million votes. The only important Democratic casualty was Congressman Franck R. Havenner of San Francisco, and Olson found a place for him on the Railroad Commission.

In the November run-offs for the Legislature, Democrats won 4 out of 5 contests for the State Senate, and 19 out of the 29 for the Assembly. Defeated for reëlection by Olson Democrats were Senator Roy J. Nielsen of Sacramento, Assemblyman Ray Williamson of San Francisco, and Roscoe W. Burson of Fillmore, all Republicans. But other Republican incumbents marked for defeat by the Olson administration were re-elected. As a result of the primary and general elections of 1940, the 1941 Legislature would include: State Senate: 24 Republicans and 16 Democrats; Assembly: 42 Democrats and 38 Republicans. With many of the Democratic senators hostile to the administration, and eight of the Democratic assemblymen recent victors over Olson in the "purge" battles of the primary, Governor Olson could look forward to no real improvement in his relations with the Legislature.

The Recall Movement

As if the three 1940 elections were not enough for one year, there was also a threat of a fourth—an attempt to recall the governor from office. Under the law, a recall election for an office such as governor could be called upon the presentation of petitions signed by qualified electors equal in number to 12 per cent of the vote cast for the office at the last general election.[33] In the case of Governor Olson, this meant 318,174 valid signatures would be necessary.

Soon after the close of the 1939 session of the Legislature a recall movement against Olson was inaugurated by J. A. ("Foghorn") Murphy, a well known Los Angeles politician, and James W. Mellen, head of the "Jeffersonian Democrats of California." Mellen vowed, "We'll recall Governor Olson if it is the last day he is in office." Mellen was something of a humorist, and did his best to coin a phrase: "We want to throw Tom, Dick and Harry—Tom Mooney, Dick Olson and Harry Bridges— out of California politics."[34] The Murphy–Mellen petitions, the first of which was filed at Santa Ana on August 4, 1939, charged Olson with incompetence, lack of leadership in state and party, and with playing politics with relief.

The first recall threat proved to be a weak one, but following the special election of 1939 the leaders of the Ham and Eggs pension movement vowed to recall Olson for his asserted treachery. The second recall movement languished in the face of general disapproval of the newspapers and of a number of prominent Republicans.

The recall movement was given a great boost by the "dictograph incident" of February 1940. Early in March a San Francisco headquarters was opened by the "Olson Recall Committee, Incorporated," which had previously functioned in southern California. This organization was headed by C. C. C. Tatum, prominent southern California real estate man, and had the support of "independent" oil operators who had defeated the administration's Atkinson oil bill at the 1939 special election.[35] Speaker Gordon Garland created some speculation about his candidacy for governor when he obtained an opinion on several points about recall procedure from the attorney general.[36] Senator Robert W. Kenny, erstwhile Olson floor leader of the upper house, announced that if the recall qualified he would run for governor, and traveled about the state apparently seeking support.[37]

Many conservatives disapproved of the third "Recall Olson" movement, as they had its predecessors. Chester Rowell suggested that sponsors of the recall, who had recently filed petitions with 256,246 signatures, give up the move in the face of the national emergency. He pointed out that if a recall election were held and a majority voted to recall Olson, the new governor might be any person who received 21 per cent of the votes cast, provided no one else got over 20 per cent. Rowell said that the third recall attempt was close to success "wholly because business men made a business of it, and put up the money."[38]

The third recall attempt ended in failure, probably because the interests backing it decided to save their money. The August primary election indicated that the upper house would remain Republican, and that the Assembly would probably be organized by the "economy bloc." The Olson administration would thus not be able to secure passage of any of its major reform measures. Furthermore, the national emergency, the presidential election, and the concern over who Olson's successor might be if he were to be recalled, all tended to make the recallers' situation quite a difficult one!

Nevertheless, the recall threat had constituted an important weapon in the arsenal of Olson's most outspoken enemies. It was an intrinsic part of the atmosphere of the frequently dramatic first half of the Olson regime, and only faded away when it was clear that the second half could not be productive of reforms.

12 *olson's second legislature*

EVEN THOUGH HIS OPPONENTS WERE MORE COMPLETELY IN control of both houses than they were in the 1939 Legislature, Olson was able to compile a greater record of success with his second legislature. In part this was because of improved economic conditions and in part because he attempted to achieve less. But most important of all, Olson himself seems to have relaxed. Recognizing that he would have to tread lightly, he did not go out of his way to pick fights. And he was even a bit more conciliatory toward the Republicans.

Certainly he could look forward to little when he surveyed the makeup of the 1941 Legislature. In the Senate, the 16 Democrats and 24 Republicans caucussed together, choosing William P. Rich (Republican, Marysville) as president pro tem.[1] The other members of the rules committee, which as before constituted also the committee on committees, were two Republicans and two anti-Olson Democrats. In the lower house, Gordon Garland was designated the candidate of the "economy bloc" by a caucus of Republicans and conservative Democrats meeting a month before the convening of the Legislature.[2] There was some Republican unhappiness at this, but the GOP simply lacked the votes to organize the Assembly without the assistance of the anti-Olson Democrats. The Republican San Francisco *Chronicle* had advocated Garland's reëlection, calling him "the natural leader of the economy bloc" and warning that any attempt to replace him with a Republican would play into the hands of Governor Olson.[3] When the Assembly met, Garland was chosen speaker by a vote of 55 to 20 over Cecil King of Los Angeles, the administration's candidate. Seventeen Democrats voted for Garland, as did all 38 Republicans. Earl D. Desmond ("economy bloc" Democrat, Sacramento) was chosen speaker pro tem over George D. Collins, Jr. (San Francisco Democrat, and candidate of the administration), by a vote of 53 to 22.[4] Garland's appointments assured the dominance of the "economy bloc" in every important committee.

In his first biennial message to the joint session of the Legislature,[5] Governor Olson contrasted the financial situation of the state with what it had been when he had submitted his last budget:

> The present World War and the prospect that the United States would now be engaged in carrying forward a National defense program involving expenditures of many billions of dollars, with resultant stimulation of industrial and commercial activities, re-employment and great reduction in the State unemployment relief load, was then unforeseen. Had the revenue measures then recommended been adopted, it now appears that by the end of the present biennium the entire State deficit would have been wiped out and we could be looking forward to a reduction in tax revenues lightening the tax burden on those least able to pay.

Olson then announced that current tax returns were sufficient to meet current expenditures and to reduce the remaining deficit, and that thus he would not be compelled to ask for additional taxes.

The governor then surveyed the activities of the various state departments during the first two years of his administration. He did not bother to read this part of his speech to the assembled legislators, simply asking them to read their copies, and skipped down to his recommendations. Reiterating his firm opposition to dole relief, he asked that "the State Relief Administration ... be provided with funds and empowered to give employment to the unemployed and training for employment." "The policy of work relief will draw the line, clearly and sharply, between the employable and the unemployable. The giving of jobs and the doing of work will eliminate the onus of public charity. Even more, it will make certain that no chiselers will be found on the relief rolls." Other recommendations of the governor included the passage of a revenue bond bill to facilitate public ownership of public utilities, a compulsory health insurance program, a state housing authority, reorganization of the state's fiscal agencies, removal of liquor control from the State Board of Equalization, a state labor relations law, broadening of unemployment insurance, exclusive state fund operation of workmen's compensation insurance, and amendments of the horse racing law.

The 1941 Budget

The new budget, sent to the Legislature on January 24, proposed the expenditure of $552,570,000.[6] This figure was $13,487,000 less than the actual and estimated expenditures for the 1939–1941 biennium. Olson estimated receipts would be $613,070,000, which would enable the state to retire its deficit and end up with a general fund surplus of $11,000,000 on June 30, 1943. But he emphasized that his estimate would be dependent upon the continuance of defense expenditures of the federal government as well as maintenance of current California tax levels. While he requested less than half as much for SRA as was being spent during the current biennium, he asked for substantial increases for general government, institutions and education. He ended on a conciliatory note: "This budget, as I have said before, is based upon what I believe to be the present requirements of our State Government. However, in the discharge of your duties as legislators, you will wish to determine for yourselves the needs of each State agency. In carrying out this task, all departments of the State Government stand ready to extend to you every facility at their disposal."

The 1941 budget fight began differently and ended differently from the 1939 struggle. The Assembly ways and means committee (headed by the bitterly anti-Olson Democrat, Seth Millington) reported out the budget bill with a reduction of $44,200,000 (including deletion of the $38,700,000 for relief).[7] Governor Olson's prediction that the legislative session would be "a very peaceful, harmonious one, finishing about May 1st,"[8] was to prove premature. As months went by without approval of the budget, the governor could not resist twitting his enemies, noting on May 8: "Just how much longer the Assembly's budget debates will be protracted by the so-called Economy Bloc's efforts to embarrass effective government is more than I can guess."[9] When the bill finally cleared the

Assembly, some $1,500,000 had been restored from the floor. An additional $2,400,000 was restored by the Senate. Two free-conference committees were necessary before the Legislature on June 3 finally passed the 1941 budget bill.[10]

The outcome of the budget fight was a severe blow to Millington, who fought against the adoption of the second conference committee report.[11] The vote on final passage in the Assembly was 62 to 12, with Millington able to win the votes of only three Democrats and eight Republicans.[12] At the same time the outcome was a triumph for Assemblyman F. Ray Bennett of Los Angeles, Olson's floor manager, who had proved to be an effective leader. The governor rewarded Bennett with an appointment to the Los Angeles Municipal Court. Only four votes were cast against the second conference report on the budget bill in the Senate, and there, curiously enough, the opposition to adoption was led by Olson's floor leader, Senator Garrison, who protested the cut in appropriations for the Department of Agriculture.[13]

The budget bill signed by Governor Olson on June 5 totalled $512,206,042, a reduction of $1,797,138 from his original request (except for the deleted $38,706,000 for relief, which was to be handled separately).[14] As Herbert L. Phillips of the Sacramento *Bee* put it: "For a man who started with two strikes on him politically when the 1941 Legislature convened last January, Governor Olson has been far luckier in his budget program for the next two years than he had any reason to expect." Phillips added that while the governor termed the cuts "deplorable" he readily signed the bill "and it was no secret in the Capitol that the administration boys were tickled pink with the outcome."[15] Admitting that the outcome was a "draw," the Los Angeles *Times* said that the governor had done better than he had in 1939, "due mainly to the State's improved financial condition, to his own foregoing of his earlier advocacy of new taxes and to a comparative absence of Olsonic controversies."[16]

The 1941 budget was also a triumph for Finance Director George Killion, who had succeeded the tempestuous John R. Richards in September 1940 and had prepared the new budget. Killion did not make the mistakes that Dewey Anderson and Olson had made in preparing the previous budget, and his work passed the scrutiny of the conservatives. Republican Senator Edward H. Tickle of Carmel, chairman of the revenue and taxation committee and member of the finance committee—and certainly no friend of the administration—noted that Killion had forced most departments to reduce their estimates, concluding, "It is my opinion that Mr. Killion has done a good job in endeavoring to economize."[17]

Governor Olson was completely successful in defeating attempts to cut taxes at the 1941 session. He announced on March 3 that he would veto measures to cut the bank and corporation franchise taxes or the personal income tax, although he said that he would consider signing bills to provide sales tax exemptions if a survey of the state's fiscal condition indicated that such exemptions would not unbalance the budget.[18] Three bills to grant sales tax exemptions passed the Assembly but died in the Senate revenue and taxation committee.[19] A bill by Senator Clarence C. Ward (Republican, Santa Barbara) providing for a reduction in income tax rates on incomes over $50,000, passed both houses, the Senate by a vote of 22 to 10, and the Assembly by 51 to 17.[20] Governor Olson vetoed the measure, saying that most of the $1,610,000 the state would lose by it would be taken by the federal income tax anyway, and that such a reduction was not in conformity with the principle of ability to pay.[21] The State Senate sustained Olson's veto by a vote of 21 to 13 (with 27 needed to override).[22] The 13 voting with the governor on this occasion included six Republicans (among them Senator Rich, president pro tem). It was notable that Senator Robert W. Kenny of Los Angeles, formerly close to the administration, voted for the Ward bill on both occasions, thus heeding Senator Ward's plea to "help keep my city from becoming a ghost town."[23]

The chief tax reduction proposal at the 1941 session was a bill by Speaker Garland and others providing a cut by approximately one-sixth of the state's principal taxes, to take effect at fixed future dates when the deficit was expected to be paid off. It was anticipated that the Garland bill would eventually provide tax cuts amounting to $22,000,000 annually.[24] Garland secured Assembly passage for his bill late in the session, by a vote of 53 (29 Republicans and 24 Democrats) to 26 (18 Democrats and 8 Republicans).[25] The Republican opponents of the Garland bill included some of the most conservative members of the lower house. The San Francisco News, which long before had become hostile to the administration, chiefly because of SRA, charged that Garland was "seeking to tear apart the whole tax structure of the state."[26] Garland's possible candidacy for governor was frequently mentioned in the newspapers, and a tax cut measure would have done much to enhance his standing with the business community. Garland found that the Senate revenue and taxation committee flatly refused to pass his measure onto the floor, and in spite of the protests of Garland and his friends against the executive session proceedings of Senate committees, there was nothing they could do.[27] Garland's successes of the past year had not made him humble and he was accustomed to ruling the Assembly, but the proud senators were in no mood to bow to his wishes.

The major fiscal reform of the 1941 Legislature was the creation of the "Joint Legislative Budget Committee," through the passage of a resolution by Senator Rich and others.[28] Administration Democrats provided only nominal opposition to this measure, which did not require gubernatorial approval. The committee was granted an appropriation of $40,000 with which to hire an expert staff, and was directed to delve into the state's finances: "It shall be the duty of the committee to ascertain facts and to make recommendations to the Legislature and to the Houses thereof concerning the State Budget, the revenues and expenditures of the State and the organization and function of the State, its departments, sub-divisions, and agencies, with a view to reducing the cost of the State government and securing greater efficiency and economy." The members of the committee were to be five Senators (including the president pro tem, and one member each from the finance, revenue and taxation, governmental efficiency, and judiciary committees selected by the committees) and five assemblymen (the speaker and four others named by him). The joint budget committee chose as the first legislative auditor Rolland A. Vandergrift, director of finance under Governor Rolph and briefly under Governor Merriam. The legislative auditor became an important figure, for he made detailed analyses for the committee and drew its attention to questionable practices and weaknesses in the executive budget.[29]

The Tenney Committee

Another investigation which was to have a permanent importance was launched by the 1941 Legislature with the establishment of the "Tenney Committee." Assemblyman Jack B. Tenney (Democrat, Los Angeles) had throughout 1940 been the second in command on the assembly relief investigating committee, headed by his friend Assemblyman Samuel

William Yorty.[30] In September, 1940, Tenney was the principal author of a bill at the fourth special session to remove the Communist party from the ballot. The measure, which had been advocated by both major parties at the state conventions, passed the Assembly with three dissenting votes and the Senate with only one (Kenny).[31] Olson signed it, saying "It is undoubtedly a fact that the Communist Party's own publications, the sworn statements of its officers, and its own actions in line with directions received from agencies in a foreign nation are relied upon to show that this party does come in the classification of a foreign controlled party and for that reason should not be entitled to legal recognition in the political life of America."[32] The State Supreme Court in 1942 declared most of the provisions of the Tenney Act to be unconstitutional.[33]

With Yorty defeated in his race for United States senator and out of the Legislature, Tenney inherited the leadership of the investigation of "un-American activities." He secured the passage, by a vote of 34 to 1 (Kenny) in the Senate and 47 to 25 in the Assembly, of a resolution setting up a "Joint Fact-Finding Committee on Un-American Activities in California," with an appropriation of $10,000.[34] At the close of the session he pushed through the lower House a similar resolution authorizing an Assembly committee to act during the interim with a grant of $15,000.[35] Tenney became the chairman of both and his work led to much controversy and many headlines in later years.

Specific legislation aimed at un-American activities was passed at the 1941 session. A bill by Tenney requiring the registration of organizations directly or indirectly advocating the overthrow of the government by force or violence, and of organizations subject to foreign control, passed both houses with but one dissent (Kenny)[36] and was signed by Olson. A bill by Senator Herbert W. Slater (Democrat, Santa Rosa) providing severe penalties for acts or attempted acts of sabotage in defense industries, and permitting the closing off of property (including streets) where deemed necessary to protect such industries, cleared both houses with little opposition and was signed by the governor. Attorney General Warren described this measure as a "model anti-sabotage bill drafted by the National Conference of Law Enforcement Officers of various states with the blessings of United States Attorney General Jackson." Particular care was taken to provide in the bill as passed that nothing in it was to be construed as curtailing or impairing the rights of employees to strike.[37]

"Hot Cargo" and "Secondary Boycott"

Labor legislation occupied much of the attention of the 1941 Legislature and provided it with its most dramatic fight.[38] A measure by three rural Republicans, with the blessings of the business community and the California Farm Bureau Federation, proposed to outlaw "hot cargo" and "secondary boycott." This "Slave Labor Bill" (as the trade union leaders quickly dubbed it) defined hot cargo as:

> . . . any combination or agreement resulting in a refusal by employees to handle goods or to perform any services for their employer because of a dispute between some other employer and his employees or a labor organization or any combination or agreement resulting in a refusal by employers to handle goods or perform any services for another employer because of an agreement between such other employer and his employees or a labor organization.

It defined secondary boycott as:

> Any combination or agreement to cease performing any services for any employer or to cause any loss or injury to such employer, or to his employees, for the purpose of inducing or compelling such employer to refrain from doing business with, or handling the products of any other employer, because of a dispute between the latter and his employees or a labor organization, or any combination or agreement to cease performing or to cause any employer to cease performing any services for another employer, or to cause any loss or injury to such other employer, or to his employees, for the purpose of inducing or compelling such other employer to refrain from doing business with, or handling the products of any other employer, because of an agreement between the latter and his employees or a labor organization.[39]

Drawn in such broad terms, the hot cargo bill soon became a symbol, and organized labor in California found itself seriously on the defensive for the first time since its fight against Proposition 1 in 1938.

As expected, the hot cargo bill had easy going in the rural Senate, where only five Democrats opposed it.[40] In the Assembly, two important amendments were adopted, limiting the life of the measure to May 1, 1943, or the duration of the national emergency, and forbidding the use by employer groups of hot cargo and secondary boycott.[41] The Assembly then passed the bill by a vote of 50 (33 Republicans and 17 Democrats) to 29 (25 Democrats and 4 Republicans).[42]

Olson returned the hot cargo bill with a long and ringing veto message, saying that he had not found any law "which has ever gone so far in attempts to defeat or circumscribe the rights of organized workers."[43] He had no patience with attempts to make the hot cargo bill appear as a defense measure:

> If constitutional guarantees are to be set aside for the safety of the Nation in war or in any of the conditions of National Emergency, it is not for the Legislature or any State to do so. That is the function of the Congress of the United States, in the exercise of its powers to provide for the common defense, or of the President under powers delegated to him by Congress. Nor should any temporary suspension of constitutional rights be confined to workers in private industries, whether they be National defense industries or all other industries to which this bill would apply. No such action was taken even by the National Government in the first World War. It was not considered expedient to do so. President Wilson, in 1917, said: "The highest and best form of efficiency is the spontaneous cooperation of free people."

Olson predicted that if the bill were enacted it would actually foment industrial strife and thus injure the defense effort.

Although the Senate at once voted 34 to 5 to override the veto, labor leaders were confident they had enough strength to sustain it in the urban lower house.[44] However, the times were not propitious. The bitter strike of CIO workers at the North American Aircraft Corporation plant at Inglewood was then approaching its climax, when troops under orders from President Roosevelt seized the plant. The strategy of the proponents of the hot cargo bill was clear enough. As the Los Angeles *Times* said, "To permit California to go into full production in this emergency, these unfair and illegitimate weapons of union labor must be banned."[45]

The Assembly battle began on June 2, when the lower house on its first roll call refused to override the veto of the hot cargo bill. Republican Floor Leader Charles W. Lyon gave notice that he would seek reconsideration, and on the next day the Assembly granted his motion. The final vote was scheduled for 9:00 P.M. on June 5. The first roll call that night showed 46 in favor of overriding and 23 opposed, with 54 necessary to pass the bill over the veto. Speaker Garland did not announce the vote, holding off until the 11 members who had not voted (including two who were due in from Washington, D.C., at 3:00 A.M.) could participate. At about 3:00 A.M. Speaker Garland turned over the gavel to Lyon, and went down onto the floor to lobby for the bill. By 3:30 A.M. the vote stood at 53 to 27, with every member voting, but Lyon refused to announce the vote. C. Don Field (Republican, Glendale) moved a "call of the house," and his motion was challenged on the ground that all members had voted and thus a call would be unconstitutional. Lyon, in the chair, overruled this objection, and a call was instituted. Earl D. Desmond (Sacramento conservative Democrat), suddenly switched from aye to no, allegedly because a special appropriation bill of his had been bottled up in committee, and then switched back to aye after a conference with Garland. Two Democrats who had voted to override then asked that their votes be changed to no, but Lyon, in the chair, refused to permit them to switch. Finally, at 4:00 A.M., Bernard A. Sheridan (Republican, Oakland), after a conference with Speaker Garland, switched from no to aye, and the bill received the required two-thirds vote.[46]

The final vote on the hot cargo bill in the Assembly was 54 aye (35 Republicans and 19 Democrats) to 26 no (23 Democrats and 3 Republicans).[47] A number of normal administration supporters among the Democrats, principally from rural areas, voted with the Republicans to override. The three Republicans voting to sustain the veto were from San Francisco, stronghold of organized labor. Only two rural Democrats voted to sustain the veto. Almost at once the California State Federation of Labor instituted petitions to hold up the hot cargo bill for referendum and thus suspend its operation until after the next general election (November 1942). With the help of the CIO, the federation was successful in this cause, and the issue remained for the voters to decide.[48]

The employer groups also took the initiative in an attempt to modify the unemployment compensation laws. A bill introduced by Assemblyman Desmond proposed to tighten provisions regarding eligibility—including ability to work and availability for work; to strengthen disqualification provisions—including voluntary quitting, misconduct, and quitting during trade disputes; and to revise procedures for filing claims and appealing from awards.[49] After the bill passed both houses (the Assembly by 44 to 28 and the Senate by 24 to 9), Governor Olson vetoed the Desmond bill with a long, detailed, and hard-hitting message.[50] He enclosed a copy of a letter from the executive director of the Social

Security Board criticizing the measure, and pointed out that its enactment would cause confusion and jeopardize grants from the federal government. Said Olson: "It is obvious that the provisions of this bill are designed to deny benefits through harsh disqualifications to many deserving unemployed workers who themselves have contributed to the fund and for whom unemployment insurance was clearly intended, and by that means to accomplish an avoidance or reduction of contribution requirements." Although no attempt was made to override the veto, employer groups could rejoice that their taking the lead with the Desmond bill had prevented any liberalization of the unemployment compensation laws.[51]

Except for the hot cargo bill, little labor legislation was enacted in 1941. A bill providing that collective bargaining agreements would be enforceable at law was passed, after considerable disagreement and numerous amendments, and signed by Olson. The Assembly refused to override the governor's veto of a bill that would have lowered from 16 to 10 years the age at which children would be permitted to sell newspapers and periodicals without a work permit. A mild version of a "Little Wagner Act" passed the Assembly only to die in Senate committee. A "Little Norris–La Guardia Act" met the same fate. Wages-and-hours bills never got out of committee in either house.[52]

An attempt was made by conservative members of the 1941 Legislature to oust Carey McWilliams, chief of the Division of Immigration and Housing.[53] McWilliams, a tireless inspector of private farm labor camps and as such a thorn to many farm operators, had long been one of the administration's most controversial figures. In spite of McWilliams' membership on the left-wing Patterson ticket at the Democratic presidential preference primary of 1940, the governor had retained the capable McWilliams in his post. Both houses of the 1941 Legislature passed a bill by Assemblyman Desmond which would have abolished McWilliams' position and transferred the functions and personnel of his division to the Department of Public Health. The Assembly vote was 48 to 17 and the Senate vote was 23 to 9. Olson pocket-vetoed the "anti-McWilliams Bill," after being advised by Director of Industrial Relations George G. Kidwell that "acquiescence in such a legislative attempt to usurp the administrative prerogative of the Governor would amount to no less than a surrender of those rights to a reactionary Legislature."[54]

The End of SRA

If the 1941 session of the Legislature was productive of little constructive legislation, it did result in the end of "the nightmare of relief." It has already been noted that the governor's request for funds for the State Relief Administration was deleted from the budget bill, to be handled as a separate measure. This meant that the Legislature was once again unwilling to subscribe to the administration's relief policies—and distrustful in the extreme of Olson's handling of the problem.

The last—and greatest—crisis in the history of the crisis-ridden SRA was precipitated by the ouster of Administrator Sidney G. Rubinow on December 8, 1940. Nine days after that event, former Finance Director John R. Richards gave a hospital bed statement to Senator Phillips and Assemblyman Wollenberg, chiefs of the joint legislative fact-finding committee on employment, in the presence of Rubinow and a court reporter.[55]

The remarks of his former finance director were most embarrassing to Governor Olson. Richards said that he had resigned because of administration attempts to force state contractors to contribute campaign funds and because of Olson's use of the SRA to provide jobs for political friends. Richards said that Dewey Anderson's resignation was "mob lynching" and that he had flatly refused to become Anderson's successor; that Walter Chambers' administration had been one of "loose management," which was what Olson really wanted; that Olson was more interested in personnel than in the proper objectives of SRA; that Deputy Real Estate Commissioner Thomas Armstrong had collected contributions from many state employees (including Richards), amounting to 10 per cent of their salaries; and that the question of soliciting or accepting contributions from contractors was frequently discussed in administration conferences at the executive mansion. Said Richards: "Governor Olson agreed usually that he wanted efficiency and did not want to break down standards, but that he couldn't see why certain positions couldn't be filled and the duties performed as well by one individual as another. So there was constant trouble, the Governor moving in and endeavoring to get control of the personnel department." He also told of Governor Olson's refusal to accept the recommendation of the finance department in his January 1940 request for relief funds, and of Olson's displeasure at Richards when the latter told a legislative committee that the state's credit would not be impaired if no new taxes were granted in 1940.

At the same time, former SRA head Rubinow made a series of similarly sensational charges before the Phillips committee.[56] He produced for the committee a stack of documents, some of them biographies of Olson candidates for SRA jobs, together with covering endorsements. He also showed a letter signed with the initials C. L. O., which was a list of SRA personnel "who must be retained" no matter how much the staff of SRA had to be cut. Rubinow said flatly, "No man recommended to me by the Governor was competent." The former SRA head told the committee that he had had a dispute over firing personnel in Alameda County with G. F. Irvine, unsuccessful Democratic candidate for Assembly in 1940, who had told Rubinow in the presence of Governor Olson, "It's you or me." Typical of Rubinow's testimony was his asserted response to Irvine and Olson: "I said they couldn't run a State agency with a sewer department. By that I meant some of the people that had been working in Alameda. One man at work in Emeryville was wanted in Illinois for murder and robbery. He was just about to get a promotion when I fired him."

The effect of the testimony of Rubinow and Richards was to place the Olson administration in a very bad position, especially in view of the fact that an already hostile Legislature was to convene in less than a month and the fate of the SRA would be at stake. Olson responded with a statement that Rubinow had been ousted upon the recommendation of the state officials comprising the SRA Board of Personnel Standards and Appeals, who considered him to be "temperamentally unfit" for his position.[57] Olson said flatly that no one had ever been employed or retained in the SRA with his approval unless his job was necessary or unless he was found to be qualified. Said the governor: "Plenty of qualified persons are available who are devoted to the cause of good government and are in sympathy with this administration's policies. Frankly, I favor the employment of such persons." Olson stated that he had consistently advocated the placing of SRA under the civil service merit system.

The already unsympathetic press made much of the Richards and Rubinow statements. The San Francisco *Chronicle* approvingly quoted Dewey Anderson's recent description of Olson: ". . . a cheap politician unable and unwilling to squarely face his duty to safeguard distribution of unemployment relief to persons who without fault of their own are without jobs and in need of food and shelter for themselves and their dependents."[58] The San Francisco *News* published an editorial entitled "Olson Administration Has Wrecked Relief with Politics," advocating that the Legislature take relief out of the hands of the governor and place it on a permanent basis with an organization like that of other state departments, with the same policies and to a large extent the same personnel.[59] The veteran political editor of the friendly Sacramento *Bee*, Herbert L. Phillips, summed up the technique of the enemies of Olson's program: " 'Batter the SRA early and late,' their strategy advisers said, in effect, 'and the rest of Olson's program will fall to pieces. Keep the public's attention on relief, and nobody will find time to put any of the rest of that stuff through the legislature.' "[60]

In time the violence of Rubinow's remarks about Governor Olson brought him the censure even of the San Francisco *Chronicle*, which ran an editorial entitled "Rubinow Confuses Issue by Calling Names," in which it said that Rubinow was "out of turn in shouting for the recall or impeachment" of Olson. The *Chronicle* said that the governor had not succeeded in explaining away Rubinow's charges, but that not enough evidence had been produced "to support the degree of Mr. Rubinow's indictment."[61]

Rubinow became an advocate of turning unemployment relief over to the counties, the favorite plan of Senator Phillips and other conservatives. In an address before the Commonwealth Club of California, Rubinow referred to the current SRA case load as "indigent," not employable "in the economic or competitive sense of the word," and stated:

> My conclusion is: the only thing that can be done at the present time to safeguard the objectives and purposes of the SRA, so far as taxpayers and relief recipients are concerned, is to return the organization to the counties as an integral part of county departments of public welfare, where the practices and operations cannot be any worse and probably will be a great deal more efficient than they have been under the Administration of the past two years.

He said that later (presumably after Olson was out of office) a joint state-county department of public welfare should be established.[62]

Meanwhile the SRA rolls continued to drop, indicating that the problem of relief was disappearing as a consequence of national defense employment.[63] Figures showing the case loads to the end of the first five months of 1941 contrast vividly with those for the preceding year:

	1941	1940
January	48,246	114,693
February	43,530	112,354
March	42,625	96,230
April	38,535	82,472
May	31,431	72,731

The Legislature made three separate piecemeal appropriations totalling $3,692,000 to carry SRA to the end of the biennium, June 30, 1941.

The great relief fight of the 1941 Legislature was over who should administer unemployment relief, the state or the 58 counties. The arguments for and against the county plan were much the same as they had been in February 1940, when a measure providing county administration had passed both houses only to be vetoed by Governor Olson. Any appropriation bill required two-thirds vote in each house for passage (27 in the Senate and 54 in the Assembly), which made a very complicated situation even more complex.

The key bill in the relief program sponsored by the Phillips committee provided for county administration of relief under the nominal supervision of the State Department of Social Welfare, with the state paying two-thirds of the cost of direct relief plus an additional amount for counties especially hard pressed by the change-over.[64] It provided further that it was not to become law unless the Legislature appropriated additional funds for old age aid and established a works program. The Senate passed the bill by a vote of 27 to 9 (with 8 Democrats and 1 Republican opposed).[65] The Assembly approved it by a vote of 43 (34 Republicans and 9 Democrats) to 36 (32 Democrats and 4 Republicans).[66]

Olson vetoed the Phillips county relief bill on May 7. He broadcast to the people of the state his opinion that it was a "regressive, reactionary measure," which had abandoned all thought of rehabilitating the unemployed, which had ignored the nationwide causes of unemployment and which took no account of the future.[67] "County lines and provincial differences are obstructions to a comprehensive, properly standardized and equitable Unemployment Relief Program." Olson noted that in spite of a "veritable campaign" against SRA "not one single act of corruption has been found to have been committed," and he blamed the confusion over SRA upon "publicity seeking individuals" and "some troublesome subversive elements." The Senate on three occasions (May 12, June 10 and June 14) refused to override Olson's veto, in spite of the pleas of Senator Phillips. With 27 votes needed to override, the roll calls were, respectively, 24 to 14, 22 to 15, and 25 to 11.[68] Following the first refusal of the Senate to pass the Phillips bill over Olson's veto, Assembly sponsors of the measure made an attempt to run through another county relief bill, introduced by Assemblywoman Daley. The lower house on May 22 by a vote of 38 aye (30 Republicans and 8 Democrats) to 33 no (30 Democrats and 3 Republicans) refused passage of the Daley bill.[69] Senator Phillips then attempted to secure passage of his relief appropriation bills, which provided $3,500,000 with which SRA was to wind up its affairs within three months, and $20,000,000 subvention to the counties to pay two-thirds of the cost of relief for the biennium. Both measures were turned down by the Senate by a vote of 21 aye (17 Republicans and 4 Democrats) to 18 no (12 Democrats and 6 Republicans).[70]

Two serious attempts to work out a compromise on relief failed in the Senate following the defeat of the Phillips appropriation bills. A bill by Democratic Senator E. George Luckey of Brawley, appropriating $3,500,000 for SRA for a final three-month period and transferring SRA's functions to the State Department of Social Welfare after that time, got 17 votes (14 Democratic and 3 Republican) while 19 votes (17 Republican and 2 Democratic) were cast against it.[71] Senator Phillips, who led the fight against the Luckey bill, said that his group "first want complete assurance that the SRA is finished," and said that the transfer of SRA personnel and functions to the Department of Social Welfare was not acceptable.[72] The other compromise bill, by Democratic Senator Jack Shelley of San Francisco, would have continued SRA for one year with an appropriation of $36,000,000 and then turned its functions over to the Department of Social Welfare, with county administration optional. This measure was turned down by the Senate, by almost the same vote with which it rejected the Luckey bill.

By this time the deadlock was complete, and tempers were frayed. The Senate then voted to adjourn *sine die*, without appropriating *any* money for relief. The roll call on the motion was 24 to 5.[73] When the

Assembly by a vote of 32 to 32 refused to pass an adjournment motion, Speaker Garland himself declared the session at an end.[74]

And thus came the State Relief Administration to its inglorious end. Finance Director Killion mailed dismissal notices to the 2,200 employees, notifying them that SRA would wind up on June 30.[75] Olson in a broadcast said that legislators who had blocked an appropriation for SRA were going to blame him for his veto of the county relief bill on May 7, but he reminded his listeners that the measure was not a relief appropriation bill, but "a bill which only contemplated the possibility that an appropriation might be made to the counties to aid the counties in assuming the burden of providing dole relief."[76] In the same speech Governor Olson announced that he would not call the Legislature back into session to solve the problem: "In view of the fact that it was impossible for the Legislature, after a session of three and one-half months, to enact any constructive measure on this subject, I am constrained to believe that nothing could be accomplished by calling them into session again."

This was the real end of the SRA, although it lingered on as a paper organization until the passage of the Johnson-Wollenberg Act of 1943. As the relief load was exceedingly light at the time appropriations ran out and the counties began taking over the residue, the financial troubles presented by the end of state relief were not overly burdensome. The San Francisco *News* excoriated both the Legislature ("the most arrant evader of grave official responsibility") and Governor Olson (for his "uncompromising attitude"), but found some light in the shadows: "There is something to be said for shaking off the barnacles of the huge SRA bureaucracy that has fastened itself upon the state during the past seven or eight years."[77] The Los Angeles *Times* blamed Olson for his veto of "a well-considered, experience-proved plan for local, short-range relief control by the counties," and concluded: "The situation is an impossible one, of course. Something must be done about it and quickly. But what? The answer seems to be up to the Governor."[78] But Olson did not call the Legislature back into session and the burden of paying the costs for relief fell upon the more populous counties. On June 30, 1941, the SRA offices throughout the state were closed, and the Department of Finance began the liquidation of SRA property. The state continued to run twelve single-men's camps, but the counties were required to pay for the keep of the men they sent to the camps.[79]

Shortly after SRA closed down, Governor Olson commuted to time served the sentences of eighteen former SRA employees convicted in Stockton of being in contempt of the Yorty committee.[80] These persons had originally been sentenced to one year in the county jail and fined $500 each for refusing to answer questions of Yorty and his colleagues. The State Supreme Court had later cut their sentences in half and dismissed the fines. As one of his last acts as governor, Olson granted full pardons to the "Stockton 18."[81]

Both Senator Phillips and Governor Olson had fought too hard for their different relief programs, and as a consequence neither was able to put his through the Legislature. Of course, the major victory was Phillips'—the SRA had ended. But the counties were forced to find additional funds in the short run for relief purposes, and county supervisors who had so long been anxious to secure control of relief policy now had to accept responsibility for paying the full costs of relief. And Olson was at last free of the burden of SRA. Job-hungry Democrats had nowhere to go, and he did not have to antagonize some of his followers who were not given the spoils they saw others getting. Now there were simply no jobs for anyone, except a few in the highest administrative positions, held by now by persons for the most part experienced and successful. SRA had outlived its usefulness as a dole-dispensing agency, and it now was discarded, "unwept, unhonoured and unsung."

13 reforms—
and attempted reforms

BUILDING AND LOAN ASSOCIATIONS, ESPECIALLY THOSE OF THE stockholding variety, had for some years been a controversial issue in California politics. In one of his last campaign speeches in 1938, Olson made clear his own attitude:

> Building and loan associations were originally formed to receive the savings of their members, in order that they might be pooled and loaned to their members for their mutual benefit in the building of their homes, and returned with interest on an amortized plan, usually paid out over a period of years.
>
> Stock promoters saw in this rich field an opportunity to institute stock-holding building and loan associations, to be controlled by stock-holding interests for their profit. For that purpose they promoted the enactment of laws under which these stockholding interests received all savings in this form of building and loan association over and above six per cent guarantee to their depositors.[1]

He charged that his opponent had been lax in the regulation of such companies: "In the case of one large company, Governor Merriam's administration permitted it to invest its funds in hotels, bars, ranches

169

and other speculative enterprises. At the same time, that association was not even paying withdrawals to its depositors, although it was permitted to receive new deposits and invest them in speculative enterprises." This was a reference to the huge Pacific States Savings and Loan Company, whose tangled affairs were to give the Olson administration one of its greatest problems.[2]

Two months after the inaugural of Olson, Building and Loan Commissioner Ralph W. Evans took possession of the PSSL by moving into its offices in San Francisco. A former assemblyman and Olson's first executive secretary, Evans was empowered under the law to check the books of each association and see that regulations were being complied with; and if an association was near collapse the commissioner had the authority to take over the management, appoint a custodian, and liquidate it or allow it to resume business under certain conditions.[3]

When he made the seizure of the PSSL, Commissioner Evans said that while his examiners were conducting their inquiry into its affairs the Pacific States Auxiliary Corporation (controlled by the same interests as PSSL) had moved its offices from the headquarters of PSSL and had denied the commissioner's men access to the books.[4] He charged that while the examination was being conducted, officials of PSSL had removed certain papers from the offices and burned them. The commissioner judged that there was an impairment of the capital of PSSL due to the use of "unsound" business practices.

The selection of a custodian presented Olson and Evans with a problem, since that person would have to be able to post a $500,000 bond. The man they chose was Norman W. Church, who had made a fortune as a dealer in bicycles, automobiles and accessories in San Francisco and Los Angeles, and as president and general manager of the Elgin Clock Company, before his retirement in the late 1920's.[5] After that he had devoted his time to horse breeding and racing, operating a stable and farm near San Jose. Church was associated with the Hollywood Turf Club, a syndicate which had started building a race track at Inglewood in competition with Santa Anita only to have its license revoked by the California Horse Racing Commission.[6] After his trainer had been suspended and his horses banned from the California tracks by the commission for alleged doping of his well-known horse "Proclivity" on New Year's Day, 1937, Church shipped his horses east and began a legal battle with the commission.[7] He hired a battery of lawyers headed by

United States Senator Burton K. Wheeler of Montana to fight for the reinstatement of his trainer, and in time succeeded with his campaign.[8] By this time the "Proclivity Affair" had become a political issue, for Senator Wheeler in statements, radio talks, and advertisements charged Governor Merriam with unfairness in his refusal to grant Church a hearing. Church contended that "Proclivity" had not been doped, and that the affair was merely a conspiracy to blacken his name on the part of those opposed to the new track, and vowed that he would never race his horses in California again as long as the present Racing Commission was in authority. Ralph W. Evans had long been Church's attorney.[9]

The other leading figure of the PSSL drama was Robert S. Odell, the company's pugnacious president. Out of town when Evans made the seizure, Odell rushed back to San Francisco only to find himself barred from his former offices. Odell at once charged that the action had been politically inspired, for "great opportunities were presented for filling positions with the politically faithful who have been clamoring at the doors of Governor Olson for jobs." He said that Norman Church had told him of contributing a large sum to the Olson campaign and had said that he hadn't given the money for "fun" but "for what I can get out of it." Odell asserted that the Pacific States Auxiliary Corporation was a holding company owning the stock of PSSL, and that as it had no bearing on the operations of PSSL the commissioner had no right to examine its books. He contended also that the burned papers were only work sheets.[10]

Odell at once telegraphed Governor Olson for an appointment and the governor wired back that he would see him on the following Monday, March 6, in Sacramento.[11] At the hearing in the governor's office, Odell repeated his charge of "political confiscation," but the governor contended that Evans was operating only in the interest of the PSSL certificate holders, and that Church had been selected because of his "financial responsibility and recognized business abilities." Odell charged that he had turned down an offer of Church's to secure the deletion of the passage referring to PSSL from the recorded speech made by Olson in exchange for a campaign contribution of $5,000.[12] Following this hearing, Odell met with newspaper reporters and made a full statement of his charges in public.[13]

While Odell at once began court proceedings to regain possession of PSSL, the battle entered the Legislature. A bill permitting Evans to hire outside counsel and aid in the case passed the Senate by a vote of 23 to 14, only to die in the Assembly, where it could muster only 37 votes to 39 opposed.[14] It had become something of a party issue, for the Democrats voted in favor of the bill 14 to 3 in the Senate and 35 to 7 in the Assembly, while the Republicans voted against it 11 to 9 in the Senate and 32 to 2 in the Assembly. In spite of this action of the Legislature, Commissioner Evans went ahead, hiring attorneys and using PSSL funds to pay them, in which course he was eventually upheld by the United States Supreme Court.[15] By February 1941, legal fees amounted to approximately $500,000, all paid out of PSSL funds (i.e., from the money invested by the certificate holders).[16]

In March 1940, following Governor Olson's request that the Legislature pass measures to give the state a larger share of the receipts of horse racing, more sensational charges were made against Norman Church. Senator D. Jack Metzger (Republican, Red Bluff), chairman of the horse race investigating committee, told his colleagues in Los Angeles that Church told him he had put $80,000 into the Olson campaign for the purpose of controlling the Horse Racing Commission, and had warned Metzger that if Santa Anita did not give up its opposition to the governor's "take" bill it would not be given any more choice winter racing dates.[17] Shortly after this, officers of the Hollywood Turf Club, currently holding summer racing, told the Metzger committee that Church and Evans had offered to arrange winter dates for them if the club would contribute $300,000 to the Democratic campaign chest.[18] These charges, denied though they were by Olson, Church and Evans, served to block approval of the legislation increasing the state's "take" from horse racing. After a stormy tenure of office, Norman Church resigned as custodian of PSSL in the fall of 1940 and was replaced by San Francisco financier Harley Hise.[19]

Meanwhile the court cases involving PSSL continued. The San Francisco *Chronicle* probably represented widespread opinion when it said: "There is little doubt that the assets of the company were seriously impaired when the State seized control for the announced purpose of protecting the certificate holders. There is no more doubt that under political management since the seizure the assets have been further seriously impaired. The longer the litigation continues the less money will be left for those who own it."[20] The Odell interests secured passage by the 1941 Legislature of a bill which would have permitted building and loan associations taken over by the state to formulate their own reorganization plans, but Governor Olson vetoed it.[21] A similar measure qualified for a place on the 1942 general election ballot as Proposition 10, but was overwhelmingly defeated by the voters.

The seizure was upheld by the courts, and in spite of the *Chronicle*'s remark, no impairment of the assets took place. The liquidation of the claims of certificate holders was finally completed under Olson's successor, who announced that the attorney general would take over all of the legal cases involving PSSL and that fees for private attorneys would be discontinued.[22]

PSSL was a headache for Olson from the outset. Odell fought back furiously. The choice of Church, no matter what his abilities may have been, was a political mistake of the first magnitude. As early as May 9, 1939, Superintendent of Banks E. W. Wilson reminded the governor that he had earlier advised him that Odell should be removed from the management of PSSL "by way of maneuvering rather than by law suit." It is hard to disagree with Wilson's description of the Evans action in instituting suit as "a business mistake and a political mistake."[23]

Norman W. Church, whose presence in the administration had brought so much grief to Olson, in 1942 contributed $1,000 to the "Warren for Governor Finance Committee."[24]

Government Reorganization

The reform of the executive department of the California state government, particularly its fiscal agencies, had long been advocated. Governor Merriam had appointed a semi-official committee to study the question of state governmental reorganization and consolidation, and that group had raised a substantial sum to finance a study by the Chicago firm of Griffenhagen and Associates. In line with the 1937 progress report of this committee, bills proposing the reorganization of fiscal responsibilities and powers were introduced in the 1937 session but failed to pass. In a message to the Legislature on May 16, 1939, Governor Olson recommended a series of measures by Senator Kenny, incorporating the major recommendations of the Merriam committee. Olson told the legislators, "I need not emphasize that the problems involved transcend partisanship."[25]

One set of Kenny reorganization measures would have taken from the controller his pre-auditing and accounting functions, and given them to the director of finance, an appointee of the governor. The controller would then become an "auditor-general," with the responsibility for post-auditing, a function at the time performed by the finance director. Another set of Kenny bills would have created a Department of Revenue, headed by a director appointed by the governor. This new department would be responsible for all state tax collection, to replace the existing system under which different taxes were collected by five different state agencies. A third set of Kenny measures would have created a Department of Alcoholic Beverage Control, which would take over liquor regulation from the Board of Equalization. The latter body would then become what it had once primarily been, a Board of Equalization of assessment of state and county taxes.

However logical these reorganization measures seemed to efficiency experts, they were enormously disturbing to powerful independent officials in the state government, who quickly allied themselves with administration opponents in the Legislature to block the reforms. The State Board of Equalization, which collected approximately 70 per cent of the state taxes (including the sales tax, chief revenue producer),[26] and enjoyed almost unlimited control over the liquor industry, fought against the proposals, and its chairman was a participant in the maneuver by which the opposition seized control of the Assembly in 1940. Few of the Kenny bills reached the floor of the Senate for consideration, and those that did were defeated. Senator Ray W. Hays (Republican, Fresno) contended that the bills were so "drastic," the Legislature should postpone action for at least two years to let the people decide whether they wanted that much centralization of authority.[27]

Governor Olson was something less than tactful in his effort to get the Legislature to pass the Kenny bills. In the midst of his great struggle with his opponents, he recounted his difficulties to his radio audience, saying:

> Notwithstanding all these differences between the reactionaries and my administration, I, as before stated, want to talk to you now in behalf of certain measures of real economy and efficiency in the State Government, on which, it seems to me, all members of the Legislature, all citizens, and all groups—from the Workers' Alliance to the Chamber of Commerce—and even all special privilege-seeking and tax dodging interests, should unhesitatingly agree.[28]

Olson in September, 1939, told a Democratic luncheon that these reorganization measures should go on the 1940 ballot as initiatives,[29] but no organized campaign in their behalf developed and they failed to qualify. In his first biennial message, the governor again asked for passage of these measures, but the proposals never reached the floor of either house for discussion during the 1941 session.

Olson was also interested in the reform of the California Legislature. During his first year in the Senate he had become an advocate of a unicameral legislature, endorsing a proposed constitutional amendment to abolish the Senate.[30] In 1936, he told the Commonwealth Club that his advocacy of a unicameral legislature was based upon his firm belief in popular democracy. "History will verify that all restraints against the realization of free popular government, locally or nationally, have been impediments to the progress of the masses of the people toward a higher order of education and social and economic well-being."[31] A 1937 unicameral intiative measure proved to be abortive, but succeeded in arousing the fervent opposition of such groups as the California Farm Bureau Federation, the California State Chamber of Commerce, the American Legion, the California Real Estate Association, the California Taxpayers' Association and the California Teachers' Association.[32] A unicameral proposal in 1939 failed to emerge from Assembly committee. An announcement by Democratic State Chairman John Gee Clark in favor of a plan for strict population-based representation met the hostility of the Sacramento *Bee*. The *Bee* contended that San Francisco, Alameda and Los Angeles counties would thereby dominate the Legislature. "And rural California would be given about as much consideration as Lazarus at the table of Dives."[33]

Following his unpleasant experiences with the Republican-dominated 1939 State Senate, Governor Olson turned once more to plans to institute a one-house legislature. The press reported that Olson's "supporters believe the time is politically at hand to place the proposal on the next ballot."[34] A "Citizens' Committee Sponsoring One House Legislature" was set up to push a measure abolishing the Senate and raising the salaries of the assemblymen from $100 to $300 per month.[35] Due to the preoccupation of the administration with other matters and to lack of campaign funds, this initiative failed to qualify. A northern California branch of the committee was set up, headed by Attorney William H. Hollander of Oakland, who asked the governor for financial aid for the campaign to qualify the petitions.[36] The governor waited over four months before replying to Hollander's letter, and then his answer on finances was not reassuring, although Olson said that he still wanted the measure on the 1942 ballot.[37] Once again the proposal failed to make the ballot, as the administration was occupied with other matters and not sure enough of its future to throw away what rural strength it had by pushing unicameralism.

Health Insurance

Advocates of compulsory health insurance looked to the Olson administration for help in the enactment of their proposal, which had been the subject of a campaign that had lasted over twenty years. Olson's advocacy of some form of health insurance had been frequently proclaimed during the 1938 campaign. Between election and the inaugural, Lieutenant Governor Patterson announced that the administration would ask the Legislature to establish compulsory health insurance.[38]

The California Medical Association did not wait until the new regime had been inaugurated before devising an appropriate defensive measure. In December 1938 it set up the California Physicians Service, a state-wide voluntary low-cost medical system. This service was launched with appropriate publicity and was obviously "an effort to forestall any legislative action which would result in lay control over medicine."[39]

The Olson administration's compulsory health insurance plan was embodied in bills introduced by Floor Leader Ben Rosenthal in the Assembly and Senator Shelley in the upper house. These bills were drawn up with the assistance of Professors Barbara Armstrong and Samuel C. May of the University of California, Chester Rowell of the San Francisco *Chronicle*, and Dr. Philip King Brown, a prominent advocate of health insurance.[40] They proposed to provide unemployment benefits payable during incapacitating illness, and to provide medical, hospital, and other care to those whose annual incomes were under $3,000.[41] The insurance was to be compulsory for employees and voluntary for farmers, professional men and small proprietors, provided their incomes did not exceed $3,000. Beneficiaries were to be allowed to choose and to change their doctors, and doctors were to be paid quarterly sums for each person on their lists, regardless of the number of calls. Doctors were to have access to laboratory tests and serums at diagnostic centers, and specialists would be available for consultations. The plan was to be financed in a manner similar to the social security program of the federal government, with 1 per cent contributions from employers and workers, plus a like amount from the state treasury, to be paid out of federal grants-in-aid if such were to be made available.

Olson appointed a committee of 21 prominent Californians to make a study and report on his health insurance plan. This group, headed by Chester Rowell, included most of the persons who had helped in the drafting of the administration's measure, as well as representatives of labor. Thus there was little doubt as to the views of the governor's committee.[42] The governor followed up with a radio speech explaining his proposed plan,[43] and a long, detailed message to the Legislature. Olson said, "I urge this health insurance measure as a central policy of my administration," although he noted that it was far more than a mere party or personal policy.

The administration had many other problems to contend with during the 1939 session, and could not give its fullest strength to the health insurance struggle. The medical profession, publicizing its new California Physicians Service, assailed the Olson-backed measure vigorously. The San Francisco *Examiner* said that the scheme "mixes politics and medicine in a dose that would soon nauseate the recipients—all persons earning $3,000 a year or less."[44]

Governor Olson had included in his 1939 budget an appropriation of $200,000 to finance diagnostic centers and provide operating expenses for the first six months of compulsory health insurance. This item was assailed as improper on the ground that the Legislature had not yet expressed itself on the subject of compulsory health insurance. Rosenthal on April 11 asked the Assembly to delete this appropriation, saying that it would be made the subject of a special bill later. The Assembly agreed overwhelmingly.[45] Opponents of compulsory health insurance had caught the administration in an attempt to "smuggle" through an appropriation. Henceforth it would be necessary to secure passage of a separate health insurance appropriation by a two-thirds vote of each house.

The administration amended the Assembly bill in various ways, in an attempt to win passage. On May 16 the Assembly turned down an amendment which would have provided for a popular referendum on the measure before it could go into effect. The roll call on this measure, which was backed by the supporters of compulsory health insurance, was 33 aye (29 Democrats and 4 Republicans) to 41 no (30 Republicans and 11 Democrats).[46] The final vote on the bill came at the end of the session, when the Assembly rejected the measure by a vote of 20 aye to 48 no, with only 19 Democrats and Republican Ray Williamson of San Francisco voting in its favor.[47] The Senate version never got out of committee.

After the 1939 session compulsory health insurance measures had no chance of passage, for both houses were controlled by administration enemies and part of the anti-Olson coalition of interest groups was the medical profession. Olson chided the California State Federation of Labor's lobbyist for his part in defeating health insurance in spite of the federation resolution in favor of it.[48] The broad groups the governor had hoped would support him never came to his aid, antagonized, perhaps, by other aspects of his program. In his first biennial message the governor repeated his recommendations for a compulsory health insurance plan, but in neither house of the Legislature could such a measure even get to the floor for a vote. The initiative taken by the California Medical Association in December 1938 appears to have been the decisive action. Compulsory health insurance was another Olson policy that got nowhere during his regime.

The Youth Authority

In the summer of 1939 the body of a 13-year-old inmate of Whittier State School was found hanging from the bar of a window in a solitary cell in the school's "Lost Privilege Cottage." Director of Institutions Rosanoff investigated at the request of Governor Olson, and exonerated the school administration from blame for the death. A committee headed by Leo Gallagher made a second investigation of the incident and likewise exonerated the institution from blame. Less than a year after the first death, a second one occurred under similar circumstances, and the Los Angeles press launched an attack on the school's administration.

Governor Olson appointed a committee of three, Judge Ben B. Lindsey (chairman), Mrs. Helen Mellinkoff, and Reverend Ernest Caldecott, to make a thorough investigation of the situation at Whittier. The committee made a long and careful study, reporting that Rosanoff's investigations had been inadequate and his recommendations "superficial."[49]

The Lindsey committee found corporal punishment prevalent and condemned the lack of counseling and vocational training, as well as the lack of responsibility and general apathy in the administration of the institution. The Lindsey group recommended that Olson appoint a committee composed of Right Reverend E. J. Flanagan (the famed Father Flanagan of Boys' Town), a representative of the federal Department of Justice, and a representative of the Osborne Society of New York, an important penology research group. The Lindsey committee suggested that the new group make an investigation and recommend a person to take charge of Whittier School on a temporary basis.

The governor followed the recommendations of the Lindsey committee, except that he was unable to secure the services of a representative of the federal government. He appointed a committee of three—Father Flanagan, William B. Cox of the Osborne Society, and Mrs. Mellinkoff. On April 4, 1941, Flanagan requested the suspension of Superintendent E. J. Milne of Whittier.[50] Rosanoff sent a notice of suspension to Milne "until charges filed against you have been acted upon by the State Personnel Board and its investigations now under way are completed."[51] The Flanagan committee in its report to Governor Olson severely criticized the management of Whittier School, and made a series of recommendations.[52] Father Flanagan and Mrs. Mellinkoff recommended that Cox be made permanent superintendent, succeeding Milne.[53]

Shortly after the Flanagan committee made its report, a special committee of the Assembly, headed by Gerald C. Kepple of Whittier, told of deplorable conditions in the city of Whittier caused by the numerous escapes from the school. The committee criticized the idea of turning the school into a sort of Boys' Town.[54] Shortly after this, Governor Olson called a conference at his office, to which came the members of the Assembly committee, Rosanoff, Cox and Mrs. Mellinkoff.[55] At this conference all phases of the problems of Whittier State School were discussed, and Cox told of his own background and experience, as well as his plans for Whittier. He apparently made a good impression on the legislators.

Cox served as superintendent of the institution, renamed the Nelles School for Boys, until November 1941, when he resigned after a series of squabbles with Rosanoff and some difficulty about his civil service status.[56] After more complications, Paul J. McCusick was made superintendent in the spring of 1942. A legislative committee headed by Senator C. H. Deuel (Democrat, Chico) made an extensive investigation of the state's penal institutions and reported to the 1943 Legislature that order had at last resulted at Whittier due largely to the work of McCusick.[57]

Out of the sorry mess at Whittier came an important reform. A bill introduced by Assemblyman James H. Phillips (Republican, Oakland) and others, setting up a "Youth Correctional Authority," passed the Legislature almost unanimously and was signed by Governor Olson on July 9, 1941. The California Youth Authority has been called "one of the most enlightened steps of recent years in the field of penology."[58] The authority, consisting of three members, was designated as the agency to which offenders aged twenty-one or less were committed by the courts. The authority, which had some jurisdiction over youth institutions, replaced the judges in the determination of whether a young offender should be confined or paroled. The Deuel committee described the authority as "a great step forward."[59] The youth authority was implemented during the Warren regime, and remains a major accomplishment of the Olson period, thoroughly in harmony with the governor's earnest humanitarian principles.

Mental Institutions

Prior to his inauguration, Olson took a tour of the state's institutions and was shocked at the overcrowded conditions prevailing.[60] As he took a special interest in the problems of mental patients, he appointed as his director of institutions Dr. Aaron J. Rosanoff, famed Los Angeles psychiatrist. Dr. Rosanoff pledged that reforms would be instituted during his regime: "California will no longer maintain its institutions as passive receptacles for end products of psychotic disease. No longer will patients be committed to these institutions as a desperate measure of last resort."[61]

Olson's 1939 budget called for substantial increases in expenditure for state mental institutions. Although the Legislature slashed the funds, Olson still was able to report in his first biennial message that 1,284 beds had been added to the capacity of the state's mental institutions. Dr. Rosanoff instituted the use of the insulin shock treatment for acute schizophrenia, which resulted in a recovery rate of 83 per cent, as contrasted with 8 per cent prior to the innovation. Furthermore, mental patients were more frequently paroled to their families. Olson reported that the number of mental patients on parole had increased 67 per cent during his first two years of office, and that as a consequence there had actually taken place a reduction in the population of the mental institutions. The new beds and the liberalizing of paroles had resulted in a reduction of overcrowding by approximately one-fourth.

An important achievement of the Olson administration was the establishment of the Langley Porter Clinic in San Francisco. This clinic was established as a center for the treatment of mental ailments in early stages, for research into mental disorders, and for the training of administrators of the state's other institutions. It was named for the recently retired Dean of the University of California School of Medicine, who had long advocated the construction of such an establishment. Governor Olson, in his address at the laying of the cornerstone, said that to him the "prime mover" was Dr. Rosanoff:

> Two years ago, after the State budget had been fixed for submission to the Legislature [a budget in the making of which he had no part], he persuaded me to include in it the cost of this project, which I did, although with but little notion that it would receive legislative approval. But thanks to his tireless efforts acquainting the Legislature with the lasting benefits that would accure to the mentally afflicted, to society in general and to the University School of Medicine; to say nothing of the substantial savings that would accrue to the Department of Institutions, the appropriation was approved.[62]

Thus the Olson administration was able to launch a significant experiment in the treatment of mental disorders, one that was to attract widespread attention in the years ahead and remain one of the outstanding contributions of the Olson regime.

Prison Reform

When he took office, Olson inherited a penal system that was both cumbersome and antiquated. California's prisons were listed second from the bottom on a recognized national rating scale.[63] Olson appointed John Gee Clark, Democratic state chairman and former assemblyman from Long Beach, to fill a vacancy on the Board of Prison Terms and Paroles, designating him chairman of that body and also director of the

Department of Penology. Clark selected as his assistant the famed penologist Kate Richards O'Hare, and the two of them set out to reform the state's prison system.

The tasks before Clark and Mrs. O'Hare were formidable indeed. The Department of Penology was a "paper" department only, for it consisted of six autonomous divisions and its director lacked authority and responsibility.[64]

The control of prisons was lodged with a five-man state board of prison directors who served ten-year staggered terms, as provided by the Constitution of 1879 (presumably "to keep the prisons out of politics"). These directors, unpaid, had authority to hire and fire prison employees, including wardens, without civil service restrictions. After he had been in office three months, Clark wrote to the governor: "Until the constitutional provisions relating to the Board of Prison Directors are abolished, the powers of the Director of Penology, with reference to penal institutions, cannot be more than advisory. . . . One of the most valuable functions and services a Director of Penology could render would be to secure the passage of such a measure."[65] A constitutional amendment granting the Legislature full authority to provide for the "establishment, governance and superintendence" of the state's prisons passed the 1939 Legislature, and went on the 1940 general election ballot.

As director of penology, Clark had the authority to investigate the prisons and make recommendations to the governor. Food riots at San Quentin Prison, as well as reports of tortures there, led to a full-scale investigation by Clark and Lieutenant Governor Patterson, who frequently visited the prison in his capacity as head of the Advisory Pardon Board. Clark instituted charges against the Board of Prison Directors, and Governor Olson himself presided at a series of hearings.[66] The care with which the governor proceeded was a matter of concern to the prison reformers. Mrs. O'Hare wrote to Olson on December 19, 1939: "Naturally our greatest anxiety is to have the hearing finished as soon as possible, within the limits of absolute fairness on your part. There has been the ever present danger that some sort of a riot or serious breach of discipline might occur in San Quentin."[67] On April 10, 1940, the governor ousted the remaining four members of the Board of Prison Directors (the term of the fifth had by then expired).[68] In a 29-page decision Olson found the board members guilty of incompetency and neglect of duty, sustaining the charges made at the long hearing that the members had countenanced flogging, had failed to keep proper records, had appointed an incompetent warden, and had permitted poor food to be served. Five days later Olson appointed Isaac Pacht, prominent Los Angeles lawyer and former superior judge, to the board, and on June 26, following court proceedings, he replaced the ousted four with new men, and Pacht became chairman.

Almost at once, the new Board of Prison Directors removed Warden Court Smith of San Quentin and replaced him with Clinton T. Duffy, on a temporary basis. Duffy, himself born at San Quentin where his father had been a guard, was a former clerk at the prison and at the time of his appointment as acting warden was assistant secretary of the Board of Prison Terms and Paroles, in which capacity he had learned of the deplorable conditions prevailing under Court Smith. Duffy said: "I had a wonderful opportunity to watch and work with men who were anxious to earn their paroles, and through them I became aware of the hell bubbling inside the walls. San Quentin trembled on the brink of riot, and we were afraid that if it came, many lives would be lost and prison progress would be turned back a hundred years."[69] In spite of the fact that Court Smith refused at first to give up the warden's office, expecting to be reinstated after Duffy's trial period was up, Duffy went ahead with a series of drastic reforms at San Quentin.[70] He fired the captain and six other guards responsible for beating prisoners, closed the ghastly underground dungeons, banned the use of all types of corporal punishment, covered over the "nine-inch circles in one of the cell blocks where offending prisoners had been forced to stand for hours at a stretch without moving or talking," abolished head shaving, eliminated the big numbers on prisoners' clothes, improved the food, and installed fresh-water showers for the prisoners. These and many other reforms had the full backing of the new Board of Prison Directors, and on September 1, 1940, Duffy was given a four-year appointment as warden by the board. Duffy's activities were widely acclaimed, and in 1943 the Deuel committee was unstinting in his praise.[71]

John Gee Clark, whose prison reform program included the centralization of administration of the penal system, the establishment of civil service for penal officers, the expansion of road camps, the reduction of overcrowding, and the greater diversification of penal institutions,[72] was aided immensely by the voters' approval of the constitutional amendment granting the Legislature jurisdiction over the prison system. This measure, Proposition 3 on the 1940 general election ballot, was passed by the narrowest of margins: Yes, 994,101; No, 991,722. It carried Los Angeles County by a majority of more than 130,000 votes, enough to put it over in the state.

A legislative committee in 1941 recommended the appointment of a full-time, well-paid director of corrections to administer the prison system, with the Board of Prison Directors acting in the capacity of a rule-making and policy-forming body.[73] A bill carrying out this recommendation, introduced by Senator Phillips and others, passed the Senate by a vote of 28 to 9,[74] but never cleared the Assembly. Such a measure advocated by the Deuel committee was passed by the Legislature in 1944.

The State Board of Prison Terms and Paroles was a paid, three-man body, serving staggered four-year terms. This board had authority to fix the exact length of prisoners' terms and to grant paroles. The governor had no power to grant paroles, but he could revoke them for cause and order the apprehension of the parolee. Until January 1941 this board was dominated by two Merriam appointees, James Stephens and Fred Esola, with Clark the sole Olson-named member. The governor intervened when this board granted a parole to Gilbert H. Beesemyer, famed embezzler of $8,000,000 of the funds of the Guarantee Building and Loan Association of Hollywood.[75] Olson, aided by the demands of some of Beesemyer's many victims, persuaded the board to revoke the parole, but a few months later it granted Beesemyer another parole, and he was released on certain conditions. This second parole was granted in the absence of Chairman Clark, and Governor Olson said, "I can't do anything about it. The parole was apparently voted by two holdovers on the board from a previous administration. All I can do is revoke his parole for cause in the future if terms have been violated."[76] On January 16, 1941, Olson was able to make a second appointment to the board, and henceforth it worked more harmoniously with the administration.

Olson was the first governor to turn over all applications for executive clemency to the Advisory Pardon Board.[77] Merriam had submitted 454 applications during 1935–1938; Olson submitted 2,173 during 1939–1942. This board was an *ex officio* body, composed of the lieutenant governor (chairman), the attorney general, the head of the Criminal Identification and Investigation Division, and the wardens of San Quentin and Folsom prisons. The body was superseded in 1944 by the "Adult Authority" in a major prison reform.[78]

The major accomplishment of the Olson administration in the field of penal reform was the minimum security prison at Chino. The 1935 Legislature had provided for "segregation from the hardened criminals, of those prisoners capable of moral rehabilitation and restoration to good citizenship."[79] A site for an institution to handle such prisoners was acquired, but the "custody minded" Board of Prison Directors had thrown away the plans and proceeded to begin a new penitentiary. In 1938, John Gee Clark met with a group including Los Angeles County Probation Officer Kenyon J. Scudder to see what could be done about getting the Chino institution back on the path the Legislature had intended for it. Scudder, at the request of Clark, made a survey of the Chino site and found that a partially completed high barbed-wire fence and a number of gun towers were its most outstanding features.

Judge Isaac Pacht, head of Olson's new Board of Prison Directors, offered the post of warden at Chino to Scudder in December 1940, promising that he would have no interference from the board in his establishment of a real minimum-security institution, and that he would be free from political pressure. After a conference with Olson, in which he told the governor that he had been ousted from the wardenship of Whittier School during the Rolph administration for refusing to accept politically-inspired personnel recommendations, and had been told by Olson that no such interference would take place at Chino, Scudder accepted the post. He found that Olson's penal philosophy was "both progressive and sound."[80]

Solidly supported by Pacht and George A. Briggs, another of Olson's appointees to the Board of Prison Directors, Scudder abandoned the gun towers and the high fence at Chino and went ahead with plans for a real minimum-security prison, the first of its kind in America. However, he almost came to grief in the business of choosing his fifty "supervisors" (the term "guard" was shunned). The positions were outside civil service and within the province of Scudder himself to fill. Scudder wanted to find young people who were in sympathy with the experiment and not "custody minded." He received 2,300 applications! Scudder had the State Personnel Board administer tests to 700 applicants, and then spent a week in interviewing the 225 who made the best scores. Scudder, himself a Republican, was "informed that the governor was very much displeased with the idea of an examination," and wanted him to accept the recommendations sent down from Sacramento.[81] However, the Board of Prison Directors, led by Pacht and Briggs, backed Scudder, who was able to pick his own men without political interference.

The Chino episode shows very clearly a conflict within Olson. As a humanitarian, he was in complete sympathy with the experiment at Chino, and he appointed a Board of Prison Directors who shared his views. As a politician, he had to pay some attention to the intense pressure placed upon him for jobs by the faithful. Unquestionably Olson was something of a Jacksonian Democrat in matters of patronage and could never see why good Democrats couldn't be found for any job. Chino was a major achievement of the Olson regime both because of and in spite of the governor's actions.

14 *defense and war*

AS THE NAZIS SWEPT THROUGH THE LOWLANDS AND INTO FRANCE, the attention of California—like that of the rest of the country—was soon drawn to the pressing need for a national defense program. Governor Olson on May 31, 1940, announced that he intended to appoint a state council of defense, saying, "I am the kind of pacifist who believes that our Nation should be prepared at all times to resist encroachment by foreign dictatorships."[1]

In June Olson, by executive order, created the California State Council of Defense "to study and plan; to organize and coordinate; to cooperate with the President's National Council of Defense; to help California to make the maximum contribution of which she is capable."[2] This council, one of the first such in the country, held its organizational meeting in Sacramento on June 24. Its members were fifty prominent Californians, including representatives of the armed forces, veterans organizations, agriculture, manufacturing, colleges and universities, labor, local government, the press and women's clubs, as well as twenty-three state officials. Governor Olson, who was himself chairman, appointed an executive committee of 11 members (later increased to 13) to act between sessions of the full council. Members of the executive committee included Professor Samuel C. May (vice chairman of the council); Attorney General Earl Warren; and Adjutant General R. E. Mittelstaedt. Executive secretary of the council was Major J. O. Donovan of the State Planning Board.[3]

Early in August 1940 the advisory commission of the Council of National Defense sent to the state a memorandum outlining policies it recommended in the establishment of state councils of defense.[4] Among the suggestions of the "model" council memorandum were these:

1 The council should be appointed by the governor.

2 The council should advise the governor, and not execute its own decisions.

3 The council "may" consist of the governor as chairman *ex officio,* an executive vice-chairman, and members appointed by or with the consent of the governor.

4 Each member should be given responsibility for a "broad functional area of subject matter," and under each a committee may be formed, consisting of appropriate state and federal officials as well as private individuals, to be appointed by the governor.

5 Others who "might well be added," formally or informally, are members of the Legislature, the head of the state planning board (if any), and a representative of organized local government.

In line with these recommendations, the California council was reorganized on September 13, 1940. Six committees, each headed by an appropriate person or persons, were set up: agricultural resources and production; civil protection; health, welfare and consumer interest; human resources and skills; industrial resources and production; transportation, housing, works and facilities.[5]

The State Council of Defense was a governor's council, and as such it had no formal legal basis and no money of its own. Unfortunately for the smooth functioning of the council, the struggle to secure legislative authorization and funds for it was long and difficult. The bitter hostility between Olson and the legislative majority, intensified by the relief problem and the 1940 elections, held up legislative action until almost the end of the 1941 session. National defense activities presented new opportunity for each side and there was a "rush by both the Legislature and the Governor to occupy and dominate this field of growing importance."[6] In September 1940 the governor asked the third special session of the Legislature to pass an act granting legal recognition to the council and appropriating $50,000 for its use.[7] "Model" bills drafted by the council and carrying out the Olson recommendations were introduced by Democratic legislators, Senator Irwin T. Quinn of Eureka and Assemblyman Cecil King of Los Angeles.[8] Republican Senator Arthur H. Breed, Jr., of Oakland introduced a bill paralleling the "model" measure except for the substitution of the attorney general (a Republican) for the governor (a Democrat) as executive head of the council! Other Republican bills provided for senatorial confirmation of the governor's appointees to the council and for an advisory committee of non-legislators, to be appointed by the Legislature. In view of the wide differences of opinion between the administration and the leaders of the Legislature, nothing was accomplished at the September and December special meetings of the Legislature, in spite of Olson's urging. The governor was forced to use money from his emergency fund to pay for the expense of the council.

The regular session of the 1941 Legislature finally passed a Council of Defense Act. As introduced by Senator Quinn, the bill provided that the principal authority within the council should be lodged in the executive committee, of which the governor would be only one member. It further provided for senatorial confirmation of the governor's appointees, with the council at large selecting from among the members the chairman and vice chairman of each committee, and the chairman choosing the other members of the committee. It provided only $10,000, to be spent by the council, which was barred from accepting money from the governor's emergency fund. Thus it represented a quite drastic departure from the "model" bill. Before it was finally passed, however, it was amended into a form more acceptable to Olson. The governor was made *ex officio* chairman, with power to appoint the vice chairman and the committees. The appropriation was raised to $25,000, and the restriction on the use of emergency funds was lifted. The council, not the executive committee, was empowered to employ personnel including an executive secretary (to be chosen either from the council or employed from outside at a maximum of $3,000 per year).[9]

As finally constituted, the State Council of Defense consisted of five *ex officio* state officers (governor, attorney general, adjutant general, state superintendent of public instruction, and director of public health) and twenty persons appointed by the governor, subject to senatorial confirmation. In addition, a legislative committee of two senators and three assemblymen (appointed by the president pro tem and speaker, respectively) was provided to participate in the work of the council. The act was made effective until September 1, 1943. As amended, the measure passed both houses without a dissenting vote, and was signed by Governor Olson on June 3, 1941. The now legalized council chose as its executive secretary Richard Graves, executive secretary of the League of California Cities, and went ahead with its work.

The State Guard

A major defense problem was presented to California by the impending induction of its National Guard into federal service. In his message to the fifth extraordinary session of the Legislature, on December 2, 1940, Governor Olson requested legislation to establish a state guard.[10] The governor sent along a letter from Adjutant General Mittelstaedt, who said that passage of the legislation was urgent because the entire National Guard would soon be called up by the federal government. The adjutant general noted that the California Military Code provided for no organization other than the National Guard. However, the session took no action on the subject.

Nevertheless, the adjutant general's office went ahead with its plan for a state guard, the need for which was acute after the induction of the 40th Infantry Division into federal service on March 3, 1941. Adjutant General Mittelstaedt resigned his state post to go with the division, and he was succeeded by Major Donovan. During the 1941 session, a bill introduced by Assemblyman Charles W. Lyon, Beverly Hills Republican, and others, providing for a state guard, passed both houses unanimously and was signed by the governor on June 17. The act directed the governor "to organize and maintain a State Guard with a minimum numerical strength of 10,000 persons and not to exceed such maximum strength as the Governor may prescribe." The governor was authorized to call the State Guard into active service for the purposes for which he could formerly have called the National Guard. A sum of $250,000 was appropriated by the act to the adjutant general to carry out its provisions during the biennium. By December 7, 1941, the strength of the State Guard was approximately 15,000.[11]

On the day of the Japanese attack, the State Guard was called into active duty at the request of the War Department, to guard plants and other places of military importance. A magazine correspondent reported one phase of the Guard's work on the night of December 7:

> The San Francisco–Oakland Bay Bridge remained lighted, but regular State Highway Patrol units were augmented by armed companies of the California State Guard. . . . A hundred men were guarding the Oakland site approaches, Toll Plaza, and the bridge span through the tunnel on Yerba Buena Island. . . Guards were also stationed along the Embarcadero guarding the state-owned belt railroad, wharves and warehouses. Altogether, about four hundred guardists on the San Francisco side. These men were ordered on duty from the state Adjutant General's office, Sacramento. An officer of the day at San Francisco Armory (guard headquarters) said exultantly: "We dare anyone to get in [Embarcadero warehouses, etc.]. They wouldn't get two feet."[12]

On December 8, Governor Olson issued a proclamation in which he called for 10,000 more volunteers for the state guard, preferably exservice men, to serve one-year enlistments. In his call the governor warned that "service in the State Guard is without compensation unless provision therefor should later be made by the Legislature of the State."[13]

Governor Olson called the Legislature into special session on December 19 to appropriate funds to meet defense expenses.[14] The governor told the Legislature of the activities of the State Guard since the 7th, reporting that a large portion of the 26,500-man guard was currently on active duty, at the request not only of the Army and Navy but also of local governments. Said Olson:

> Whether the full present strength of the Guard will be required on duty throughout the next year or during the rest of this biennium, or when, if at all, the Federal Government may make provision for guard duty at plants and places of military and strategic value in this State, I do not know. Nor could anyone know definitely at this time. But it is certain that plants and places of military and strategic value are also plants and places of great value to the State, as well as are other plants and places requiring protection from destruction.

The governor said that the adjutant general had advised him that the cost of maintaining the full guard on active duty for one year would be $37,090,881, provided the statutory pay scale for non-commissioned officers was raised and other benefits increased in line with the recommendations of Adjutant General Donovan. But Olson asked the Legislature to appropriate only $17,500,000, saying that he anticipated that the full strength of the guard might not be needed on active duty throughout the year and that the federal government might make provision for some of the guard duty. Olson also asked the Legislature to appropriate an additional $9,250,000 for the emergency fund, to bring it up to a full $10,000,000.

The California State Guard on December 17, 1941, was composed of thirteen infantry regiments, a small air force, cavalry, and service units, including engineers, a signal corps, medical corps, and a quartermaster organization. Many guards, when called to active duty, spent their own funds for uniforms, although Olson made available to them some materials formerly in the possession of the State Relief Administration. The $250,000 appropriated by the 1941 Legislature was soon exhausted. Few received the pay to which they were nominally entitled (for officers, the same as their equivalent rank on federal duty; for enlisted men, two dollars per day).[15]

The guard appropriation bill introduced by Senator Quinn and others, granting a sum of $10,000,000 for the State Guard as constituted by the Lyon Act of June 17, 1941, passed the Senate on December 21, 1941, by a vote of 34 to 1.[16] When the bill got to the Assembly, it was promptly held up in committee. Republican Assemblyman C. Don Field of Glendale inserted in the journal editorials opposing hasty action from the two Sacramento newspapers.[17] The *Bee* (December 18) had cautioned the Legislature to make sure necessity existed before approving a "vast" amount. The *Union* (December 19) had said, "The talk of formation of a State Guard sounds like an attempt to build up another political machine." And the *Bee* (December 20) asked the Legislature to vote a token sum and then study the problem. Two supporters of the guard in the Assembly, Lee T. Bashore (Republican, Glendora) and George D. Collins, Jr. (Democrat, San Francisco), gave notice that they would move to withdraw the bill from committee, but the Legislature instead recessed until January 12.

Olson was then in a difficult position with the State Guard (which by now had inevitably been dubbed "Olson's Army" by his enemies). But he found an unexpected and exceedingly unlikely ally in the person of William Randolph Hearst. The Olson-Hearst honeymoon, short-lived as all honeymoons, is one of the most curious episodes of the entire ad-

DEFENSE AND WAR

ministration. On January 4, 1942, the San Francisco *Examiner* said: "California should be looking out for itself and for Californians, and the Governor should be given the appropriation he asks for without delay." The *Examiner* had confidence that the governor would see that the proper persons were commissioned in the guard and that they would be properly trained.

When the Legislature reconvened, Assemblyman Bashore (who will be remembered as one of the governor's main opponents in the SRA struggles of 1940) made an attempt to withdraw the Quinn State Guard appropriation bill from committee. His motion fell short of success by two votes, securing 39 ayes (33 Democrats and 6 Republicans) to 35 noes (30 Republican and 5 Democratic).[18] The six Republicans supporting withdrawal included some of the most conservative members of the lower house. Speaker Garland and four of his "economy bloc" colleagues comprised the Democratic opposition.

After this roll call, the San Francisco *Examiner* attacked the anti-Olson bloc in the Assembly most violently, virtually endorsing the governor for reëlection: "Governor Olson has been very wise and patriotic in his attitude, very temperate and very judicious. He has made himself a great many friends and probably has assured his re-election. The lower house of the legislature has shown itself incompetent in peace and improvident in war."[19]

When it was evident that the Assembly would not pass the Quinn bill, alternative measures were brought up for consideration. A bill by Republican Assemblymen Randal F. Dickey of Alameda and Clyde A. Watson of Orange proposed a drastic overhauling of the State Guard's structure, which supporters of the Guard said "establishes merely a night-watchman organization."[20] This bill lost when the Assembly failed to accord it the necessary two-thirds vote in adoption of the urgency clause. The roll call was 45 aye (35 Republicans and 10 Democrats) to 24 no (all Democrats).[21] A second compromise measure introduced by Senator Ed Fletcher (Republican of San Diego) and others passed the Senate on January 20 by a vote of 31 to 3.[22] On the next day administration supporters blocked passage in the Assembly, but on the following day it passed, 63 to 5.[23] The governor said that he would sign the Fletcher bill "since it is the best we have been able to get out of an opposition intent on destroying the guard."[24] The Oakland *Post-Enquirer* (Hearst) assailed the Legislature in an editorial entitled "Why Do Legislators

Sabotage Democracy at Such a Time."[25] Another Hearst paper, the San Francisco *Call-Bulletin,* thought that the anti-administration bloc "took a sound and WELL DESERVED TROUNCING," contending that it had had to yield on the important points.[26]

Governor Olson was not pleased with the Fletcher Guard bill, although he was forced to sign it. The measure appropriated approximately $8,000,000 for the Guard, but limited the number of men who could be called to active duty to 7,000 and eliminated most of the non-infantry units. Furthermore, not more than 60 members out of each infantry company of 220 could be called up for active duty. Olson pointed out that the State Guard troops had been inspected and approved by the War Department, which had then given them uniforms, new rifles, ammunition and other equipment. Olson also noted that the "model" (Lyon) State Guard Act of June 1941 had called upon the governor to organize a guard of at least 10,000 men, seven months before the outbreak of war.[27] The governor sought a writ of mandate from the California Supreme Court, contending that the limitations of the Fletcher act upon his powers as commander-in-chief were unconstitutional, but the court upheld the Legislature and thus the guard had to be reorganized in accordance with the act. The governor hinted that he might call more men to duty under the original provisions of the Military Code, saying that it could not be reasonably anticipated that "anything but further uncertainty, confusion and doubt" would ensue if he called another session of the Legislature.[28] The San Francisco *Chronicle* charged that the governor "wanted the guard to be an Olson army, an instrument for his re-nomination and reelection as Governor," and that when the Legislature had rejected his plan, the governor had blocked "a proper bill" and signed "an unsatisfactory makeshift" so that he could then attack the Legislature.[29] The State Guard, plagued by a rapid turnover principally because its members were being taken away by Selective Service, became a great issue in the 1942 elections.

The Olson-Warren Feud

Soon after the outbreak of war the long-smouldering feud between Governor Olson and Republican Attorney General Earl Warren broke into the open. Warren, in his capacity as the state's chief law enforcement officer, had become keenly interested in defense activities. Early in 1940 he attended the federal-state conference on law enforcement problems of national defense. Upon his return, he passed on its recommendations to California law enforcement officers. In the summer of 1940 he called a state national defense law enforcement conference, the first of its kind, at which all problems relating to war were studied by state and local officials and specialists. Participating in this conference were army, navy, and FBI representatives. Warren persuaded the Legislature in 1940 to pass the Mutual Assistance Act, which enabled fire departments to cross city and county lines, and the Uniform Sabotage Prevention Act. Warren's campaign biographer explains the origin of the attorney general's feud with Olson as follows: "Governor Culbert Olson distrusted all Republicans, reasoning that their one objective was to defeat him at the next election. He knew very little about the character and background of Earl Warren, and very soon he came to the conclusion that the Attorney General's movements throughout the state were aimed at building a political machine which would enable Warren to supplant him in 1942."[30] Olson appointed the attorney general to the first State Council of Defense in June 1940. In the reorganization of the Council in September 1940, the governor designated Warren as chairman of the committee on civil defense, in which post Warren was continued after the Council was given statutory authority in June 1941. But while Olson had thus obeyed the amenities, it had never been a secret that the attorney general and the governor were not fond of each other.

On December 14, 1941, the governor issued a "state of emergency" proclamation in which he omitted any specific mention of the role of the attorney general.[31] He designated "the duly constituted officers of the State" and local governments as: "the officers to take charge of this emergency in their respective jurisdictions, and to carry into effect plans for civil protection adopted by the State Council of Defense and by local councils of defense in accordance therewith, in cooperation with the duly constituted authorities of the Government of the United States in the prosecution of the war and in provisions for civilian protection." Five days later, in ignorance of this order, Lieutenant General John L. De-Witt, commander of the Western Defense Command and the Fourth Army, wrote to Olson asking him to

> . . . designate some responsible and competent State official to co-ordinate, supervise and direct the activities of all regular peace

DEFENSE AND WAR   195

and other law enforcement officers of your State in all matters, to coordinate all measures for State and civilian defense in cooperation with the Armed Forces of the United States, to direct and complete the Voluntary Civilian defense organization of your State and to expedite the enrollment and training of personnel for civilian protection services. . ..[32]

As soon as he learned of Olson's proclamation, DeWitt said that it "substantially" complied with the suggestions in his letter, and concluded: "Your prompt and vigorous action in thus proclaiming the existing state of war and in setting in motion the defense forces of your State is a source of much gratification."[33]

However, Attorney General Warren promptly challenged Olson's authority to issue the proclamation. At a meeting of the State Council of Defense in Sacramento on December 18—the day before the special session of the Legislature was to meet—Warren said that the language of the proclamation was "remarkably similar" to a 1929 statute which permitted the governor to rule by decree in such emergencies as fires, floods, earthquakes and other natural calamities, but not in war. Warren said that under the law, as interpreted by the attorney general's office, the governor's proclamation might even permit Olson to "name any State Guard officer to supplant local authorities to rule by decree." Warren implied that the governor's request for funds might run into difficulty: "If the money is to be used to supplant local government or divest State officials of their discretion, it would unquestionably bear upon the judgment of the Legislature as to how funds shall be spent." In reply, the governor pointed out that his proclamation had designated the "duly constituted officers" of the state and local governments as the ones to take charge of the emergency in their "respective jurisdictions," and denied that he had any intention of interfering with local law enforcement officers. Olson said that he had issued the proclamation in order to set up machinery whereby uniform regulations issued by the state council of defense might be put into effect.[34]

This disagreement between the governor and his Republican attorney general has been accurately called "the final parting of the ways" for the two men.[35] Warren's attack might have been avoided if the governor had consulted him freely and sought his advice. But one of the things Olson never was nor could have been was truly diplomatic. Each man was wilful and determined to play his proper role in the state's war effort, and each distrusted the other. While it is foolhardy to say that anything in history is "inevitable," the Olson-Warren feud probably was just that.

The consequences for the administration were disastrous. It is true that, after hearing the debate between the attorney general and the governor, the defense council approved a resolution urging the Legislature to vote whatever appropriation for defense Olson asked. But the actions of the Legislature in refusing to pass the appropriation asked by the governor and in drastically altering the State Guard can be attributed, in part at least, to Warren's pronouncement. Furthermore, at Warren's request, the Legislature tacked onto a bill appropriating additional money for the emergency fund the provision that "no money be used in exercising any powers under the Statutes of 1929 which might be interpreted as bestowing emergency powers."[36]

By now Olson was goaded almost beyond even his monumental capacity for endurance. He reduced the legislative contingency appropriation bill from $35,000 to $5,000.[37] He pocket-vetoed a bill appropriating $214,000 for the attorney general's office. This measure was one of several passed to provide additional funds for state agencies whose resources were being taxed by the war emergency, and had passed both houses with but one dissenting vote. Warren told the press that the appropriation was entirely intended "to meet the additional costs of my office due to the war," and said that he would be forced to request funds from the emergency fund controlled by the governor, although he doubted if he could get any.[38] Six weeks later Warren formally announced his candidacy for governor. His campaign biographer, contending that Warren had "no ambition to become governor," says that Olson "by his own effort created the only opposition that could possibly have arisen to his reëlection."[39] This view is somewhat curious, inasmuch as Olson by this time had the most formidable and comprehensive collection of enemies of any public official in recent California history. It was really only a question of whom Olson's opponents would choose to unite behind. Warren turned out to be the choice. He agreed to run after his full break with the governor.

Governor Olson ran into other difficulties over the State Council of Defense. Richard Graves resigned as executive secretary following the outbreak of war and the moving of Council headquarters to Sacramento. When at its January 8 meeting the Council failed to choose his successor,

Olson designated Director of Natural Resources Kenneth I. Fulton as acting executive secretary. Under Fulton's direction, a staff for the Council was selected, principally from persons who had completed the Office of Civilian Defense School at Stanford. Olson did not call a meeting of the Council until April 18, in spite of current problems. "Although the Governor's attention had been called to the fact that only the Council could appoint the executive secretary and staff members, he preferred to wait until he could present a going organization which the Council would ratify, and accordingly he did not call the Council."[40]

When the Council did meet in April, it refused to approve Fulton as executive secretary, although it did accept the staff he had chosen. Fulton had been an active participant in the 1938 campaign, and had held continuous office in the administration, occupying successively all three of the governor's chief secretarial positions and finally becoming director of natural resources. The principal student of the California State Council of Defense contends: "The Council's rejection of Fulton was definitely an attempt to keep the Council functioning on the high, non-partisan plane adhered to before January 1942. The actions of the Governor in building up a staff from January through May was a knowing usurpation of the Council's authority and the subsequent charges of 'spoils' tactics are thus justifiable."[41]

Following the August 1942 primary election campaign, in which charges and countercharges concerning the State Guard and the State Council of Defense made headlines, Warren and Olson once more clashed at a Council meeting.[42] The attorney general said that it was "strange" that a series of radio broadcasts on civil defense, scheduled to begin the following week, should have been left until the final two months of the election campaign, when the chairman of the Council (Olson) was seeking office. Warren said that the chairman of the committee on civil protection—himself—had never been consulted on the subject matter to be used in the broadcast, and indeed had not been advised of anything that was to be presented to the Council since the first of the year. He said further that matters would not be so bad if members of the council staff included persons "competent in the basic services," but pointed out that no member of the staff had been "trained as a law enforcement officer." Admitting that the members of the Council could not be improved upon, he contended that the Council had been immobilized during the early months of 1942 while Olson refused to call meetings. Returning to the forthcoming broadcasts, Warren pointed out that they were to be put on by "Hollywood Players," and asked: "What do these Hollywood broadcasters know about Civilian Protection, and—"

At this point Olson broke in: "I am compelled to say here, with sincere regret, that it is because of his candidacy that the only dissident note, the only political injection has come into the whole preparation of the civilian and military defense of California." The governor then reviewed the history of the State Council of Defense, contending that California was the first state really to begin preparation for civil defense and that its pattern had largely been adopted by the Office of Civilian Defense. He said that Warren had been obstructing the work of the Council since its first meeting in June 1940, and noted that, although Warren had been criticizing the Council staff in his campaign, he had never before criticized the staff at a Council meeting. The governor said that the staff had been recruited without any regard for politics and that at the Council meetings at which the staff had been interviewed neither Warren nor any other member had uttered a word against the selection or competency of the members. He referred also to Warren's opposition to the "emergency" proclamation of December 14, 1941, terming it "political obstruction."

After the meeting, at which a staff representative made a vigorous reply to Warren's charges against the competency of his group, Olson told the press that Warren was "unfit for the office of Governor as well as his present office."[43] The Sacramento Bee took Warren severely to task for his charges on the broadcasts, pointing out that they had been arranged by the general manager of the California Newspaper Publishers Association. "In trying to smear Olson by voicing a trifling criticism," said the Bee, "Warren smeared every member of the state defense council. Surely a candidate for governor of California should be more broad gauged than that!"[44] Following his own inauguration as governor, Warren described the State Council of Defense as "cumbersome," "wholly unworkable," and "unwieldy" and secured its replacement by a smaller council with fuller responsibility and ample funds. Warren, by the same legislation (the War Powers Act of January 30, 1943) was given larger emergency powers.[45]

Olson and DeWitt

Another phase of Olson's wartime administration was his relationship with Lieutenant General DeWitt. At DeWitt's request, Olson ordered local law enforcement officers to close down houses of prostitution.[46] DeWitt asked the governor to have state authorities forbid the sale of liquor to military personnel except between the hours of 6 and 10 p.m., and Olson promptly complied.[47] Shortly after this, again at the request of the general, Olson asked the Board of Equalization to relax the restriction on liquor sales to military personnel on beer only.[48] The general asked that "necessary action be taken to prohibit fires on the beaches, except during daylight hours."[49] On these and similar matters, the governor was prompt in carrying out the polite but firm "suggestions" of the military commander.

On one matter, concerning the four state highway bridges across the Colorado River, Governor Olson was not able to comply with the wishes of General DeWitt. On December 23, 1941, Olson requested that the military assign troops to guard these bridges. In January, DeWitt sent the governor a letter, reporting that army men were doing so, and that representatives of state inspection services were also on duty at the bridges. Said the general:

> At all of these state controlled immigration stations a detailed inspection of all articles transported by vehicle is made. However, since such inspections are customarily made after crossing the bridges, it is conceivable that an enemy sympathizer might be able to conceal an appreciable quantity of explosives in an innocent appearing cargo and detonate same on the bridge.
>
> I believe that this protection of these bridges against acts of sabotage would be materially increased if all detailed inspections as to cargo contents, etc., were made before crossing rather than afterward as at present.
>
> It would be appreciated if you and Governor Osborne of Arizona, to whom I have addressed a similar letter, could arrange some agreement to carry out the proposed plan.

After the DeWitt suggestion had been made the subject of a number of letters between the governor and some members of his cabinet, DeWitt was forced to clarify his request: "It is my suggestion that by general agreement between the States of California and Arizona, the California Inspection Service be moved across the bridges into Arizona, and the

Arizona Inspection Service be moved across the bridges into California, where each will continue to make the same type of inspection as is now being made of all vehicles." Director of Agriculture William J. Cecil advised the governor of the many problems that this border inspection service would face in such a move (including lack of authority to stop cars in Arizona, lack of authority to carry arms, lack of compensation insurance and lack of money). Olson thereupon asked DeWitt for written instructions to move the inspectors across the bridge. DeWitt told the governor that the army lacked the authority to issue such instructions: "However, in view of the present emergency it is urgently requested that this transfer be effected as soon as possible."

DeWitt's project ended when Olson informed the general that the attorney general had advised the director of agriculture he had no authority to carry on inspection work on the Arizona side, and that the controller would be unable to pay the men for their work if they were sent across the bridges! This episode, humorous as it sounds in retrospect, well illustrates the relationship Olson had with the military commander and some problems that ensued during the early months of the war.[50]

The Japanese Evacuation

The presence in California of substantial numbers of alien Japanese and native-born persons of Japanese ancestry was a matter of some concern in many quarters. Shortly before the attack on Pearl Harbor, Governor Olson noted: "If the friction aroused by relations with Japan should generate much heat, in dealing with them I shall rely upon the fact that recognition and protection of the rights and safety of minorities has always been a basic tenet of American government and the American sense and practice of fair play."[51] On December 8, 1941, he suggested to the State Council of Defense that all alien enemies be ordered to remain indoors as a means of avoiding riots, but the Council did not approve this suggestion because it feared the effect it might have on the state's food supply.[52] In 1940 there were in the state 5,135 Japanese-operated farms, producing 42 per cent of the state's produce crops.[53] On December 14 the governor broadcast a plea for tolerance, saying that he had had assurances from "every racial group" of their loyalty and devotion to the United States.[54]

Indeed, the first reaction of Californians generally seemed to be friendly toward the Japanese.

> For two months after December 7, 1941, the people of the West Coast, facing as they thought an attack from the sea, showed less prejudice toward the local Japanese than at any time in their history. While all the adjectives of melodrama were being applied to the enemy, people went out of their way to assure the Nisei that they were not included or identified with the enemy. Many Nisei noted the fact with gratitude at the time.[55]

The State Council of Defense, meeting on January 8, 1942, recommended that enemy aliens be allowed to remain on their farms, under proper surveillance, so that they might continue to produce food.[56]

Lieutenant General DeWitt, designated head of the Western Defense Command when that entity was created by the War Department on December 11, 1941, is said to have declared, "I am not going to be a second General Short."[57] It seems likely that the experiences of the luckless army commander of the Hawaiian Department had made a strong impression on many military men in addition to General DeWitt.

In his letter to Olson of December 19, in which he requested the proclamation of a state of emergency, DeWitt emphasized the menace presented by the large number of enemy aliens and possible fifth columnists. He noted that there were in California in 1940: 71,727 persons born in Germany; 100,910 persons born in Italy; 33,569 persons born in Japan; and 60,148 persons born in the United States of Japanese extraction. This DeWitt letter is significant, for it indicates that *all* persons of Japanese extraction were being considered separately from persons of German or Italian ancestry by the military commander, less than two weeks after the attack on Pearl Harbor. In this same letter DeWitt warned Olson of the danger to California, saying: "Already, since the beginning of hostilities against this country, proof has mounted of fifth column activity and sabotage, particularly in Hawaii and the Philippines, which have caused serious property and military damage and have contributed to the loss of many American lives."

Carey McWilliams has called anti-Oriental agitation "California's Bloody Shirt."[58] In recent decades that agitation had primarily been directed at the Japanese and "for nearly fifty years prior to December 7, 1941, a state of undeclared war existed between California and Japan."[59]

In view of the long political history of anti-Oriental activity, it was not surprising to find politicians re-discovering the "Yellow Peril" after Pearl Harbor. The chief vehicle for this agitation was the California Joint Immigration Committee, formed in 1919 by V. S. McClatchy with the sponsorship of the Native Sons of the Golden West, the California State Grange, the California State Federation of Labor, and the American Legion.[60] McClatchy resigned as editor and publisher of the Sacramento *Bee*, his family property, to devote all of his energies to this committee. On February 7, 1942, at the first meeting of this organization following the outbreak of hostilities, Attorney General Earl Warren was present as a guest. He told the anti-Orientalists that they had to recognize that the problem of the Japanese in California was a military and not a political problem, and advised them to put pressure upon the military authorities, who would not be adverse to such activity.[61]

Professor Eric Bellquist, University of California political scientist and one of the leading opponents of Japanese evacuation, describes how the anti-Japanese agitation began: "In January, the commentators and columnists, 'professional patriots,' witch hunters, alien-baiters, and varied groups and persons with aims of their own began inflaming public opinion."[62] In mid-January the legislators passed a resolution introduced by Senators John Harold Swan (Democrat, Sacramento) and D. Jack Metzger (Republican, Red Bluff) calling upon the State Personnel Board to take steps to prevent disloyal persons from holding state jobs. This resolution passed the Senate without a dissent, although the vote in the Assembly was 41 (25 Democrats and 16 Republicans) to 22 (15 Republicans and 7 Democrats).[63] This roll call would indicate that the "conservatives" had remained more friendly to the Japanese state employees than had some of the "liberals." After some confusion, the State Personnel Board unanimously resolved on April 2 that "all state civil service employees of Japanese ancestry employed by any department, agency, board or commission be suspended effective immediately." Attorney General Warren, who had acted as strategy adviser to the state's chief anti-Japanese organization, declared that this action of the board was illegal.[64] This apparent contradiction has been explained by one of the students of the evacuation: "Attorney General Warren's record is characterized, on one side, by a scrupulous regard for the legal status of resident Japanese and, on the other, by a determination to foster the evacuation by every possible lawful means...."[65] As late as February

6, the San Francisco *Chronicle,* reporting a lack of "hysteria" at the grass roots level, said that excitement about the resident Japanese was visible chiefly "in political and journalistic quarters, which presumably are not themselves excited at all." ,

Carey McWilliams, chief of the Division of Immigration and Housing, became concerned about the anti-Japanese sentiment in the state, and suggested to the Tolan committee of Congress (the "Select Committee Investigating National Defense Migration") that it hold some hearings on the west coast, to study the Japanese situation at close range and possibly to soothe ruffled feelings. The arrangements of the Tolan committee to go to the west were completed on February 14, one day after the entire west coast congressional delegation recommended to the president "the immediate evacuation of all persons of Japanese lineage."[66] On the same day General DeWitt recommended such an evacuation to the president.

The recommendation of General DeWitt was embarrassing to Governor Olson. On February 2, the governor, following a meeting with DeWitt, said that mass evacuation would not be necessary.[67] On February 4, Olson told his radio audience about the conference: "At our conference on Monday, general plans were agreed upon for the movement and placement of the entire adult Japanese population in California at productive and useful employment within the borders of our State, and under such surveillance and protection for themselves and the State and Nation as shall be deemed necessary." At the same time, Olson said, "To lose the benefit of this Japanese labor in agricultural production would be a serious loss to our war economy."[68] President Roosevelt on February 19 signed an executive order authorizing the War Department to prescribe military areas and to exclude any persons from those areas, and on the following day Secretary of War Henry L. Stimson delegated the responsibility to General DeWitt.[69]

Thus when the Tolan committee arrived on the west coast the most important decisions had already been made. Persons favoring evacuation "were prepared for the occasion and dominated the hearings." Carey McWilliams found two considerations uppermost with pro-evacuation witnesses before the committee: "In the first place, there was an almost unanimous assumption that Japanese should be placed in a separate category from German and Italian nationals; and, second, every one assumed that sabotage had been practiced by resident Japanese in

Hawaii."[70] Attorney General Warren told the committee that there was greater potential danger from Japanese born in America than from elderly ones born in Japan, that unless federal authorities acted quickly vigilantism would occur, that it was "more than coincidence" that Japanese had "completely surrounded aircraft plants," and that the mere fact that no sabotage had so far been noticeable was "part of a pattern to lull us into a sense of false security and is inviting another Pearl Harbor."[71]

General DeWitt went ahead with his evacuation plans. On March 2, he issued his Proclamation No. 1, which declared that western Washington, western Oregon, western California and southern Arizona constituted Military Area #1, from which would be removed all Japanese (citizens and aliens), but only those German and Italian aliens and individuals suspected of espionage and sabotage. Following the setting up of the War Relocation Authority by presidential executive order, General DeWitt ordered the evacuation of the Japanese from the whole of the west coast states, in a series of orders beginning March 24.[72]

The die was thus cast, with the military authorities taking the decisive steps. General DeWitt, in his *Final Report,* contended that "the evacuation was impelled by military necessity."[73] But an indication of the way military necessity was explained to the general by civilian authorities is indicated by a passage from the testimony of Mayor Fletcher Bowron of Los Angeles before the Dies Committee:

> I may say that I was quite active in getting the Japanese out of Los Angeles and its environs. I held various conferences with Tom Clark, now Assistant U. S. Attorney General, who was designated in charge of enemy alien activities on the Pacific Coast, and together with him and the then Attorney General, now Governor Warren, we held a long conference with General DeWitt relative to the situation, and I hope we were somewhat helpful in General DeWitt making his decision.[74]

Morton Grodzins, a leading student of the subject, contended that "military necessity" was but a pretext: "The judgments made on the West Coast in the winter of 1942 were largely nonmilitary in character; the reasons adduced to link resident Japanese to military dangers were sociological (the Japanese are 'almost wholly unassimilated'); anthropological ('the racial strains are undiluted'); and political (many Japanese were 'dual citizens, owing allegiance to the Emperor')."[75]

Governor Olson appears to have had less influence than Warren and Bowron with General DeWitt, if results are to be the criterion. Like Warren and Bowron, Olson feared sabotage, was convinced it was impossible to tell a loyal from a disloyal Japanese, and feared vigilantism, but Olson was less willing to condemn the Japanese as a group. Olson's position wavered, however:

> The governor's statement that mass evacuation was unnecessary was followed in a matter of days by an Army announcement of just such a program. He later demanded complete evacuation of Japanese from the entire state, at a time when the War Department was committed to a program of evacuating only the coastal area; but, when the Army assumed the task of evacuating the entire state, Governor Olson made the futile request that Japanese in inland farm areas be allowed to remain to help harvest growing crops.[76]

In the period before the decision to evacuate was made, Governor Olson was calm and moderate, allowing his chief political rival to take the initiative by urging the evacuation of all Japanese from the state. He thus cannot be charged with any responsibility for the evacuation itself, no matter what he declared *after* the evacuation was begun.

The evacuation of the Japanese from California, which occurred during the Olson administration, thus in actuality had very little to do with that regime. In reality the governor probably could not have stopped the evacuation even if he had wanted to. Apparently he did not want to do so. Carey McWilliams says that a social "fault," similar to earthquake faults, existed along the coast separating the Japanese minority from the rest of the people. The shock of the attack on Pearl Harbor thus "sent tremors throughout the entire Pacific area" and the local Japanese were "victims of this social earthquake."[77]

In retrospect the evacuation of the Japanese appears both cruel and unnecessary, and the politicians who urged it seem petty and self-seeking. That Olson took no stronger line than he did is clear evidence that even a man of liberal instincts and genuine humanitarianism could be bewildered by the forces set in motion by the waving of "California's Bloody Shirt."

15 *defeat*

IN THE EARLY MONTHS OF 1942 OLSON COULD LOOK BACK UPON three years of political frustration. His enemies were almost without number, and their economic and political power was enormous. In the absence of any appreciable amount of patronage, he had not been able to build a machine and he found himself much worse off in campaign finance than four years before. Even his efforts to lead California's defense and war effort had met with hostility in the Legislature. Probably no governor in California history had ever had such a hostile press.

Yet, characteristically, Olson was incorrigibly optimistic. Democratic politicians took comfort from the registration figures, which showed their party the three-to-two choice of California voters. Furthermore, the fiscal condition of the state was excellent. The governor considered his administration as a phase of Franklin Delano Roosevelt's New Deal, and as such virtually invincible.

That Olson would seek reëlection in 1942 was never in doubt, but for some time it was by no means certain that he could avoid an intra-party fight for the nomination. His chief rival was Senator Kenny of Los Angeles, his floor leader during the 1939 session. Witty and popular, Kenny was a former judge of the Superior Court (1932–1939), to which he had been appointed by Governor Rolph. He had entered Democratic politics as a leader of the Olson primary campaign in 1938 and won for himself the Senate seat Olson had vacated to run for governor. The first evidence that Kenny and Olson were not in entire harmony came during the 1938 primary election, when Kenny endorsed Earl Warren for attorney general and Olson issued a statement saying that Kenny was speaking for himself only.[1] Following the 1938 general election, Kenny was not called in for consultations by the governor-elect, and indeed did not see Olson until the time of the inauguration.[2] In the interval between election and inauguration, Kenny broke into the news with the announcement of a plan to abolish the initiative. The political editor of the San Francisco *News* reported on January 13, 1939, that there was "much eyebrow raising" when Kenny, the administration floor leader of the Senate, introduced bills to exempt individual trusts and holding companies from payment of the state corporation franchise tax, at a time when the governor was supposed to favor heavier taxation for them.[3] Before many months had passed it was clear that Kenny was not going to be an administration stalwart. At the close of the 1939 session of the Legislature, Kenny turned down an Olson appointment to the Court of Appeals, preferring to remain in the Senate.[4]

Kenny first got into the race for governor early in 1940, when he announced that he would be a candidate in case the recall petitions qualified and a special election was held.[5] Olson was, not unexpectedly, somewhat displeased at this announcement by the Democratic senator from Los Angeles! Nevertheless, Kenny was given a position on the Ickes-Olson third-term slate in the 1940 presidential preference primary. He gave the governor no aid in the great "purge" campaign. At the 1941 session, his place as administration leader of the Senate was taken by J. C. Garrison of Modesto, the governor's old friend and colleague. By early 1942, Kenny had obtained support in his campaign for governor from such persons as George Creel, District Attorney John F. Dockweiler of Los Angeles, and former Finance Director John R. Richards.[6] Kenny is also said to have been the choice of the California leadership of the CIO.[7]

However, Kenny could have won the 1942 Democratic nomination for governor only after a hard fight with Olson, and, six weeks after Earl Warren entered the gubernatorial race, Kenny withdrew "in the interest of unity" and ran for attorney general.[8]

Two other Democratic state officials had considered making the race for attorney general, but withdrew "in the interest of unity" upon Kenny's announcement. These two, Lieutenant Governor Patterson and Secretary of State Peek, ran instead for reëlection. Patterson and Olson had got along much better since the 1940 elections than before. In May 1941 Patterson told a Jackson Day dinner gathering that Olson was one of the few California governors "who has endeavored to live up to his party's platform," and predicted Olson's reëlection in 1942 if he sought it.[9]

Olson was concerned with the unbalance of the ticket if Patterson were to be his running-mate, for Patterson had moved his residence from King City to Los Angeles. For some time it appeared that Senator Garrison, a northern California farmer, would be the administration's choice. Indeed, his announcement of candidacy was drawn up. But it was not issued when it was clear that the leaders of organized labor wanted Patterson and wouldn't accept Garrison as a substitute, in spite of the senator's pro-labor voting record.[10] The "official" statewide Democratic ticket included, in addition to Olson, Patterson, Kenny, and Peek, M. Leland Stanford for controller, and Superintendent of Banks George J. Knox for treasurer.

For some time it was not clear who would be the major conservative candidate against Olson. Early in March 1940, the candidacy of Speaker Gordon Garland was advanced by a newspaper in his home district, which called him "the most available man in California to complete the term of the incumbent Democratic governor in the event of a recall."[11] Garland, a registered Democrat and leader of the "economy bloc" in the Legislature, might well have become the candidate backed by the business community had the recall ever qualified. On February 26, 1942, Garland announced that he would seek the Democratic nomination for governor, addressing his appeal "to the overwhelming mass of voters who are sick and tired of extremists on both side [sic] and who believe with me that the interests of minority pressure groups must be subordinated to the welfare of our people." Garland assailed the Olson administration vigorously, and promised that if elected he would ask the Legislature for an immediate tax cut.[12]

But Garland's brief years of glory were near their end. However great their gratitude to Garland—and it should have been great considering his services—the California conservatives could not afford to back him for governor in the 1942 primary. Ironically, his greatest asset as a leader of the "economy bloc"—his Democratic registration—was the one thing that made him impossible as a conservative candidate for governor. Under the law, a candidate had to win the nomination of his own party to remain on the general election ballot, and no one had the slightest delusion that Garland could win the Democratic nomination. And if he had won the Republican without the Democratic, he would have been disqualified! Of course, he could have changed his registration to Republican. But then he would have been just another Republican and much of the bi-partisan glamor of the "economy bloc" would thereby have evaporated. Garland held on for a long while, even after Warren announced his own candidacy for both nominations, but at last he saw the handwriting on the wall. He withdrew from the gubernatorial race to run for a seat on the State Board of Equalization against a recent Olson appointee.[13] The conservatives, with an almost audible sigh of relief, backed Garland to the hilt in his new race, into which no Republican candidate ventured.

Warren in the Running

Earl Warren's candidacy for governor had long been anticipated.[14] Although two Republicans had already announced themselves when he entered the race in April 1942, they both soon withdrew. Warren said that he would seek both Republican and Democratic nominations, becoming the first serious candidate to do so since Mayor Rolph in 1918. The attorney general said that he had been persuaded by "persistent urgings" for the "past year or more." He noted that his own governmental experience had been in the "field of non-partisan government," and pledged that if elected governor he would conduct a "non-partisan administration." "I believe in the party system and have been identified with the Republican party in matters of party concern, but I have never found that the broad questions of national party policy have application to the problems of state and local government in California," Warren said.[15] The Republican state-wide ticket was soon worked out, with the party presenting a united front against the Democrats except for the office of lieutenant governor, where there was a contest.

Earl Warren was fifty-one years old when he entered the race for governor. Born in Bakersfield, he graduated from the University of California in 1912 and took a law degree at Boalt Hall in 1914. After three years of law practice, he entered the Army and served until 1919, although he did not go overseas. Upon his discharge, he secured the post of minute clerk of the Assembly judiciary committee, and in that same year was appointed deputy city attorney of Oakland. From 1920 to 1925, Warren served as deputy district attorney of Alameda County, and in the latter year he was appointed district attorney by the Board of Supervisors. Repeatedly reëlected, Warren served as district attorney until his inauguration as attorney general. In 1938 he won both major party nominations, in part because of Democratic factionalism, and thus he could say in 1942 that he had held "non-partisan" offices exclusively.[16]

Earl Warren had long been known as a Republican politician, for he had held the positions of Republican state chairman and Republican national committeeman. He had been the nominal head of the 1936 delegation to the Republican national convention. When he ran for attorney general in 1938, however, he did not run as a partisan but rather as an experienced law enforcement officer, and as such he won the support of many Democrats, including Robert W. Kenny. As a long-time local law enforcement officer, Warren in his political philosophy emphasized "local government and the decentralization of power."[17] Opinions vary as to Warren's performance as attorney general. His campaign biographer says: "He gradually weeded out any misfits in the office and gathered round him fifty young and energetic lawyers. He departmentalized the work into divisions of taxes, litigation, collections, criminal work and opinions for the state. The deputies who were most interested and talented in these divisions were made specialists in their fields. Thousands of antiquated cases were disposed of and the calendar brought up to date."[18] Carey McWilliams, a political enemy, considers that Warren was "a very mediocre Attorney General of California," citing especially Warren's failure to intervene when local law enforcement broke down at Westwood during the 1939 lumber strike vigilantism.[19]

Before the relations between Governor Olson and Attorney General Warren were completely severed following their jurisdictional dispute over defense activities, Warren and Olson had had two memorable disagreements. One came when Warren (as a member of the Qualifications Commission) voted against confirmation of Olson's appointment of Max Radin to the State Supreme Court. Radin, professor of law at the University of California, was a member of Olson's "brain trust." When the governor named Radin to the court, the Republican San Francisco *Chronicle* acclaimed him a "distinguished liberal" with a "high degree of judicial temperament and a passion for justice," saying that he should be confirmed "with no more of the scurrilous attack that arises from inability to distinguish between liberal faith and subversive character."[20] However, the Qualifications Commission voted 2 to 1 against confirmation and Olson was forced to withdraw the nomination.[21] Radin had written letters to the city attorney of Stockton and to another Stockton attorney, asking them to seek clemency for eighteen SRA employees who had been convicted of contempt of the Yorty committee for refusing to state whether they were Communists and to turn over their CIO union membership lists.[22] Warren cited these actions of Radin as evidence of his unfitness for the high court.

The other great clash between the governor and the attorney general came over the celebrated "Ship Murder Case."[23] Three maritime unionists, Earl King, E. G. Ramsay, and Frank Connor, had been successfully prosecuted by Warren's office while he was district attorney of Alameda County and convicted of second degree murder for having dispatched thugs to beat up the chief engineer of the ship "Point Lobos," (who died as a result of his beating). King, Ramsay, and Connor, as well as one of the thugs (the other was never found), were given twenty-six year sentences in San Quentin. The CIO had long sought their pardon, and in October 1940 Olson visited San Quentin, talked with the four men, described the evidence upon which they were convicted as "largely conflicting and impeached," and said: "I can't figure them out as the type of men who would deliberately participate in the murder of anyone."[24] Warren, not surprisingly, resented the governor's remarks and said so: "Heretofore I have never said one word against the governor on any of his official acts, but silence on my part in this matter would be cowardice. These men are assassins—proved to be so."[25] Olson did not pardon the men, but in December 1941 the Board of Prison Terms and Paroles released King, Ramsay and Connor on parole.

"Leadership, Not Politics," was the keynote of Warren's campaign for both nominations for governor. He undertook an intensive tour of the state, on which he was accompanied by his good friend, the well known movie actor Leo Carrillo.[26] His campaign was managed by that ablest of professional managers, Clem Whitaker of San Francisco.[27]

In his first major speech—on June 6 to a Republican gathering—Warren set the tone for his campaign. He called for an end to "petty partisan politics" which he said had "hamstrung our state government in meeting its war obligations and which has let vital, critical jobs go undone while the State Administration at Sacramento haggled and struggled for political advantage."[28] On June 17 he assailed the Olson administration for its SRA "scandals."[29] He assured a convention of Republican women that he firmly believed in the two-party system, but pointed to President Roosevelt's request for an adjournment of partisan politics for the duration of the war.[30] On June 21, he told a convention at Sacramento that he favored an increase in old age pensions to fifty dollars a month, and said that pensions at 65 should be a matter of right and not a dole.[31] On August 7, Warren charged that "there never has been an honest effort by the Governor of this state to build up the State Guard." He declared himself in favor of repeal of the state income tax, a measure to be voted upon by the people at the 1942 general election. He contended that Olson was not interested in tax reductions: "The Governor does not believe in tax reduction because he says that after the war he will need this money to take care of postwar problems, and, perhaps, with another SRA."[32]

"Olsonism" became the favorite target of the Warren supporters. The attorney general himself said that the people did not want any more of it. He contended that the conflict in the Legislature was not a party issue but an issue between Olson and everybody else. In the same address he assailed the governor for not calling a meeting of the State Council of Defense during the opening months of the year, and charged that the council's staff had been selected for political reasons.[33] On August 19, Warren told an AFL meeting in Santa Rosa that he was "neutral" on the hot cargo issue, scheduled for popular referendum at the general election. But Warren solicited the support of the unionists by identifying himself as a member of the AFL Musicians' Union, and saying that he had spoken against the application of the anti-sabotage law to labor disputes. He maintained that "the right of workers to form unions for collective bargaining upon wages, hours and conditions of employment is no longer a subject of debate."[34] Warren, however, won little support from trade union leaders. His labor campaign was headed by Charles Real, Oakland teamsters' official, who had backed Governor Merriam against Olson in 1938.

In the last days of the primary campaign, Warren summed up his charges against the Olson administration, and made commitments himself. On August 20, he charged that the administration expected civil servants to contribute to campaign funds.[35] He repeated his charge that

Olson opposed tax cuts, announcing his own belief that it would be possible to reduce the sales tax, as a supplement to the anticipated repeal of the income tax.[36] In his election eve broadcast, Warren repeated his pledge of "non-partisan" government, and again assailed the administration's handling of defense matters, especially the State Guard.[37]

Warren had the support of nearly all of the state's metropolitan newspapers, who referred to him in news stories as "non-partisan candidate for governor."[38] The only important newspapers supporting Olson were Manchester Boddy's Los Angeles *Daily News* and *Evening News*, while the Sacramento *Bee* remained neutral and reported both sides of the campaign fully. The Scripps-Howard San Francisco *News*, neutral like the *Bee* in 1938, in 1942 ardently supported Earl Warren. The *News* ran a series of three editorials entitled "Culbert Olson Should Be Defeated," in which it bitterly excoriated the administration and nearly all of its actions.[39] Said the *News:* "Mr. Olson as governor provides a definite menace to the progress and welfare of this state. He has failed miserably in providing progressive leadership. He has laid the palsying hand of politics on every public problem, has dealt with every public question in the light of what he could get out of it for his own political advantage." It charged that Olson had "mishandled" the State Guard and State Defense Council, that he had played politics in SRA, that he had surrounded himself with "yes men," and that he had made "deals" (such as the veto of the hot cargo bill) to win labor support. The *News* minimized Olson's financial accomplishments, saying that "the present surplus could have been built up in the state treasury if a cocker spaniel had been governor. . . ."

The Republican San Francisco *Chronicle* said that Earl Warren had leadership, honesty of purpose, courage, unselfish devotion to the welfare of the people, reasonable foresight, and a clear intellect, and contended that Olson had none of these. The *Chronicle*, which frequently ran short, biting editorials entitled "Olsonism," said that Olson had no claim to statesmanship: "We doubt if Governor Olson has any very clear idea of what goes on in the world, or in California as a part of the world, except as events may relate to the welfare of Culbert Olson."[40]

Olson's Campaign

In contrast to his opponent, Governor Olson made only a token campaign for the Democratic nomination, the only nomination he sought.

He made a few radio speeches, but undertook no tour and in most areas there was no Democratic campaign at all. Party-minded as he was, Olson never thought that Warren represented any serious threat in the Democratic primary. The governor was content to save his energies for the general election campaign.[41]

The governor began his reëlection campaign with a speech delivered at a testimonial dinner given in his honor on April 6, shortly before Warren entered the race. Olson took pride in the administration's fiscal accomplishments, saying "We have given an economical administration in the true sense of a sound economy." He said that he had tried to cut governmental costs in proposing a reorganization of the state government's fiscal agencies and a program of self-help for the unemployed, but that the Legislature had refused to approve his plans, making small, injurious cuts in his budgets, crippling some agencies and then passing larger special appropriation bills. He spoke of his administrative reforms and of the humanitarian reforms in the treatment of the mentally ill and of the state's prisoners. Olson referred to his messages to the Legislature for documentary evidence of his faithfulness to the 1938 platform and called the roll of his enemies: lobbyists and "special interests," "racketeers," "party betrayers in office," and the daily press of the state, and said that his administration had been "sniped at and sabotaged from the rear by Communists." He concluded:

> I am here to tell you that we stand squarely on the record we have made during the three years and three months of our Administration; that we would not change any of that record (except by avoiding two or three bad appointments which were soon terminated) if we had it to do over again. By this time the Democrats and people of California generally know, or should know, what kind of an administration of the affairs of our great State we now have and may anticipate in the future if we are continued in office.[42]

Olson, however, did not begin his real campaigning for renomination until late in July. Then he defended "politicians" against "special interest groups" who, the governor charged, in reality only wanted to place in office another set of "politicians." He tied his administration to President Roosevelt:

> The great majority of the voters of California are Democrats because they know our Democratic Party is the party of the people

and that the Republican Party is the party of predatory interests, opposed to social gains and progressive economic policies.

Our state and national administrations have proved their fidelity to the people's trust, and we Democrats go before the people squarely on our record of faithful performance.[43]

A week later Olson assailed the initiative measure taking away from the Legislature the power to levy an income tax, describing any supporter of the proposal as a "confirmed reactionary" interested in helping a minority avoid its just share of taxation.[44]

During the last week of the primary campaign, Governor Olson, seemingly aroused at last, made three major radio broadcasts.[45] On August 20, he spoke to Democrats "to briefly remind you of the ever-present fundamental issues upon which we *challenge* Republican party opponents who are hypocritically seeking Democratic votes by getting their names on Democratic ballots in the Democratic primaries." Olson listed some of those "fundamental issues": taxation, taking profits out of war, protection of the consumer, public ownership of public utilities, low interest farm credit, and "greater social gains." Olson contended that the California Republicans "studiously avoid" those issues, except for their support of the income tax repeal initiative. He said that the majority of California's people had learned "through bitter experience" that the Republican party was the party of "predatory interests" and of "an aristocracy of wealth." He charged that the major publishers of the state were aiding Warren's campaign of "sinister innuendo, fraud, misrepresentation and false publicity," and asked Democrats to "vote only for Democrats and not for any Republican whose name you may find on your ballot."

Three nights later, Olson lashed out at Warren's criticism of the administration's defense and war policies, saying that Warren had never coöperated fully, and referring to his opponent as "the puppet pretender." On the next night, election eve, Olson again warned Democrats against voting for "cross-filing Republicans" and lashed out at the "non-partisan" campaign of Warren: "Anyone who is so cowardly as to put on the cloak of non-partisanship in an election like this, either acknowledges that he is a political eunuch and does not know what it is all about, or that he is a political hypocrite. This non-partisan, non-political propaganda is a piece of colossal deceit. It is essentially a lie."

The Primary Results

The outcome of the primary election of August 25, 1942, was a severe setback for Olson. Winning the Republican nomination over only nominal opposition, Warren ran up an imposing total in the Democratic primary as well—404,778 votes to 514,144 for Olson. Olson's statewide percentage was 52.03, and Warren's 40.96. Of the major counties, Olson ran best in Warren's home county of Alameda (60.46 per cent) and worst in Los Angeles (53.25 per cent).

Olson told reporters that he considered Warren's large vote in the Democratic primary was "the result of old sores created by pressure groups," and said: "I do not think the opposition will succeed when the full voting strength is brought out in November in spite of antisocial and reactionary forces."[46] The Republican press hailed Warren's "two to one victory,"[47] which it of course arrived at by totalling Warren's vote on both tickets and comparing it with Olson's vote in the Democratic. It was the opinion of many of Olson's advisors that he had made a grave error in not cross-filing, for the primary result made the Democratic incumbent look like a certain loser in November.[48] It was observed that many of the Democratic votes for Warren were cast in pension-minded areas, where the Ham and Eggs leaders' campaign against Olson apparently had had some effect. The Ham and Eggers had their own candidate in Roy G. Owens, but concentrated on attacking Olson.

Warren's strong showing in the Democratic primary elated conservatives. The San Francisco *Chronicle* said editorially: "Warren's strength was a welcome surprise even to his friends. Olson's weakness was greater than his sternest critics expected. A million and a quarter Democrats did not vote. They did not care enough about Olson to show up, or knowing his unfitness, were restrained by habit from voting in a Democratic primary against a Democratic incumbent."[49] The neutral Sacramento *Bee's* veteran political editor, Herbert L. Phillips, considered that Olson's campaign speeches had over-emphasized partisanship and the differences between the parties: "Tuesday's election seems to highlight an error in Governor Olson's reasoning. How can Warren be a 'reactionary Republican' and some 400,000 Democrats who voted for him be essentially progressive? The governor can hardly be right on both counts."[50] Helen Fuller reported that organized labor had not given Olson its full voting support, in spite of its endorsement of the governor: "Labor did not do its part in the primaries. Perhaps the lightest bloc of the very light Democratic vote cast was in the left-wing, labor ranks. To too great an extent the attitude here was one of being *against* Earl Warren rather than *for* Olson."[51] The total vote cast was only 47.2 per cent, as compared with 59.9 in 1938 and 59.3 in 1934.

Governor Olson received a number of letters from supporters who tried to explain the primary result. The San Diego County Democratic chairman reported: "One thing that did hurt here was the fact that the Ham and Egg people waged a bitter contest against you and I think that they made more votes for Warren than they did for Owens."[52] State Fire Marshal Lydell Peck contrasted the economic and social characteristics of 1942 California with those of 1938 California and said: "Today those for whom you fought so courageously—and I mean specifically the labor element—no longer have empty stomachs and shacks in which to live, but are enjoying the fruits of a great social and economic progress. Loyalty of organized labor has always been about as lasting as an earthquake, and the loyalty of organized labor to you in the last election was nowhere indicated."[53]

Of the statewide Democratic ticket, only three persons in addition to Olson survived. Ellis E. Patterson and Robert W. Kenny easily won the Democratic nominations for lieutenant governor and attorney general, respectively, although neither was able to win the Republican nomination. Secretary of State Paul Peek won the nomination and as he did not cross-file, he, too, had to face Republican opposition at the general election. The Democratic candidates for controller and treasurer lost their own party's nomination to Republican incumbents.

The chief consolation of the primary election for the Olson administration was the defeat of the bitterly anti-Olson Speaker Gordon Garland. He lost the Democratic nomination for the State Board of Equalization (second district) to Ivan C. Sperbeck, incumbent Democrat. Garland won the Republican nomination overwhelmingly (no Republican had sought it), but as he had lost the nomination of his own party to Sperbeck, under the election laws he was disqualified and the Republican State central committee would have to fill the vacancy with a Republican.

The results of the nomination contests for the state Legislature showed that the Republicans would again control the upper house but left the outcome for the Assembly in some doubt. Four run-offs for state senator remained after the primary, where 8 Democrats and 8 Republicans had won both nominations and thus were elected. Twenty-eight run-offs for assemblyman were scheduled for the general election, for 27 Republicans and 25 Democrats had been elected at the primary by winning both major party nominations. As several of the Democrats elected to the Legislature at the 1942 primary were members of the "economy bloc," the governor could count on at least two more years of legislative opposition even if he were himself reëlected. Two of Olson's bitterest Democratic enemies, Senator Peter P. Myhand of Merced and Assemblywoman Jeanette E. Daley of San Diego, were defeated for renomination by Olson-endorsed candidates, and were eliminated from the ballot in spite of the fact that they had both won Republican nominations. Of the 13 superior judges appointed by Olson since the 1940 elections, 10 were retained at the 1942 primary and three defeated.

The Final Campaign

Following his very impressive showing at the primary, Earl Warren soon made it clear that he was going to retain his "non-partisan" stratagem. He told the Republican state convention on September 17 that the campaign was: ". . . not a contest between the Republican and Democratic parties, for Governor Olson, by his arrogance, his blundering and his selfish manipulation of State Government during a period of gravest emergency, has jeopardized the safety and welfare of the people of California."[54] The convention put the party squarely in line with Warren's campaign by adopting a platform that never mentioned the New Deal, but somehow suggested that the Republican Party of California was the party of Franklin D. Roosevelt: "In a critical situation such as now confronts us, party politics has no place and must be eliminated, so that we may give to President Roosevelt our unqualified support in prosecuting the war to a victorious conclusion no matter what the cost may be." It also charged that under Olson the state lacked leadership:

> Partisan politics and spoils system have been the dominant factors in the Governor's office—liberation of known criminals has become a common practice. Competency and efficiency were abandoned, and the administration of public affairs left to flounder among philosophies and "isms" destructive of sound business administration of state affairs. No state can carry on and do its part in winning the war under such an administration.

The Republican platform of 1942 was brief and vague in its commitments.[55] It pledged, in its first policy plank, to abolish "the practice of permitting dangerous and depraved criminals to be released from our penal institutions and turned loose to again prey upon a trusting public." It pledged to "streamline" state government, to institute "humane rather than political administration" of state institutions, to accord full civil service protection to state employees, to support "adequate old age pensions as a matter of right," to plan for postwar conversion, to maintain the right of labor to organize and bargain collectively, and to assure agriculture "that labor will be available when and as required," and that the price of agricultural products would at least guarantee a fair return over the cost of production. This last plank on agriculture may have been intended as a vague "straddle" on the issue of "hot cargo," and it is notable that among labor's rights the Republicans agreed to maintain was not the right to strike. The Republican platform closed with a pledge of "Non-Political Government," and a request for support: "We call on all loyal citizens of the great State of California to forget partisan politics and unite with us in bringing to California the kind of leadership and government which will insure to our people the efficiency in administration and the protection of our homes which are so essential if we are to survive the ordeal through which we are now passing. By so doing we will insure peace at home and victory abroad."

As was shown by their action in making it their first platform plank, the Republicans attacked the administration's parole policies. On October 22, Warren charged that the handling of parole was "the darkest chapter of the Olson Administration," and said that of the 5,904 "criminals" paroled under Olson, 207 had been convicted of rape and 285 of other sex crimes. He said that only 5.8 per cent of convicted criminals had been paroled under Merriam, but that under Olson the number had been raised to 28 per cent.[56] Olson vigorously defended his administration's prison and parole record. After discussing the ouster of the Board of Prison Directors and the reform work of Warden Duffy of San Quentin, Olson said: "This humane program does not appeal to the Republican candidate for Governor, who has been a prosecutor during his entire life, and whose capacity for bias and prejudice against his fellow men is unlimited."[57] Warden Duffy himself took a part in the 1942 general election by making an address in defense of the administration's prison and parole policies.[58]

Warren brought the "Ship Murder Case" into the 1942 election campaign when he charged that Olson had released "Communist radicals" in order to "curry labor votes," and said that Olson's action was "an insult to the intelligence of organized labor."[59] Olson replied by saying that Warren was attempting to mislead the people into the belief that King, Ramsay and Connor had murdered the engineer. He said that he had declined to pardon the men when the Advisory Pardon Board reported against it, but that the Board of Prison Terms and Paroles had decided to parole them after they had served nearly six years of their terms, on the grounds that the three were not present at the murder, that they did not know that a murder had been contemplated or committed, and that no witnesses had testified that there had been any conspiracy to commit murder. Olson said that Warren had disregarded his duty to uphold the law, for by the law the parole board was given "the duty of exercising honest and courageous justice."[60]

The leaders of the Ham and Eggs pension movement supported Warren in the 1942 general election, scheduling four statewide broadcasts every week in his behalf, and offering "a photostatic copy of Earl Warren's signed pension statement" upon request.[61] A leader of the Olson campaign charged that Warren was responsible for keeping the Ham and Eggs movement alive, because his party had allegedly contributed $25,000 to "purchase" the endorsements of Lawrence and Willis Allen.[62] Olson fought hard to detach the old age pension enthusiasts from the Ham and Eggs leaders. He told the Ham and Eggers that while he didn't ask them to forget that he had opposed their plan, he did ask them to remember that he had consistently supported the objectives they sought, and told them that they had nothing to hope for from a Republican victory.[63] Late in the campaign Will H. Kindig, former Ham and Eggs leader, appeared on a broadcast with Olson, and asked the pension supporters to vote for the governor. Olson said that Lawrence Allen had come to him with a request for $50,000, with which he proposed to put on a pro-Olson radio program. Olson said that when he turned Allen down, the Ham and Eggs leader then made a deal with Warren.[64] In the early part of the campaign, Olson did have the support of George H. McLain, another erstwhile "Ham and Eggs" leader and currently head of the "Citizens Committee for Old Age Pensions," which sponsored a "sixty-at-sixty" pension plan. Early in October McLain sent a letter to Olson, revealing that his group, "cooperating with the Governor's Committee for election," had received $3,850 for its expenses. McLain presented a budget of $16,473.32 for the general election campaign, and closed his letter with, "Yours for success."[65] After the Democratic leaders let it be known that they were unable to meet McLain's financial request, he switched sides and came out for Warren!

Through all of the campaign Warren pledged a "non-partisan" administration if he were to be elected. On one occasion he offered as evidence of his non-partisanship the fact that three of his five "key assistants" as attorney general were registered Democrats.[66] More impressive than this was the number of Democrats who deserted their party to support Warren. Notable among these was George Creel, who had campaigned vigorously for Olson in 1938 and had long been close to President Roosevelt. In his autobiography Creel relates the breakdown of his friendship with the President to his own endorsement of Warren: "Not only was Earl Warren, the Republican, a vastly superior person in every way, but I had sickened of the crackpot demagoguery that passed for liberalism. Marvin McIntyre, the President's secretary, called on three occasions, urging me to withdraw my endorsement of Warren, and my refusal left a distinct chill in the air."[67] Speaker Garland, defeated in his race for the State Board of Equalization, pleaded with "rank and file Democrats" to vote for Warren in order to put the "welfare of the people of California above partisan politics during this time of crisis."[68] Senator-elect Jack B. Tenney of Los Angeles, chairman of the joint fact-finding committee on un-American activities, assailed Olson, and his remarks were published in newspaper advertisements by the "Loyal Democrats Warren for Governor" committee. Said Tenney: "You either take the entire program and promise to go the devious political route with Olson or you are out. There is no room for independent thinking or wholesome opposition to the machine once you have exchanged your political birthright for the Olson blessing."[69] Leo Carrillo headed the "Loyal Democrats" organization supporting Warren. This group attacked Olson more violently than did any other organization or individual during the 1942 campaign. Its final advertisement in the Los Angeles *Daily News* included the following:

> Warren served his country in World War I.
> Warren is a veteran of the last conflict.
> Mr. Olson, we have searched the record. . . .
> Mr. Olson, where were you in 1898—
> where in 1917?

In 1942 you prattle patriotism.
We remember the familiar old quotation:
The cloak of patriotism is the last refuge
of a Scoundrel.[70]

In a radio broadcast on October 30, Warren summarized his campaign promises. These included (foremost) making the war the main concern of his administration; working with the Legislature and not against it, and calling special sessions whenever necessary; giving financial support to the State Guard while freeing it from "politics"; staffing the Defense Council with "experienced men"; seeking legislation to establish more child day nurseries; coöperating with the federal government to secure more out-of-state labor; reducing taxes "for non-essential purposes"; insisting upon "rigid economy"; creating a postwar planning commission; and "improving" the state's pension system.[71]

Olson's general election campaign never really got going. A bitter contest developed at the Democratic state convention over who should be vice-chairman of the Democratic state central committee. The administration threw its support to George R. Reilly of San Francisco, who had been reëlected at the primary to the State Board of Equalization. Reilly was victorious over San Francisco County Chairman William M. Malone, the outgoing state chairman, by a vote of 218 to 182.[72] This episode, which has been termed "Olson's swan song blunder,"[73] left its mark on the campaign, as the Malone faction thereafter lost much of its enthusiasm for the administration and Reilly turned out to be something less than a success.

The Democratic state platform of 1942 was much longer and more detailed than its Republican counterpart.[74] It expressed pride in the "wartime leadership of both state and nation," and in "the salutary improvements wrought in both the finances and general conduct of the State Government under the administration of Governor Culbert L. Olson." It assailed the Republican leaders of the state: "Loose pledges of aid are unreliable, and victory slogans are meaningless unless tied to definite commitments. In this State, Republican leadership is compromised by appeaser and isolationist alliances. Republican candidates for State offices must be silent on the dominant issues and policies which alone can make victory possible." The Democratic platform specifically advocated the establishment of a "State War Production Board," equal pay for women in war work, state-financed child care centers, protection for agriculture (including labor supply and "cost plus" price ceilings), democratically administered rationing, postwar planning for heavy industry, state enforcement of fair employment practices, and the reorganization of the state's fiscal system. The platform flatly opposed the hot cargo bill. It recommended: "Immediate reduction and revision of the sales tax and increased exemptions from the state income tax consistent with the maintenance of a balanced budget and a reasonable surplus." On the crucial subject of old age pensions, the platform pledged the party "to introduce legislation as soon as the legislature convenes and press such legislation through to successful enactment into law" to establish pensions of at least sixty dollars per month at age sixty, and to eliminate family responsibility for the support of the elderly.

While Warren's well-financed campaign was conducted with smoothness and polish by Clem Whitaker, Olson's never recovered from the shock of the primary election returns. As late as October 9, John B. Elliott turned down an offer from the governor and State Chairman Alfred W. Robertson to take charge of the campaign! Elliott, a wealthy oil man and the manager of Sheridan Downey's successful campaign for the United States Senate in 1938, said that the offer had come too late. "Also," said Elliott—in what must have been the unkindest remark of all to Olson—"I am very considerably influenced in the matter by President Roosevelt's declaration against purely partisan political activities during the war, as tending to bring friction and disunity among the people."[75] The chairman of the Democratic county central committee in one of the Los Angeles Assembly districts pleaded with the governor for help, pointing out that Warren's supporters had already opened two headquarters in the district and had ten paid workers in the field, and that the Ham and Eggs people were working for Warren. He described the Democratic campaign in his district: "We've so far had NO Literature, NO Cards: No nothing—As the Old Saying Goes: NOTHING from NOTHING leaves NOTHING."[76] In the rural areas, the Democrats were handicapped by the stand of Olson and the party platform on the hot cargo referendum. Farmer-assemblyman S. L. Heisinger of Fresno, a general supporter of Olson in the Legislature, wrote a personal letter to Olson, Patterson and Robertson, in which he said that the party's stand on hot cargo had driven "rural California" away from the Democrats, although he said that he himself would continue to support the governor "because I don't want the State to return to a reactionary Government."[77]

Olson, almost always on the defensive, tried to tie his administration to the Roosevelt regime. He charged that Warren had not supported the Roosevelt foreign policy, selective service or lend-lease, and had not been known as a supporter of the national defense program before Pearl Harbor. Olson also repeated his charge that Warren had "obstructed" the work of the State Council of Defense and the State Guard. In the same speech Olson said that General DeWitt had reported to President Roosevelt that Olson and the California State Council of Defense had cooperated "100%" in civil defense organization. Said the governor: "Mr. Warren has overstepped the due bounds set by patriotic consideration of the national safety in his unwarranted and untruthful attacks upon our State government's civilian defense efforts." He noted that California had three times given Roosevelt "the warm handclasp of support," and said: "We Democrats urge you to renew that handclasp by voting for the Democratic candidates you will find on the November ballot."[78]

Olson's only important newspaper supporter, Manchester Boddy, was not ardent in his advocacy of the Democratic ticket in 1942. The endorsement editorial in his Los Angeles *Daily News* did not say anything about Olson's own administration or qualifications, and declared its reasons for supporting Olson: "All of them spring exclusively from our own intense desire to do anything and everything within the scope of our limited ability to help defeat the Axis powers and win the war." And this same editorial said kind things about Warren! Said the *Daily News* of Warren and his advisers:

> They have not advanced a single argument against our national war effort, they have attempted from the beginning to escape the stigma of "out" party affiliation by constantly calling themselves non-partisan. They have gone far afield in pledging support and full cooperation with the war administration in Washington. But they failed to take the one and only step that would have preserved our democratic unity: in view of his own declaration of policy, Earl Warren should have registered and stood for office as a member of the party now in full charge of our united effort to win the war.[9]

The paths of the two gubernatorial candidates crossed only once during the course of the 1942 general election campaign. This was when they participated in a unique debate on October 11 at the Curran Theater in San Francisco, sponsored by the San Francisco *News* and radio station KYA.[80] For an hour and fifteen minutes the debate raged, and it was both detailed and acrimonious. Olson hammered away at Warren's motto, "Leadership—Not Politics," asking his opponent what he meant by the "use of Hitler's slogan." Olson also asked what was meant by the Republican platform contention, "State Government must be and remain non-political." Said the governor: "As there can be no such thing as non-political government in a democracy, such a strange declaration needs explanation." He reiterated his belief in the fundamental differences between the two major parties, and concluded: "To talk of non-partisanship in the presence of these sharp and fundamental differences is sheer nonsense. Moreover, to profess non-partisanship is to confess a lack of honest, firmly-held convictions, without which no man is fit or competent to be a Governor." Warren, in his statement, defended his concept of "non-partisanship" and censured Olson for the latter's asserted mixing of politics with relief and the State Guard. When pressed by Olson for his views on the hot cargo measure on the general election ballot, Warren said:

> I am taking a neutral position on the hot cargo bill because I believe it is absolutely imperative that bitterness and controversy should be avoided at this time on any issue which tends to divide our people. . . . The hot cargo and secondary boycott question is on the referendum ballot—in the hands of the highest authority in this State, the voters of California—and in this period of grave crisis, it should not be made a political football in the governorship campaign.

Olson's supporters were very pleased with their candidate's showing at the San Francisco debate. The governor challenged his opponent to more such meetings, but Warren never accepted.[81]

Olson's Defeat

After the primary it was evident that only a miracle could save Olson, and that miracle never materialized. The result of the general election was a decisive victory for Earl Warren, the vote being Warren 1,275,287 and Olson 932,995. Warren received 57.07 per cent of the total vote cast for governor, while Olson received only 41.75 per cent. Olson ran somewhat better in Los Angeles County, where he received 44.64 per cent and Warren 54.12 per cent, but even there Warren held a majority of almost 100,000 votes. Of the counties, only mountainous and intensely

Democratic Plumas gave Olson a majority. The Warren trend was unmistakable from the beginning of the count, and at 11:30 on election night Olson sent the following telegram to Warren: "Early and incomplete returns indicate your election is a distinct victory for the Republican Party of California. Accept my sincere assurance of complete support and cooperation in maintaining unity of all parties and peoples in the performance of California's important part in winning the war. No election controversies or differences in internal policies can be permitted to obstruct the accomplishment of that purpose." Olson also issued a statement reflecting his pride in his accomplishments as governor:

> I am not unhappy over this result from the standpoint of my own personal well-being. But I naturally regret this Republican Party victory and the defeat of the Democratic principles and policies which my record as governor represents. I believe that official record will stand the test of time and the future appreciation of my party and of the people. It establishes fidelity to the platform of the progressive Democracy of California.[82]

The other members of the statewide Democratic ticket ran ahead of Olson. Both Lieutenant Governor Patterson and Secretary of State Paul Peek failed of reëlection by exceedingly narrow margins. Senator Robert W. Kenny, candidate for attorney general, alone of the statewide Democratic candidates was victorious. He had conducted his campaign independently of the other members of his ticket, and had gathered substantial support, including that of Mayor Fletcher Bowron of Los Angeles, former Attorney General U. S. Webb, and the San Francisco *News*. Ivan C. Sperbeck, Olson's appointee to the State Board of Equalization, was defeated by James H. Quinn, who was designated the Republican candidate after Speaker Gordon Garland was disqualified.

As a consequence of the 1942 election, the Republicans won a clear majority in the Assembly for the first time since 1934. Of the 28 run-offs, 17 were won by Republicans and 11 by Democrats, and a number of Democratic incumbents went down to defeat. All four contests for state senator were won by Republicans. Thus the new governor could count on Republican majorities in both houses of the Legislature. The people, by a vote of 1,124,624 to 909,061, approved the Hot Cargo Act, but rejected the constitutional amendment taking from the Legislature the authority to levy an income tax.

The defeat of Olson in 1942 was in line with a national trend against the Democratic party. The Republicans almost won control of the House of Representatives, and substantially increased their number of United States Senate seats and governorships. The 1942 elections were held during the first rather disorganized year of the Second World War, a year in which many persons had had their ways of living drastically altered.

> The factor of total war affected the 1942 election much more than that of 1918. The mushroom war industries drew workers from all over the United States. Not only were those in the armed service unable to vote, but a high percentage of the great army of industrial workers, both men and women, were disqualified on the basis of residential qualifications. Incidentally, these disqualifications affected the Democrats vitally, for labor was preponderantly behind the Roosevelt program. For the first time since 1930, the Republican vote was greater than that for the Roosevelt party.[83]

The San Francisco *Chronicle,* in a post-mortem editorial on the election entitled "Dissatisfaction Was the Voters' Urge," said, "It is management, not general policy that they find wanting."[84] As Olson had repeatedly tied in his administration with that of President Roosevelt, it follows that he, like other Democrats, had been made to suffer by those who cast ballots in a manner that would express displeasure at the way things were going.

Herbert L. Phillips summed up Olson's plight shortly before the election: "Boiled down to the final analysis, it appears, as the campaign edges toward its final week, that only (1) a heavy vote, (2) Democratic loyalty to party at the polls and (3) united Organized Labor support can win for Governor Olson."[85] The vote cast at the election was far below normal. Many Democrats apparently accepted the indictment of their party's administration as drawn up by most newspapers and by Earl Warren, or else (like the Ham and Eggers) had a special grievance against Olson and were voting *against* Olson rather than *for* Warren. Trade union members, preoccupied with war work, would not even come to the Democratic rallies in sizable numbers. Thus none of Phillips' three conditions seems to have prevailed.

In addition, Olson's 1942 campaign was not expertly managed. Lou N. Small, campaign director of the Democratic State Central Committee, and Chairman Robertson were not in accord. In a post-election letter,

Small told Olson: "Anyway, you will please me by taking the attitude that the State Committee's deficit is the responsibility of Robertson and his so-called good Democratic friends, who incidentally I didn't see or hear of during the campaign."[86] The wounds left by the Reilly-Malone fight over the vice-chairmanship did not heal. As Olson had almost no newspaper support, the factor of inexpert campaign management alone was vital.

Finally, Earl Warren was no Frank Merriam. He entered vigorously into the campaign and was on the road "day and night from July to November."[87] And he chose his own weapons and terrain. "Earl Warren is a shrewd politician with a well developed ability to conduct a campaign on his own issues, avoiding questions of a highly controversial nature and emphasizing his own most decisive arguments."[88] Warren's "non-partisan" campaign, which neatly avoided basic economic and social issues while hammering away at administrative weaknesses of the Olson regime, seems to have struck just the right note with most Californians who bothered to go to the polls in 1942. Also, Warren had the support of the many interest groups antagonized by the often blunt-spoken Olson. And, having defined his own issues by taking the initiative, and with nearly the whole of the press to back him and the accomplished campaign direction of Clem Whitaker, Warren forced Olson to take an essentially defensive position. Whatever his talents, Olson had no real enthusiasm for the defensive. An advocate himself, he became the victim of a rival advocate.

16 *the significance*

GOVERNOR CULBERT L. OLSON, ELECTED ON A PLATFORM PLEDGING a long, detailed program of reforms, was unable to secure the passage of his principal measures by the Legislature. Thus, while he was able to achieve administrative changes and to block some measures antithetical to his beliefs by use of the veto, his regime cannot be considered a great reform administration. Olson's place in California history is primarily that of an educator, not necessarily ahead of his times but blocked by the political conditions of his era—and his own limitations—from being the great crusading governor he so ardently wished to become.

Why was Olson unable to do what he proposed in such major fields as unemployment relief, public ownership of public utilities, and taxation?

First, the reform era was largely over. California, like the rest of the nation, had been drastically altered, both socially and economically, by Roosevelt's New Deal. California's role in this reform period was primarily passive, more so perhaps than that of any other major state. Under the gay and jaunty Rolph and the meek and plodding Merriam, the state had fallen into line and participated as a state in the New Deal programs—*after* those programs had been sought by the national adminis-

230

tration and passed by the Congress. The 1938 elections brought serious reverses to the New Deal, and, supplemented by the President's increasing preoccupation with foreign affairs and national defense, marked an end to New Deal expansion. At precisely the same moment, Culbert L. Olson was winning the governorship and preparing to launch his reform program. The first Democratic administration in forty years had clearly come too late.

Second, Olson's program was too inclusive, detailed and specific. The platform, when backed by his record of courage and tenacity in the State Senate, showed rather precisely what the candidate would attempt to do if elected. Thus his astute opponents were placed upon their guard. Some of them, such as the doctors with their California Physicians Service, promptly proceeded to undercut Olson's program by making concessions in the form of counter-reforms. Others laid their plans for the legislative session, where an anti-administration coalition was soon formed, representing *all interests* desirous of blocking *any aspect* of the Olson program.

Third, Olson had bad luck. His illness, beginning at the end of his first week in office, left his administration leaderless at its most crucial period, and the death of his wife, at the time of the critical preliminary skirmishes of the 1939 budget struggle, forced the grief-stricken governor to withdraw once more. Indeed, he continued to be plagued by ill health during the whole of his administration.

Fourth, Olson had only limited means of attracting popular support for his program. He had no consistent newspaper backing and, of the major papers, only the Sacramento *Bee* reported fully, fairly and consistently his administration's endeavors. The unpredictable San Francisco *News*, professing always a desire for most of the reforms advocated by Olson, seldom approved Olson's methods, and ended in bitter opposition. Manchester Boddy's Los Angeles newspapers gave little space to Sacramento news. Olson thus had to fall back on the use of the radio. Here his voice was scarcely an asset, for, in spite of its obvious sincerity in tone, it suffered by comparison with that of Franklin Delano Roosevelt.

Fifth, Olson was the victim of his own illusions about the party system in California. He looked upon himself as the leader of the great Democratic party of the state, and upon the more than two million registered Democrats as his followers. With very little exaggeration, Raymond Moley noted in 1940: "No one can control the 'Democracy' of California because no one knows what it is. Its habitat is indeterminate; its size problematical, and its various purposes, unlimited in number and completely contradictory one to the other."[1] But to Olson, his platform (accepted by the Democratic party at its state convention as official dogma) was both a sacred pledge and a solemn obligation. When Democrats in the Legislature refused to help him carry it out, he looked upon them as traitors and asked the "members" of his party to oust them at the primaries. His "black and white" categorizing left out of account the fact that there were persons who could not stomach *either* Merriam *or* health insurance. Olson's attitude ignored both the fundamental nature of California politics (individualism tempered by pressure groups) and the spirit of California's old-line progressivism. This progressivism still shone brightly in the columns of the Sacramento *Bee* and occasionally in the San Francisco *News,* and might well have been cultivated by Olson to advantage, had he been more willing to make appropriate bows to its deities and dogma, and had he been less party-conscious.

Sixth, Olson was frequently heavy-handed. One of his closest associates told the author that "Olson was about as diplomatic as a pair of brass knucks." He was abrupt and quick to anger. He frequently took to the air to excoriate his opponents. The opposition legislators, better aware than Olson of the limitations of the powers of the governor as party leader, did not fear him, and Olson, like any leader, suffered from the opposition's knowledge of his own lack of power.

Seventh, and largely a consequence of several of the above reasons, Olson managed to acquire a formidable roster of powerful enemies. These, when they coalesced at Sacramento, had ample strength to block the governor's program. And, when they fought the governor in the "purge" campaign, they decisively routed him at the local level. Furthermore, Olson had an insignificant amount of patronage to bestow and an enormous block of "hungry," job-seeking followers, thousands of whom had done yeoman service in the 1938 campaign. Many of these turned on the governor with fury when he was unable to give them the jobs into which Republicans had already been blanketed by the civil service regulations.

Finally, Olson was not an able administrator. He was temperamentally unsuited for public administration, being a frequent bad judge of character and intolerant of routine. He was handicapped by the inexperience of both himself and his associates, by the eagerness with which the latter proceeded (at first), and by the presence in the administration of such persons as Norman W. Church. More than anything else, it was Olson's shortcomings as an administrator that brought on his downfall in 1942, for his opponent flatly refused to join battle on the issue of Reform versus Reaction, at which Olson had bested Merriam.

Thus Culbert L. Olson's achievements as governor—humanitarian changes in the state's penal and parole systems and in the treatment of the mentally ill; scrupulous and often courageous protection of civil liberties and the rights of labor and minority groups; appointments of distinguished liberals to the courts; the pardon of Mooney and commutation of the sentence of Billings; and the training of a number of Democratic administrators—amounted to but a fraction of what he had set out to accomplish.

Olson at once faded from the limelight of California politics. He never again ran for public office and, in spite of his efforts and those of his friends, he never received a federal judicial appointment.[2] He remained as Democratic national committeeman until the 1944 convention, when he made a last-ditch fight for the renomination of Vice President Henry A. Wallace, in opposition to his old enemy Robert W. Kenny, who supported Harry S. Truman. He became a dignified elder statesman of the Democratic party, always available for help and advice to those who needed it—and California Democrats always needed help, even if unwilling to take the advice.

Ten full years after his defeat it was quite clear that Olson's most lasting contribution was that of an educator. He paved the way, through his speeches, messages and planning, for reforms achieved—or at least sought—by his successor. A popular Sacramento story, current years later, said that conservatives considered that their chief difficulties with Earl Warren stemmed from the fact that Olson had departed without cleaning out the governor's desk!

notes

CHAPTER 1: THE RISE OF THE CALIFORNIA DEMOCRATS

[1] *Confessions of a Congressman* (Garden City, 1947), p. 17.
[2] *Upton Sinclair's EPIC News*, August 25, 1934.
[3] *Rebel at Large* (New York, 1947), pp. 285–286.
[4] Upton Sinclair, *I, Candidate for Governor And How I Got Licked* (Pasadena, 1935), pp. 100–104.
[5] "Future of EPIC," *Nation*, 139 (November 28, 1934), 617.
[6] *California: The Great Exception* (New York, 1949), p. 182.

CHAPTER 2: THE RISE OF CULBERT L. OLSON

[1] Frank Scully, *The Next Governor of California* (campaign pamphlet, n.d., n.p.).
[2] *I, Candidate for Governor And How I Got Licked*, p. 101.
[3] Los Angeles *Times*, November 9, 1934.
[4] Luther Whiteman and Samuel L. Lewis, *Glory Roads* (New York, 1936), p. 241.
[5] *Ibid.*, p. 239.
[6] Hichborn memo, June 28, 1938, Hichborn Papers.
[7] T. William Goodman, "Culbert L. Olson and California Politics, 1933–1943" (M.A. thesis, University of California, Los Angeles, 1948), pp. 27–40.
[8] California State Legislature, Legislative Counsel, *Proposed Amendments to Constitution, Propositions and Proposed Laws to be Submitted to the Electors of the State of California At the General Election To Be Held Tuesday, November 3, 1936, Together With Arguments Respecting the Same* (Sacramento, 1936) Part I, pp. 10–11; Part II, pp. 7–9. Hereafter termed "voter's handbook."
[9] *One Hundred Votes; An Analysis of the 1937 Session of the California Legislature* (Los Angeles, 1938), pp. 33–34.
[10] "Why I Shall Vote For Culbert L. Olson For Governor," Hichborn Papers.
[11] Author's interview with Olson, October 27, 1949.
[12] San Francisco *Chronicle*, April 6, 1937.
[13] Olson to McKeage, June 17, 1937, Olson Papers.
[14] San Francisco *Chronicle*, August 2, 1937.
[15] Scully, *op. cit.*, p. 18.
[16] *Platform of Senator Culbert L. Olson, Democratic Candidate for Governor of California*, copy in Olson Papers.
[17] San Francisco *Chronicle*, September 8, 1937.
[18] *Ibid.*, September 9, 1937.
[19] August 12, 1938.
[20] Los Angeles *Evening News*, August 29, 1938.
[21] *Ibid.*, June 3, 1938.
[22] Statement of Irving Fig Newton in *ibid.*, June 14, 1938.
[23] Governor Elmer Benson to Olson, May 5, 1938, Olson Papers.
[24] *Sam Clark's Hollywood Red Ink and Hollywood Life,* of which there is a partial file in the Olson Papers, published Neblett's speeches.
[25] Carey McWilliams, *Southern California Country* (New York, 1946), pp. 242–246.
[26] H. R. Philbrick, *Legislative Investigative Report* (Sacramento, 1939) Part II, pp. 25–39.

[27] *Sam Clark's Hollywood Red Ink and Hollywood Life,* August 26, 1938.
[28] *Southern California Country,* p. 304.
[29] Winston and Marian Moore, *Out of the Frying Pan* (Los Angeles, 1939), p. 77.
[30] Los Angeles *Evening News,* July 27, 1938.
[31] Olson radio speech, December 3, 1939, Olson Papers.
[32] Olson speech, August 28, 1938, Olson Papers.
[33] Olson radio speech, August 29, 1938, Olson Papers.
[34] Los Angeles *Examiner,* April 19, 1938.
[35] *Democratic Leader* (Olson campaign paper), August 4, 1938. Copy in Olson Papers.
[36] Photostatic copy in Olson Papers.
[37] Los Angeles *Daily News,* August 27, 1938.
[38] Los Angeles *Evening News,* June 8, 1938.
[39] *United Progressive News,* August 1938. Copy in Olson Papers.
[40] Rena M. Vale, "Stalin Over California," *American Mercury,* 49 (April 1940), 413.
[41] "The Democratic Front in California," *The Communist,* 17 (July 1938), 663.
[42] Olson radio speech, July 24, 1938, Olson Papers.
[43] Olson radio speech, July 25, 1938, Olson Papers.
[44] Olson radio speech, July 26, 1938, Olson Papers.
[45] Olson radio speech, July 29, 1938, Olson Papers.
[46] Olson radio speech, August 5, 1938, Olson Papers.
[47] Olson radio speeches, August 12 and 19, 1938, Olson Papers.
[48] Olson radio speech, August 26, 1938, Olson Papers.
[49] *Rebel at Large,* p. 308.
[50] *Southern California Country,* p. 306.
[51] Los Angeles *Daily News,* August 26, 1938.
[52] Author's interview with Olson, October 27, 1949.
[53] San Francisco *Chronicle,* November 6, 15, and 18, 1936.

CHAPTER 3: VICTORY

[1] Sinclair, *I, Candidate for Governor And How I Got Licked,* pp. 114–118; "Men Under the Moon," *Time* 32 (October 24, 1938), 12–14.
[2] Whiteman and Lewis, *Glory Roads,* p. 2.
[3] Richard V. Hyer, "California, the First Hundred Years," *in* Robert S. Allen, ed., *Our Sovereign State* (New York, 1949), p. 386.
[4] Philbrick, *Legislative Investigative Report,* Part IV, pp. 1–36, 44–47; Part V, pp. 2–51.
[5] Los Angeles *Evening News,* June 17, 1938.
[6] *Democratic Leader* (n.d.), copy in Olson Papers.
[7] Los Angeles *Examiner,* September 16, 1938.
[8] *Loc. cit.*
[9] San Francisco *News,* September 16, 1938.
[10] *Ibid.,* September 21, 1938.
[11] *Ibid.,* September 26, 1938.
[12] *Ibid.,* September 29 and October 1, 1938.
[13] Copy in Olson Papers.
[14] San Francisco *Chronicle,* September 15, 1938.
[15] Olson speech (undated), Olson Papers.
[16] Olson speech, October 11, 1938, Olson Papers.
[17] Olson radio speech, October 27, 1938, Olson Papers.
[18] Olson radio speech, November 2, 1938, Olson Papers.
[19] Olson radio speech, September 5, 1938, Olson Papers.
[20] Olson radio speech, September 7, 1938, Olson Papers.
[21] Winston and Marian Moore, *Out of the Frying Pan,* p. 92.

[22] Olson radio speech, November 7, 1938, Olson Papers.
[23] Olson radio speech, November 3, 1938, Olson Papers.
[24] Sacramento *Bee,* October 26, 1938.
[25] San Francisco *News,* September 2, 1938.
[26] Los Angeles *Evening News,* November 4, 1938.
[27] *Ibid.,* November 1 and 3, 1938.
[28] *Platform of the California Republican Party—1938* (mimeographed), in possession of author.
[29] Sacramento *Bee,* November 3, 1938.
[30] San Francisco *News,* October 26, 1938.
[31] August Raymond Ogden, *The Dies Committee* (2d ed., Washington, 1945), pp.
79, 83.
[32] Edith Claire Dresdner, "The Dies Committee Investigations, With Special
Reference to Labor" (M.A. thesis, University of California, 1947), pp. 25–34.
[33] Paul Y. Anderson, "Investigate Mr. Dies!" *Nation,* 147 (November 5, 1938), 471.
[34] Olson speech, October 26, 1938, Olson Papers.
[35] San Francisco *News,* November 7, 1938.
[36] Los Angeles *Daily News,* October 27, 1938.
[37] *The California Volunteer* (Olson campaign paper), November 3, 1938. Copy in
Olson Papers.
[38] Los Angeles *Daily News,* October 19, 1938.
[39] San Francisco *News,* October 10, 1938.
[40] Sacramento *Bee,* November 5, 1938.
[41] Form letter signed by Anderson, October 29, 1938, Hichborn Papers.
[42] Olson speech, October 26, 1938, Olson Papers.
[43] Los Angeles *Daily News,* October 18, 1938.
[44] *Loc. cit.*
[45] *Ibid.,* October 19, 1938.
[46] San Francisco *News,* October 22, 1938.
[47] *Ibid.,* November 10, 1938.
[48] Paul Y. Anderson, "What the Election Means," *Nation,* 147 (November 19, 1938),
527.
[49] Jerry Saul Caplan, "The CIVIC Committee in the Recall of Mayor Shaw" (M.A.
thesis, University of California, Los Angeles, 1947).
[50] Transcript of broadcast in Olson Papers.

CHAPTER 4: BEGINNING THE REGIME

[1] Los Angeles *Examiner,* November 9, 1938.
[2] San Francisco *Chronicle,* November 10, 1938.
[3] November 12, 1938.
[4] San Francisco *News,* November 16, 1938.
[5] *Ibid.,* December 28, 1938.
[6] *Ibid.,* November 10, 1938.
[7] Winston Crouch and Dean E. McHenry, *California Government* (2d ed., Berkeley and Los Angeles, 1949), p. 105.
[8] Los Angeles *Examiner,* December 8, 1938.
[9] Interviews of author with M. Stanley Mosk, April 26, 1949, and Carey McWilliams, April 27, 1949.
[10] San Francisco *News,* November 16, 1938.
[11] *Ibid.,* November 21 and 22, 1938.
[12] Los Angeles *Examiner,* December 8, 1938.
[13] San Francisco *News,* December 9, 1938.
[14] *Ibid.,* November 21, 1938.
[15] Los Angeles *Evening News,* January 13, 1939.

[16] San Francisco *News*, November 30, 1938.
[17] Olson to Hichborn, November 30, 1938, Hichborn Papers.
[18] January 3, 1939.
[19] San Francisco *News*, December 19 and 21, 1938.
[20] Los Angeles *Examiner*, December 24, 1938.
[21] Olson, *State Papers and Public Addresses* (Sacramento, 1942), pp. 3–11.
[22] January 4, 1939.
[23] January 4, 1939.
[24] January 3, 1939.
[25] January 4, 1939.
[26] January 4, 1939.
[27] January 3, 1939.
[28] January 3, 1939.
[29] San Francisco *News*, December 19, 1938.
[30] Los Angeles *Examiner*, September 17, 1938.
[31] San Francisco *News*, November 15, 1938.
[32] *Ibid.*, November 30, 1938.
[33] Author's interview with Peek, March 24, 1950.
[34] *Assembly Journal* (January 2, 1939), 5–6.
[35] Hichborn memo, September 1938, Hichborn Papers.
[36] Author's interview with Patterson, February 2, 1950.
[37] San Francisco *Examiner*, December 17, 1938.
[38] San Francisco *News*, December 20, 1938.
[39] *Senate Journal* (January 2, 1939), 7.
[40] Sacramento *Bee*, January 3, 1939.
[41] *Senate Journal* (January 2, 3, and 4, 1939), 13–14, 40, 60–61.
[42] San Francisco *News*, January 18, 1939.

CHAPTER 5: THE END OF THE MOONEY CASE

[1] Ernest Jerome Hopkins, *What Happened in the Mooney Case* (New York, 1932); San Francisco *Chronicle*, January 8, 1939.
[2] Mooney to Mayor James J. Walker of New York, quoted in San Francisco *Chronicle*, January 8, 1939.
[3] *Assembly Journal* (March 10, 1937), 773.
[4] *Senate Journal* (March 16, 1937), 825.
[5] *Ibid.*, pp. 826–841.
[6] *Assembly Journal* (March 31, 1937), 1421; *Senate Journal* (April 7, 1937), 1507.
[7] *Assembly Journal* (March 8, 1938), 46.
[8] *Ibid.*, p. 131; *Senate Journal* (March 12, 1938), 147.
[9] March 13 and 18, 1937.
[10] Anna Louise Strong, *My Native Land* (New York, 1940), p. 61.
[11] Hichborn memo, June 28, 1938, Hichborn Papers.
[12] San Francisco *News*, August 19, 1938.
[13] *Tom Mooney's Message to Organized Labor, His Friends and Supporters, and All Liberal and Progressive Voters of California on the 1938 Election* (San Francisco: Tom Mooney Molders Defense Committee, 1938). Copy in Olson Papers.
[14] Mooney to Olson, September 22, 1938, Olson Papers.
[15] Press Release, October 12, 1938, Mooney Papers.
[16] Los Angeles *Examiner*, November 10, 1938.
[17] San Francisco *Chronicle*, November 10, 1938.
[18] San Francisco *Examiner*, January 3, 1939.
[19] Oakland *Tribune*, January 8, 1939.
[20] January 6, 1939.

[21] Sacramento *Bee,* January 7, 1939.
[22] Original in Mooney Papers.
[23] *Christian Science Monitor,* February 14, 1939. Clipping in Olson Papers.
[24] Mooney Papers.
[25] Shipler to Olson, no date, Mooney Papers.
[26] A. F. Sweeney to Olson, January 8, 1939, Mooney Papers.
[27] Holmes to Olson, January 9, 1939, Mooney Papers.
[28] Ickes to Olson, January 11, 1939, Mooney Papers.
[29] January 7, 1939.
[30] 148 (January 14, 1939), 49.
[31] 97 (January 18, 1939), 297.
[32] Various dates, Mooney Papers.
[33] F. M. Hooper to Olson, January 7, 1939, Mooney Papers.
[34] Rev. Vincent J. Toole to Olson, January 9, 1939, Mooney Papers.
[35] Anonymous to Olson, postmarked San Diego, January 9, 1939, Mooney Papers.
[36] Sacramento *Bee,* January 9, 1939.
[37] Fresno *Bee,* January 27, 1939.
[38] San Francisco *Chronicle,* January 8, 1939.
[39] *Ibid.,* January 9, 1939.
[40] "22 Years After," *Time,* 33 (January 16, 1939), 18.
[41] San Francisco *Chronicle,* March 9, 1942.
[42] *Ibid.,* February 24, 1939.
[43] *Ibid.,* October 18, 1939.

CHAPTER 6: THE LEGISLATURE DISPOSES

[1] Oakland *Tribune,* January 8, 1939.
[2] January 27, 1939.
[3] San Francisco *News,* February 27 and 28, 1939.
[4] *Senate Journal* (March 6, 1939), 437–438.
[5] *Assembly Journal,* pp. 273–275.
[6] *Ibid.,* p. 76.
[7] Sacramento *Bee,* January 13, 1939.
[8] San Francisco *News,* January 13, 1939.
[9] *Assembly Journal* (January 17, 1939), 218.
[10] Sacramento *Bee,* January 18, 19 and 25, 1939.
[11] *Senate Journal* (January 25, 1939), 360–361.
[12] *Ibid.* (March 12, 1939), 442–443.
[13] Olson radio speech, March 12, 1939, Olson Papers.
[14] *Budget of the State of California for the Biennium, July 1, 1939 to June 30, 1941 . . .* (Sacramento, 1939).
[15] Author's interview with Olson, October 27, 1949.
[16] Sacramento *Bee,* January 25, 1939.
[17] Hichborn memo, January 23, 1939, Hichborn Papers.
[18] Oakland *Tribune,* March 12, 1939.
[19] Olson radio speech, March 12, 1939, Olson Papers.
[20] Olson Papers.
[21] Los Angeles *Times,* March 30, 1939.
[22] San Francisco *Examiner,* April 1, 1939; San Francisco *Chronicle,* April 11, 1939.
[23] April 6, 1939.
[24] *Assembly Journal,* pp. 1117–1119.
[25] Olson Papers.
[26] San Francisco *Chronicle,* April 12, 1939.
[27] Los Angeles *Times,* April 12, 1939; *Assembly Journal,* pp. 1137–1140.

[28] *Assembly Journal* (April 13, 1939), 1188–1189.

[29] Sacramento *Bee*, April 18, 1939.

[30] *Assembly Journal*, p. 1309.

[31] *Ibid.*, p. 1492.

[32] *Ibid.*, p. 1716.

[33] May 4, 1939.

[34] Olson radio speech, May 7, 1939, Olson Papers.

[35] *Senate Journal* (May 5, 1939), 1872–1873.

[36] *Ibid.*, p. 2345.

[37] *Ibid.*, p. 2416.

[38] *Assembly Journal* (June 3, 1939), 2710–2711.

[39] *Tabulation of Votes Upon Selected Legislative Measures by the Fifty-Third Session of the California State Legislature* (San Francisco, 1939).

[40] Olson radio speech, May 28, 1939, Olson Papers.

[41] Olson radio speech, June 4, 1939, Olson Papers.

[42] *Assembly Journal* (June 9, 1939), 2903–2904; *Senate Journal* (June 19, 1939), 3192.

[43] *Assembly Journal* (May 29, 1939), 2555; *Senate Journal* (June 20, 1939), 3290.

[44] *Assembly Journal* (May 31, 1939), 2642.

[45] *Ibid.* (June 8, 1939), 2813–2853.

[46] *Ibid.* (June 13, 1939), 3075.

[47] Neill Davis, "Who Won the Budget Battle—and Why," *Building-Loan Journal*, 12 (July 1939), 81.

[48] June 20, 1939.

[49] Hichborn memo, May 25, 1939, Hichborn Papers.

[50] San Francisco *News*, December 30, 1938.

[51] Sacramento *Bee*, January 4, 1939.

[52] *Senate Journal* (January 4, 1939), 62.

[53] Sacramento *Bee*, January 16, 1939.

[54] San Francisco *Chronicle*, February 18, 1939.

[55] *Senate Journal* (April 5, 1939), 1104.

[56] Sacramento *Bee*, May 9, 1939.

[57] San Francisco *News*, April 27, 1939.

[58] *Assembly Journal*, p. 1976.

[59] Olson radio speech, May 21, 1939, Olson Papers.

[60] *Assembly Journal* (March 20, 1939), 650; *Senate Journal* (June 9, 1939), 2820.

[61] *Assembly Journal* (May 22, 1939), 2341.

[62] *Ibid.* (June 20, 1939), 3369.

[63] *State Papers and Public Addresses*, pp. 30–33.

[64] *Assembly Journal* (April 5, 1939), 1022.

[65] *Ibid.* (June 5, 1939), 2736.

[66] Olson radio speech, June 25, 1939, Olson Papers.

[67] Los Angeles *Examiner*, April 14, 1939.

[68] Olson radio speech, Olson Papers.

[69] Olson radio speech, Olson Papers.

[70] Olson radio speech, Olson Papers.

[71] June 23, 1939.

[72] *State Papers and Public Addresses*, pp. 28–29.

[73] April 29, 1939.

[74] *Oakland Tribune*, July 26, 1939.

[75] San Francisco *Examiner*, July 24, 1939.

[76] April 19, 1939.

[77] *Assembly Journal* (June 8, 1939), 2866.

[78] Olson radio speech, June 25, 1939, Olson Papers.

[1] Crouch and McHenry, *California Government, Politics and Administration*, p. 360.

[2] *Unemployment Relief in California, July–December 1939* (Los Angeles, 1940). This is the source for all SRA statistics, 1938–1939.

[3] Public Administration Service (Chicago), *Administrative Evaluation of the California State Relief Administration* (Chicago, 1938), p. 39.

[4] Dewey Anderson to Olson, August 14, 1939, published in *Senate Journal* (January 30, 1940), 35.

[5] Leigh Athearn,*Unemployment Relief in Labor Disputes* (Los Angeles, 1939).

[6] San Francisco *Chronicle*, January 13, 1939.

[7] January 14, 1939.

[8] Sacramento *Bee*, January 16, 1939.

[9] Olson Papers.

[10] *Reemployment: Report of the Governor's Commission on Reemployment* (Sacramento, 1939), p. 1.

[11] Jack E. Thomas, "Digest of Testimony and Briefs Submitted to the Assembly Interim Committee on Unemployment Relief" (unpublished MS, University of California, Bureau of Public Administration, 1939).

[12] Los Angeles *Times*, February 11, 1939.

[13] *Ibid.*, March 29, 1939.

[14] *Loc. cit.*

[15] Sacramento *Bee*, January 16, 1939.

[16] Stanley Paul Faustman, "Pressure Groups and the California State Relief Administration" (M.A. thesis, University of California, 1942).

[17] *Ibid.*, pp. 47–48.

[18] Mary Helen Williamson, "Unemployment Relief in Kern County, California, 1935–1940" (M.A. thesis, University of California, 1941), pp. 138–147.

[19] *Assembly Journal*, pp. 643–644.

[20] San Francisco *Chronicle*, March 26, 1939.

[21] Faustman, *op. cit.*, p. 83.

[22] San Francisco *News*, March 23, 1939.

[23] Affidavit, March 28, 1939, Olson Papers.

[24] San Francisco *Chronicle*, March 30, 1939.

[25] *Ibid.*, April 4, 1939.

[26] Los Angeles *Examiner*, March 31, 1939.

[27] San Francisco *Chronicle*, April 5, 1939.

[28] *Loc. cit.*

[29] San Francisco *News*, April 5, 1939.

[30] April 5, 1939.

[31] San Francisco *Chronicle*, April 8, 1939.

[32] Anna Louise Strong, *My Native Land*, p. 68.

[33] Oliver Carlson, *A Mirror for Californians* (Indianapolis, 1941), p. 163.

[34] Victor Jones, *Transients and Migrants* (Berkeley: University of California, Bureau of Public Administration, 1939), p. 21.

[35] San Francisco *Chronicle*, October 11, 1938.

[36] Athearn, *op. cit.*, pp. 10–12.

[37] *Ibid.*, p. 24.

[38] *Assembly Journal* (May 31, 1939), 2634.

[39] *Farm Wage Boards* (Berkeley: University of California, Bureau of Public Administration, 1941), pp. 19–20.

[40] Los Angeles *Times*, March 4, 1939.

[41] *Ibid.*, March 8, 1939.

[42] San Francisco *Chronicle*, May 9, 1939.

[43] *Assembly Journal*, pp. 1139–1140.
[44] San Francisco *Chronicle*, April 25, 1939.
[45] *Senate Journal* (May 24, 1939), 2301–2305.
[46] Phillips, *Inside California* (Los Angeles, 1939), pp. 113–143.
[47] Olson speech, May 4, 1939, Olson Papers.
[48] Olson radio speech, June 11, 1939, Olson Papers.
[49] *Senate Journal*, p. 2863.
[50] *Assembly Journal* (June 13, 1939), 3092.
[51] *Ibid.* (June 19, 1939), 3245–3289.
[52] *Ibid.*, pp. 3405–3409.
[53] San Francisco *Examiner*, June 23, 1939.
[54] *Assembly Journal* (June 20, 1939), 3424–3425.
[55] Neill Davis, "Who Won the Budget Battle—and Why," *Building-Loan Journal*, 12 (July 1939), 81.
[56] Olson speech, Olson Papers.
[57] San Francisco *Chronicle*, April 15, 1939.
[58] Los Angeles *Examiner*, March 31, 1939.
[59] San Francisco *Chronicle*, July 13, 1939.
[60] Long Beach *Press-Telegram*, July 7, 1939.
[61] San Francisco *Chronicle*, July 17, 1939.
[62] *Ibid.*, August 11, 1939.
[63] Published in *Senate Journal* (January 30, 1940), 34–41.
[64] San Francisco *Chronicle*, August 15, 1939.
[65] *Ibid.*, August 17, 1939.
[66] August 16, 1939.
[67] Los Angeles *Evening News*, August 15, 1939.
[68] San Francisco *Chronicle*, August 18, 1939.
[69] Richard V. Hyer, "California, the First Hundred Years," *in* Robert S. Allen (ed.), *Our Sovereign State*, p. 387.
[70] Alden Stevens, "100,000 Political Footballs," *Nation*, 153 (July 19, 1941), 53.

CHAPTER 8: THE FIGHT FOR PUBLIC POWER

[1] Mary Montgomery and Marion Clawson, *History of Legislation and Policy Formation of the Central Valley Project* (Berkeley: United States Department of Agriculture, Bureau of Agricultural Economics, 1946), pp. 46–64.
[2] Robert de Roos, *The Thirsty Land* (Stanford University, 1948), pp. 30–35.
[3] Merrill Randall Goodall, "Administration of the Central Valley Project" (M.A. thesis, University of California, 1942), p. 137.
[4] de Roos, *op. cit.*, p. 36.
[5] Montgomery and Clawson, *op. cit.*, pp. 65–92.
[6] Goodall, *op. cit.*, p. 103.
[7] Margaret Rohrer and Kenneth Decker, *Water Resources Problems in California* (Berkeley: University of California, Bureau of Public Administration, 1949), p. 34.
[8] William True, "Some Aspects of the Conflict over Central Valley Project Power" (M.A. thesis, University of California, 1949), pp. 76–77.
[9] Arthur Desko Angel, "Political and Administrative Aspects of the Central Valley Project of California" (Ph.D. dissertation, University of California at Los Angeles, 1941), pp. 139–156.
[10] Sacramento *Bee*, May 8, 1937.
[11] Angel, *op. cit.*, p. 153.
[12] *Ibid.*, pp. 154–156.
[13] Sacramento *Bee*, January 2, 1939.
[14] Olson's letter and Ickes' reply are published in Montgomery and Clawson, *op. cit.*, pp. 95–96.

[15] Sacramento *Bee,* May 3, 1939.
[16] True, *op. cit.,* p. 84.
[17] Angel, *op. cit.,* p. 143.
[18] *Senate Journal,* p. 2573.
[19] San Francisco *Chronicle,* June 3, 1939.
[20] *Senate Journal,* p. 2651.
[21] June 8, 1939.
[22] Olson Papers.
[23] Sacramento *Bee,* June 17, 1939.
[24] *Ibid.,* June 21, 1939.
[25] Los Angeles *Times,* June 21, 1939.
[26] Los Angeles *Evening News,* June 21, 1939.
[27] Los Angeles *Times,* June 21, 1939.
[28] San Francisco *Examiner,* June 23, 1939.
[29] *Ibid.,* June 22, 1939; Sacramento *Bee,* June 22, 1939.
[30] *Assembly Journal* (June 20, 1939), 3409.
[31] San Francisco *Examiner,* June 23, 1939.
[32] June 22, 1939.
[33] June 23, 1939.
[34] "Governor Olson Will Carry on Fight to Bring People Water and Power at Cost," *California Highways and Public Works,* 17 (October 1939), 4.
[35] Sacramento *Bee,* June 29, 1939.
[36] Author's interview with Peek, March 24, 1950.
[37] Garrison to Olson, December 26, 1939, Hichborn Papers.
[38] Montgomery and Clawson, *op. cit.,* pp. 99–101.
[39] Olson radio speech, January 28, 1939, Olson Papers.
[40] *State Papers and Public Addresses,* pp. 58–59.
[41] Los Angeles *Times,* January 24, 1940.
[42] *State Papers and Public Addresses,* pp. 266–269.
[43] *Ibid.,* pp. 116–117.
[44] Angel, *op. cit.,* p. 165.
[45] Sacramento *Bee,* January 27, 1941.
[46] Montgomery and Clawson, *op. cit.,* pp. 102–104.
[47] Sacramento *Bee,* March 31, 1941.
[48] Montgomery and Clawson, *op. cit.,* pp. 105–107.
[49] Sacramento *Bee,* October 30, 1941.
[50] Angel, *op. cit.,* pp. 163–164.

CHAPTER 9: HAM AND EGGS, LOAN SHARKS, AND OIL

[1] Winston and Marian Moore, *Out of the Frying Pan,* p. 133.
[2] *Ibid.,* pp. 143–146.
[3] San Francisco *Chronicle,* April 24, 1939.
[4] Olson Papers.
[5] May 19, 1939.
[6] Olson radio speech, Olson Papers.
[7] *Assembly Journal* (May 26, 1939), 2467.
[8] Los Angeles *Evening News,* June 5, 1939.
[9] *Ibid.,* June 26, 1939.
[10] *State Papers and Public Addresses,* pp. 403–405.
[11] Winston and Marian Moore, *op. cit.,* pp. 169–171.
[12] Text in voter's handbook (1939 special election), Part II, pp. 1–14.
[13] August 5, 1939.
[14] *California Democrat,* August 11, 1939. Copy in Olson Papers.
[15] *Ibid.,* August 25, 1939.

[16] "Lament for Ham-and-Eggs," *American Mercury*, 49 (January 1940), 95.

[17] 149 (November 18, 1939), 538.

[18] Phillips, *Inside California*, pp. 147–158.

[19] *United Progressive News*, October 23, 1939. Copy in Olson Papers.

[20] Oakland *Tribune*, November 5, 1939.

[21] Olson Papers.

[22] Olson radio speech, November 19, 1939, Olson Papers.

[23] November 24, 1939.

[24] Sacramento *Bee*, December 9, 1939.

[25] Jack E. Thomas, *Small Loan Legislation* (Berkeley: University of California, Bureau of Public Administration, 1939), pp. 1–8.

[26] Jack E. Thomas, "Small Loan Regulation in California" (M.A. thesis, University of California, 1939), pp. 40–72.

[27] Olson radio speech, Olson Papers.

[28] *State Papers and Public Addresses*, pp. 24–25.

[29] Thomas, "Small Loan Regulation in California," pp. 63–64.

[30] *Ibid.*, pp. 65–68.

[31] *Ibid.*, p. 72.

[32] Los Angeles *Times*, July 26, 1939.

[33] Fred A. Weller, "Confidential Report on the Loan Shark Situation and the Activities of the Division of Corporations with Reference Thereto," August 14, 1939, Olson Papers.

[34] Thomas, "Small Loan Regulation in California," p. 162.

[35] Olson radio speech, October 16, 1939, Olson Papers.

[36] Dated October 25, 1939, Olson Papers.

[37] Crouch and McHenry, *California Government, Politics and Administration*, p. 295.

[38] Author's interview with Olson, January 26, 1950.

[39] Author's interview with Paul Peek, March 24, 1950.

[40] Text in voter's handbook (1939 special election), Part II, pp. 40–48.

[41] Los Angeles *Evening News*, June 15, 1939.

[42] Author's interview with Peek, March 24, 1950.

[43] San Francisco *Chronicle*, June 16, 1939.

[44] Author's interview with Peek, March 24, 1950.

[45] *Assembly Journal* (June 13, 1939), 3086–3087.

[46] *Senate Journal* (June 19, 1939), 3189.

[47] Olson radio speech, June 25, 1939, Olson Papers.

[48] Voter's handbook (1939 special election), Part I, pp. 10–11.

[49] "Whose Little Pig IS This?" (campaign document). Copy in Olson Papers.

[50] November 6, 1939.

CHAPTER 10: THE REVOLT OF THE ASSEMBLY

[1] Olson radio speech, Olson Papers.

[2] Garrison to Olson, December 26, 1939, Hichborn Papers.

[3] Oakland *Tribune*, October 30, 1939.

[4] San Francisco *Chronicle*, December 7, 1939.

[5] *Ibid.*, January 29, 1940.

[6] San Francisco *Examiner*, January 30, 1940.

[7] *Assembly Journal*, p. 6.

[8] San Francisco *Examiner*, January 30, 1940.

[9] Author's interview with Peek, March 24, 1950.

[10] San Francisco *Examiner*, January 30, 1940.

[11] Los Angeles *Evening News*, January 29, 1940.

[12] Visalia *Times-Delta*, March 1, 1940. Clipping in Olson Papers.

[13] San Francisco *Chronicle*, October 8, 1939.
[14] *Ibid.*, January 31, 1940.
[15] *Assembly Journal*, pp. 110–111.
[16] Sacramento *Union*, February 2, 1940.
[17] January 30, 1940.
[18] Sacramento *Union*, February 2, 1940.
[19] San Francisco *Chronicle*, February 22, 1940.
[20] *Assembly Journal*, p. 336.
[21] *Ibid.* (May 24, 1940), 870–889.
[22] San Francisco *Call-Bulletin*, April 8, 1940.
[23] San Francisco *Chronicle*, April 17, 1940.
[24] *Assembly Journal* (May 24, 1940, 1st extraordinary session), pp. 870–885.
[25] *Ibid.*, pp. 885–888.
[26] The Governor's Commission on Reemployment, *Reemployment* (Sacramento, 1939).
[27] Statistics for 1939 are from SRA, *Unemployment Relief in California;* those for 1940 are from SRA, *Monthly Statistical Summary.*
[28] Olson Papers.
[29] Olson radio speech, Olson Papers.
[30] *Senate Journal* (January 30, 1940), 34–52.
[31] *State Papers and Public Addresses*, pp. 43–45.
[32] Olson radio speech, February 11, 1940, Olson Papers.
[33] Assembly Journal (February 1, 1940), 100–101.
[34] San Francisco *Chronicle*, February 2, 1940.
[35] Hichborn memo, February 9, 1939, Hichborn Papers.
[36] Los Angeles *Evening News*, January 8, 1940.
[37] *Ibid.*, February 2, 1940.
[38] *Ibid.*, January 27, 1940.
[39] *Ibid.*, February 1, 1940.
[40] San Francisco *Examiner*, February 3, 1940.
[41] Los Angeles *Evening News*, February 5, 1940.
[42] *Assembly Journal*, pp. 209–215.
[43] *Senate Journal* (February 3, 1940), 113.
[44] Olson radio speech, January 7, 1940, Olson Papers.
[45] San Francisco *Examiner*, February 4, 1940.
[46] Olson radio speech, February 4, 1940, Olson Papers.
[47] San Francisco *Examiner*, February 4, 1940.
[48] *Assembly Journal*, p. 364.
[49] *Senate Journal*, p. 342.
[50] *Ibid.*, pp. 347–348.
[51] *Loc. cit.; Assembly Journal* (February 23, 1940), 394.
[52] *Assembly Journal*, p. 417.
[53] *Senate Journal*, pp. 359–361.
[54] Olson radio speech, February 25, 1940, Olson Papers.
[55] Olson radio speech, May 5, 1940, Olson Papers.
[56] *Assembly Journal* (May 21, 1940, 1st extraordinary session), 553–558.
[57] *Senate Journal* (May 13, 1940, 1st extraordinary session), pp. 391–411.
[58] *Assembly Journal* (May 24, 1940, 1st extraordinary session), 814–861.
[59] *Ibid.*, p. 868.
[60] Olson radio speech, May 26, 1940, Olson Papers.
[61] Los Angeles *Times*, January 14, 1940.
[62] "Richards and Rubinow" (unpublished holographic MSS [1950]), Olson Papers.
[63] San Francisco *Chronicle*, August 10, 1940.
[64] Sacramento *Bee*, September 14, 1940.

[65] *Assembly Journal* (3d extraordinary session, Sept. 13, 1940), 34.
[66] Sacramento *Bee,* September 14, 1940.
[67] Olson to Richards, July 12, 1940, Olson Papers.
[68] Richards to Olson, July 17, 1940, Olson Papers.
[69] Olson Papers.
[70] San Francisco *Chronicle,* December 4, 1940.
[71] Los Angeles *Examiner,* December 10, 1940.
[72] *Loc. cit.*
[73] December 12, 1940.
[74] Anderson to Olson, December 18, 1940, Olson Papers.

CHAPTER 11: ELECTIONS—AND THREATS OF ELECTIONS

[1] Copies of these speeches are in Olson Papers.
[2] Author's interview with Olson, October 27, 1949.
[3] Patterson to Peek, Olson Papers.
[4] Ickes, "My Twelve Years with FDR," Part VI, *Saturday Evening Post,* 220 (July 10, 1948), 32–33 *et passim.*
[5] Author's interview with Patterson, February 2, 1950.
[6] San Francisco *Chronicle,* March 15, 1940.
[7] Boddy to Olson, March 15, 1940, Olson Papers.
[8] San Francisco *Chronicle,* March 21, 1940.
[9] John B. Elliott to Olson, March 20, 1940, Olson Papers.
[10] McWilliams to Olson, March 25, 1940, Olson Papers.
[11] Author's interview with Olson, October 27, 1949.
[12] "Chaos in California," *Newsweek,* 15 (April 15, 1940), 72.
[13] *Democrat News* (n.d.). Copy in Olson Papers.
[14] San Francisco *Chronicle,* May 6, 1940.
[15] *Ibid.,* May 1, 1940.
[16] *Ibid.,* June 4, 1940.
[17] *Ibid.,* July 16, 1940.
[18] *Ibid.,* July 17, 1940.
[19] Author's interview with Olson, October 27, 1949.
[20] Los Angeles *Evening Herald-Express,* July 17, 1940.
[21] San Francisco *Chronicle,* July 19, 1940.
[22] *Ibid.,* July 20, 21, and 22, 1940.
[23] Author's interview with Olson, October 27, 1949.
[24] Rae L. Shoemaker to Olson, February 25, 1940, Olson Papers.
[25] Author's interview with Peek, March 24, 1950.
[26] Olson Papers.
[27] Sacramento *Bee,* August 24, 1940.
[28] August 26, 1940.
[29] *Assembly Journal* (1st extraordinary session, September 22, 1940), 934. The letter is dated May 1940.
[30] Los Angeles *Daily News,* August 23, 1940.
[31] Speeches in Olson Papers.
[32] Olson form letter to Democratic leaders, October 29, 1940, Olson Papers.
[33] Crouch and McHenry, *California Government, Politics and Administration,* p. 120.
[34] Santa Ana *Register,* August 5, 1939. Clipping in Olson Papers.
[35] San Francisco *Chronicle,* March 4, 1940.
[36] *Ibid.,* March 12, 1940.
[37] *Ibid.,* March 10, 1940.
[38] *Ibid.,* July 19, 1940.

[1] Sacramento *Bee,* January 6, 1941.
[2] San Francisco *Chronicle,* December 5, 1940.
[3] December 26, 1940.
[4] *Assembly Journal* (January 6, 1941), 4–5.
[5] *State Papers and Public Addresses,* pp. 93–120.
[6] *Ibid.,* pp. 121–132, contains Olson's budget message.
[7] A. O. Lefors, "California's State Spending Plan: Budget and Special Appropriations Listed," *Tax Digest,* 19 (August 1941), 257.
[8] Sacramento *Bee,* March 3, 1941.
[9] Olson radio speech, Olson Papers.
[10] Lefors, *loc. cit.*
[11] Sacramento *Bee,* June 4, 1941.
[12] *Assembly Journal* (June 3, 1941), 3816.
[13] *Senate Journal* (June 3, 1941), 2248; Sacramento *Bee,* June 4, 1941.
[14] Lefors, *loc. cit.*
[15] June 7, 1941.
[16] June 15, 1941.
[17] "A Senator Looks at California," *Tax Digest,* 20 (May 1942), 177.
[18] Sacramento *Bee,* March 3, 1941.
[19] "Highlights of the 1941 Legislature," *California State Chamber of Commerce Bulletin,* 2:5 (July 1, 1941).
[20] *Senate Journal* (May 14, 1941), 1696; *Assembly Journal* (May 30, 1941), 3721.
[21] *Senate Journal* (June 14, 1941), 2772–2774.
[22] *Ibid.,* p. 2781.
[23] Los Angeles *Times,* June 16, 1941.
[24] "Highlights of the 1941 Legislature," *op. cit.*
[25] *Assembly Journal* (May 23, 1941), 3491.
[26] May 28, 1941.
[27] San Francisco *Chronicle,* June 16, 1941.
[28] *Senate Journal* (April 2, 1941), 910; *Assembly Journal* (June 5, 1941), 3964.
[29] Crouch and McHenry, *California Government, Politics and Administration,* p. 91.
[30] Edward L. Barrett, Jr., *The Tenney Committee* (Ithaca, 1951), pp. 1–13.
[31] *Senate Journal* (4th extraordinary session, September 22, 1940), 21.
[32] *State Papers and Public Addresses,* pp. 253–256.
[33] *Communist Party v. Peek,* 20 Cal. 2d 536 (1942).
[34] *Senate Journal* (January 25, 1941), 285; *Assembly Journal* (January 22, 1941), 361–362.
[35] *Assembly Journal* (June 16, 1941), 4328–4330.
[36] *Senate Journal* (April 9, 1941), 1068.
[37] Edward Gorham McGrath, "California Labor Legislation Concerning Industrial Disputes, 1941–1947, With Special Reference to 'Hot Cargo' and Secondary Boycott" (M.A. thesis, University of California, 1948), pp. 8–11; Irving Stone, *Earl Warren* (New York, 1948), pp. 108–109.
[38] McGrath, *op. cit.,* pp. 16–32.
[39] Quoted in *State Papers and Public Addresses,* p. 137.
[40] *Senate Journal* (March 25, 1941), 692.
[41] McGrath, *op. cit.,* pp. 17–18.
[42] *Assembly Journal* (May 13, 1941), 2974.
[43] Text in *State Papers and Public Addresses,* pp. 137–146.
[44] McGrath, *op. cit.,* p. 21.
[45] June 3, 1941.
[46] McGrath, *op. cit.,* pp. 26–29, contains an excellent eyewitness account.
[47] *Assembly Journal* (June 5, 1941), 3989.

[48] McGrath, *op. cit.*, pp. 29–32.

[49] "Highlights of the 1941 Legislature," *op. cit.*

[50] *State Papers and Public Addresses*, pp. 147–162.

[51] "Highlights of the 1941 Legislature," *op. cit.*

[52] *Loc. cit.*

[53] Samuel Egerton Wood, "The California State Commission of Immigration and Housing: A Study of Administrative Organization and the Growth of Function" (Ph.D. dissertation, University of California, 1942), pp. 138–142.

[54] Kidwell to Olson, May 26, 1941, Olson Papers.

[55] San Francisco *Examiner*, December 18, 1940; *Assembly Journal* (January 6, 1941), 36–51.

[56] Transcript of testimony in Olson Papers.

[57] Copy of statement in Olson Papers.

[58] December 26, 1940.

[59] December 20, 1940.

[60] December 28, 1940.

[61] January 15, 1941.

[62] "What's Wrong With State Relief?" *Transactions of the Commonwealth Club of California*, 35 (February 18, 1941), 403–406.

[63] State Relief Administration's *Monthly Statistical Bulletin* gives statistics for relief loads.

[64] "Highlights of the 1941 Legislature," *op. cit.*

[65] *Senate Journal* (April 24, 1941), 1328.

[66] *Assembly Journal* (April 24, 1941), 2246.

[67] Olson radio speech, May 8, 1941, Olson Papers.

[68] *Senate Journal*, pp. 1647, 2500, 2822.

[69] *Assembly Journal*, p. 3443.

[70] *Senate Journal* (June 12, 1941), 2608–2609.

[71] *Ibid.* (June 14, 1941), 2808.

[72] San Francisco *Chronicle*, June 14, 1941.

[73] *Senate Journal* (June 14, 1941), 2851.

[74] *Assembly Journal* (June 14, 1941), 4537, 4541.

[75] Los Angeles *Times*, June 18, 1941.

[76] Olson radio speech, June 19, 1941, Olson Papers.

[77] June 18, 1941.

[78] June 18, 1941.

[79] San Francisco *Chronicle*, July 1, 1941.

[80] *Ibid.*, July 4, 1941.

[81] *Ibid.*, December 28, 1942.

CHAPTER 13: REFORMS—AND ATTEMPTED REFORMS

[1] Olson radio speech, November 2, 1938, Olson Papers.

[2] Articles by Floyd Healey, San Francisco *Chronicle*, February 4–8, 1941.

[3] Crouch and McHenry, *California Government, Politics and Administration*, p. 326.

[4] San Francisco *Chronicle*, March 5, 1939.

[5] John L. LeBerthon, "The Pacific States Savings & Loan Squabble," *News Letter and Wasp*, 83 (March 10, 1939), 2.

[6] San Francisco *Chronicle*, January 18, 1937.

[7] *Ibid.*, October 12, 1937.

[8] *Ibid.*, November 9, 1937.

[9] *Ibid.*, March 10, 1940.

[10] *Ibid.*, March 5, 1939.

[11] Odell to Olson and Olson to Odell, March 5, 1939, Olson Papers.
[12] Partial transcript of hearing in Olson Papers.
[13] Copy of Odell statement in Olson Papers.
[14] *Senate Journal* (June 13, 1939), 2919; *Assembly Journal* (June 20, 1939), 3429.
[15] San Francisco *Chronicle*, April 20, 1940.
[16] *Ibid.*, February 4, 1941.
[17] *Ibid.*, March 2, 1940.
[18] *Ibid.*, March 10, 1940.
[19] *Ibid.*, October 31, 1940.
[20] November 22, 1940.
[21] Sacramento *Bee*, May 24, 1941.
[22] San Francisco *Chronicle,* January 21, 1943.
[23] Wilson to Olson, Olson Papers.
[24] Report of Warren for Governor finance committee, November 18, 1942, in Secretary of State Archives.
[25] *State Papers and Public Addresses,* pp. 36–40.
[26] Margaret S. Culver, *State Tax Administration* (Berkeley: University of California, Bureau of Public Administration, 1939), p. 4.
[27] San Francisco *News,* November 31, 1939.
[28] Olson radio speech, May 7, 1939, Olson Papers.
[29] Olson speech, September 9, 1939, Olson Papers.
[30] Olson radio speech, October 23, 1935, Olson Papers.
[31] Olson speech, May 15, 1936, Olson Papers.
[32] C. C. Young, ed., *The Legislature of California* (San Francisco, 1943), pp. 102–103.
[33] April 3, 1939.
[34] *Christian Science Monitor,* July 19, 1939. Clipping in Olson Papers.
[35] Harry Graham Balter to Olson, June 25, 1940, Olson Papers.
[36] Hollander to Olson, November 8, 1940, Olson Papers.
[37] Olson to Hollander, March 31, 1941, Olson Papers.
[38] Raymond Edward Donnelly, "The Health Insurance Movement in California, 1938–1948" (M.A. thesis, University of California, 1949), pp. 10–13.
[39] Don Jensen, "The Development of the Health Insurance Movement in California" (M.A. thesis, University of California, 1939), p. 123.
[40] *Ibid.,* p. 124.
[41] Olson message to Legislature, April 13, 1939, *State Papers and Public Addresses,* pp. 15–20.
[42] Fern E. Scneder, *Health Insurance and Medical Care* (Berkeley: University of California, Bureau of Public Administration, 1939), p. 17.
[43] April 9, 1939, Olson Papers.
[44] April 21, 1939.
[45] Donnelly, *op. cit.,* pp. 21–22; Los Angeles *Times,* April 12, 1939.
[46] *Assembly Journal,* p. 2122.
[47] *Ibid.* (June 13, 1939), 3013.
[48] Olson speech, September 27, 1939, Olson Papers.
[49] "Report of the Governor's Committee on Conditions at Whittier School" (unpublished MS), Olson Papers.
[50] Flanagan to Olson, Olson Papers.
[51] Rosanoff to Milne, April 4, 1941, Olson Papers.
[52] Governor's Committee on Whittier School to Olson, April 18, 1941, Olson Papers.
[53] Mrs. Mellinkoff and Father Flanagan to Olson, April 18, 1941, Olson Papers.
[54] *Assembly Journal* (April 21, 1941), 2131–2133.
[55] Transcript of conference on Whittier School, Olson Papers.

[56] Olson to Cox, November 18, 1941, Olson Papers.

[57] *Senate Journal* (March 17, 1943), 565.

[58] Crouch and McHenry, *op. cit.,* p. 339.

[59] *Senate Journal* (March 13, 1941), 561.

[60] Author's interview with Olson, January 26, 1950.

[61] Los Angeles *Evening News,* January 26, 1939.

[62] *State Papers and Public Addresses,* pp. 289–293.

[63] Kenyon J. Scudder, *Prisoners Are People* (Garden City, 1952), p. 17.

[64] Milton Chernin, *Probation—Prisons—Parole* (Berkeley: University of California, Bureau of Public Administration, 1941).

[65] Clark to Olson, April 13, 1939, Olson Papers.

[66] San Francisco *Chronicle,* February 11, 1940.

[67] Olson Papers.

[68] San Francisco *Chronicle,* April 11, 1940.

[69] Clinton T. Duffy (as told to Dean Jennings), *The San Quentin Story* (Garden City, 1950), pp. 59–60.

[70] *Ibid.,* pp. 65–76.

[71] *Senate Journal* (March 17, 1943), 562.

[72] San Francisco *Chronicle,* February 11, 1940.

[73] Chernin, *op. cit.,* p. 8.

[74] *Senate Journal* (May 7, 1941), 1566.

[75] On Bessemeyer, see San Francisco *Chronicle,* December 12, 1930 ff.

[76] San Francisco *Chronicle,* January 8, 1940.

[77] Marcie Hancock Wolf, "The Pardoning Power of the Governors of California" (M.A. thesis, University of California, 1943), pp. 35, 49.

[78] Crouch and McHenry, *op. cit.,* p. 338.

[79] Scudder, *op. cit.,* p. 16.

[80] *Ibid.,* p. 20.

[81] *Ibid.,* p. 34.

CHAPTER 14: DEFENSE AND WAR

[1] San Francisco *Chronicle,* June 1, 1940.

[2] *State Papers and Public Addresses,* pp. 249–252.

[3] Alten Bigler Davis, "The California State Council of Defense" (M.A. thesis, University of California, 1949), pp. 14–18.

[4] *State Councils of Defense* (Berkeley: University of California, Bureau of Public Administration, 1943), p. 1.

[5] Davis, *op. cit.,* pp. 25–26.

[6] *Ibid.,* p. 50.

[7] *State Papers and Public Addresses,* p. 76.

[8] Davis, *op. cit.,* pp. 52–61, discusses the various 1940 bills.

[9] *Ibid.,* pp. 62–69.

[10] *State Papers and Public Addresses,* pp. 88–90.

[11] *Ibid.,* p. 165.

[12] Suzanne Hammond *in* Correspondents of *Time, Life* and *Fortune, December 7: the First Thirty Hours* (New York, 1942), p. 93.

[13] *State Papers and Public Addresses,* pp. 454–455.

[14] *Ibid.,* pp. 165–170.

[15] Olson radio speech, December 17, 1941, Olson Papers.

[16] *Senate Journal* (December 21, 1941), 56.

[17] *Assembly Journal* (December 21, 1941), 94–97.

[18] *Ibid.* (January 15, 1942), 248.

[19] January 21, 1942.

[20] *Assembly Journal* (January 21, 1942), 417.

[21] *Ibid.,* p. 416.

[22] *Senate Journal,* p. 226.

[23] *Assembly Journal,* p. 425.

[24] Sacramento *Bee,* January 24, 1942.

[25] January 23, 1942.

[26] January 23, 1942.

[27] Olson speeches, January 27 and February 20, 1942, Olson Papers.

[28] Olson radio broadcast, April 2, 1942, Olson Papers.

[29] April 14, 1942.

[30] Irving Stone, *Earl Warren,* pp. 105–110.

[31] *State Papers and Public Addresses,* pp. 458–459.

[32] DeWitt to Olson, December 19, 1941 (1), Olson Papers.

[33] DeWitt to Olson, December 19, 1941 (2), Olson Papers.

[34] San Francisco *Chronicle,* December 19, 1941.

[35] Stone, *op. cit.,* p. 114.

[36] Transcript of meeting of State Council of Defense, August 28, 1942, Olson Papers.

[37] *Statutes of California* (1st extraordinary session, 1941–1942), chapter 23.

[38] San Francisco *Chronicle,* February 28, 1942.

[39] Stone, *op. cit.,* p. 110.

[40] Davis, *op. cit.,* p. 161.

[41] *Ibid.,* p. 162.

[42] Transcript of meeting of August 28, 1942, Olson Papers.

[43] Sacramento *Bee,* August 28, 1942.

[44] August 31, 1942.

[45] Davis, *op. cit.,* p. 164.

[46] DeWitt to Olson, December 18, 1941; Olson to "Attorney General and All Law Enforcement Officers," December 23, 1941; Olson Papers.

[47] DeWitt to Olson, December 20, 1941; Olson to Board of Equalization, December 23, 1941; Olson Papers.

[48] DeWitt to Olson, January 9, 1942; Olson to Board of Equalization, January 13, 1942; Olson Papers.

[49] DeWitt to Olson, February 25, 1942, Olson Papers.

[50] DeWitt to Olson, February 2, 1942; Cecil to Olson, March 9, 1942; Olson to DeWitt, March 11, 1942; DeWitt to Olson, March 20, 1942; Olson to DeWitt, April 13, 1942; Olson Papers.

[51] Quoted in Eric C. Bellquist, "Tolerance Needed," *California Monthly,* 43 (April 1942), 43.

[52] Morton Grodzins, *Americans Betrayed: Politics and the Japanese Evacuation* (Chicago, 1949), p. 107.

[53] Carey McWilliams, "Moving the West-Coast Japanese," *Harper's,* 185 (September 1942), 359–369.

[54] Olson Papers.

[55] Bradford Smith, *Americans from Japan* (Philadelphia, 1948), p. 261.

[56] Grodzins, *op. cit.,* p. 121.

[57] *Ibid.,* p. 278.

[58] *California: The Great Exception,* p. 183.

[59] Carey McWilliams, *Prejudice: Japanese-Americans: Symbol of Racial Intolerance* (Boston, 1944), p. 15.

[60] *Ibid.,* p. 54.

[61] Grodzins, *op. cit.,* p. 47.

[62] Bellquist, *op. cit.,* p. 8.

[63] *Assembly Journal* (1st extraordinary session, January 18, 1942), 320.
[64] Grodzins, *op. cit.*, pp. 125–127.
[65] *Ibid.*, p. 93.
[66] *Ibid.*, p. 328.
[67] *Ibid.*, p. 93.
[68] Olson MSS.
[69] McWilliams, *Prejudice,* p. 108.
[70] *Ibid.*, pp. 117–118.
[71] San Francisco *Chronicle*, February 22, 1942.
[72] McWilliams, *op. cit.*, p. 109.
[73] United States Army, Western Defense Command and Fourth Army, *Final Report: Japanese Evacuation from the West Coast, 1942* (Washington, 1943), vii.
[74] Quoted in McWilliams, *op. cit.*, p. 116.
[75] Grodzins, *op. cit.*, pp. 301–302.
[76] *Ibid.*, p. 106.
[77] *Op. cit.*, p. 106.

CHAPTER 15: DEFEAT

[1] Los Angeles *Examiner*, July 30, 1938.
[2] Author's interview with Kenny, April 26, 1949.
[3] January 13, 1939.
[4] Author's interview with Kenny, April 26, 1949.
[5] Los Angeles *Times*, February 25, 1940.
[6] San Francisco *Chronicle*, February 16, 1940.
[7] Author's interview with Paul Peek, March 24, 1950.
[8] San Francisco *Chronicle*, May 26, 1942.
[9] Oakland *Post-Enquirer*, May 16, 1941.
[10] Author's interview with Olson, October 27, 1949; draft of Garrison's announcement of candidacy is in Olson Papers.
[11] Visalia *Times-Delta*, March 4, 1940. Clipping in Olson Papers.
[12] San Francisco *Chronicle*, February 27, 1942.
[13] *Ibid.*, June 5, 1942.
[14] "Politics on the West Coast," *Fortune*, 21 (March 1940), 140.
[15] San Francisco *Chronicle*, April 10, 1942.
[16] Irving Stone, *Earl Warren,* pp, 92, 134.
[17] Richard Foote Pedersen, "Governor Earl Warren As Seen Through His Speeches" (M.A. thesis, Stanford University, 1947), p. 26.
[18] Stone, *op. cit.*, p. 95.
[19] "Warren of California," *New Republic*, 109 (October 18, 1943), 517.
[20] June 28, 1940.
[21] San Francisco *Chronicle*, July 23, 1940.
[22] *Assembly Journal* (1st extraordinary session, September 22, 1940), 935–936.
[23] Stone, *op. cit.*, pp. 85–88.
[24] San Francisco *Chronicle*, October 16, 1940.
[25] Sacramento *Bee*, October 16, 1940.
[26] Stone, *op. cit.*, p. 117.
[27] McWilliams, *California: The Great Exception,* pp. 206–207.
[28] Quoted in Pedersen, *op. cit.*, p. 8.
[29] *Ibid.*, pp. 10–11.
[30] *Ibid.*, p. 43.
[31] *Ibid.*, p. 92.
[32] Los Angeles *Examiner*, August 8, 1942.
[33] Quoted in Pedersen, *op. cit.*, pp. 8–10.

[34] *Ibid.,* p. 14.
[35] *Ibid.,* p. 54.
[36] *Ibid.,* p. 117.
[37] *Ibid.,* p. 10.
[38] San Francisco *Chronicle,* August 21, 1942.
[39] August 17, 18 and 19, 1942.
[40] August 21, 1942.
[41] Author's interview with Olson, October 27, 1949.
[42] Olson Papers.
[43] Olson radio speech, July 30, 1942, Olson Papers.
[44] Olson radio speech, August 6, 1942, Olson Papers.
[45] Copies in Olson Papers.
[46] Sacramento *Bee,* August 29, 1942.
[47] Oakland *Tribune,* August 26, 1942.
[48] Author's interview with Paul Peek, March 24, 1950; with M. Stanley Mosk, April 26, 1949.
[49] August 27, 1942.
[50] August 29, 1942.
[51] "Voting for Victory," *New Republic,* 107 (October 12, 1942), 465.
[52] Thomas E. Moss to Olson, August 28, 1942, Olson Papers.
[53] Peek to Olson, August 27, 1942, Olson Papers.
[54] Quoted in Pedersen, *op. cit.,* p. 9.
[55] A copy is in the Bancroft Library.
[56] Quoted in Pedersen, *op. cit.,* p. 10.
[57] Olson radio speech, October 8, 1942, Olson Papers.
[58] Los Angeles *Daily News,* October 30, 1942.
[59] Quoted in Pedersen, *op. cit.,* p. 9.
[60] Olson radio speech, October 8, 1942, Olson Papers.
[61] Los Angeles *Daily News,* October 13, 1942.
[62] Sacramento *Bee,* October 31, 1942.
[63] Olson radio speech, October 1, 1942, Olson Papers.
[64] Olson radio speech, October 29, 1942, Olson Papers.
[65] McLain to Olson, October 8, 1942, Olson Papers.
[66] Pedersen, *op. cit.,* p. 42.
[67] *Rebel at Large,* p. 326.
[68] San Francisco *Chronicle,* October 15, 1942.
[69] Los Angeles *Daily News,* October 21, 1942.
[70] *Ibid.,* November 2, 1942.
[71] Pedersen, *op. cit.,* pp. 11–13.
[72] San Francisco *Chronicle,* September 20, 1942.
[73] Author's interview with Robert W. Kenny, April 26, 1949.
[74] Copy in Bancroft Library.
[75] Elliott to Olson, October 9, 1942, Olson Papers.
[76] Franklin P. Buyer to Olson, October 6, 1942, Olson Papers.
[77] Dated September 24, 1942, Olson Papers.
[78] Olson radio speech, October 15, 1942, Olson Papers.
[79] November 2, 1942.
[80] San Francisco *News,* October 12, 1942.
[81] Sacramento *Bee,* October 24, 1942.
[82] *Ibid.,* November 4, 1942.
[83] Cortez A. M. Ewing, *Congressional Elections, 1896–1944* (Norman, Oklahoma, 1947), p. 35.
[84] November 5, 1942.
[85] Sacramento *Bee,* October 24, 1942.

[86] Small to Olson, December 20, 1942, Olson Papers.

[87] Frank J. Taylor, "Man With a New Broom: California's Governor Warren," *Saturday Evening Post*, 216 (August 7, 1943), 92.

[88] Pedersen, *op. cit.*, p. 7.

CHAPTER 16: THE SIGNIFICANCE

[1] "Chaos in California," *Newsweek*, 15 (April 15, 1940), 72.

[2] There is considerable correspondence on this in the Olson Papers.

bibliography

COLLECTED PAPERS

Culbert L. Olson Papers. Bancroft Library, University of California. An extensive collection of the governor's correspondence, speeches, and press clippings. Included are numerous reports of state officials, legislative committees, and governor's commissions.

Franklin Hichborn Papers. University of California Library, Los Angeles. Correspondence of the veteran California journalist as well as his vast collection of documents and campaign ephemera.

Thomas J. Mooney Papers. Bancroft Library, University of California. Correspondence and court records of the famous prisoner. Includes also the correspondence of the Mooney defense committees and letters received by Governor Olson following the pardon of Mooney.

STATE OF CALIFORNIA DOCUMENTS

Laws. *Constitution of the State of California.* Revised after each election at which amendments are adopted.

————. *California Statutes and Amendments to the Codes.* Published at the end of each regular and special session of the Legislature.

Legislature. *Final Calendar of Legislative Business.* Published at the close of each session.

————. *Journals of the Assembly and Senate.* Published daily during sessions; collected and indexed at the close of each session. Includes all governor's messages and reports of the committees.

————. Legislative Counsel. *Proposed Amendments to Constitution, Propositions and Proposed Laws to be Submitted to the Electors of the State of California . . . Together With Arguments Respecting the Same.* Distributed by the secretary of state prior to each state election at which propositions are voted upon.

————. *List of Members, Officers and Committees, and the Rules of the Two Houses of the California Legislature at Sacramento.* Popularly known as the "Handbook," published early in each regular session.

Olson, Culbert L. *Budget for the Biennium, July 1, 1939 to June 30, 1941.*

————. *Budget for the Biennium, July 1, 1941 to June 30, 1943.*

————. *Full and Unconditional Pardon for Thomas J. Mooney (1939).*

————. *State Papers and Public Addresses.* Selected by Stanley Mosk, executive secretary to the governor (1942).

————. The Governor's Commission on Reemployment. *Reemployment; Report of the Governor's Commission on Reemployment* (1939).

Rolph, James, Jr. *In the Matter of the Application Made on Behalf of Thomas J. Mooney for a Pardon* (1932).

Secretary of State. Executive record of the State of California. Unpublished official record of the appointments of the governor.

Secretary of State (*Continued*)

------. Statements of campaign receipts and expenditures (titles vary). Official reports signed by candidates and campaign committees in conformity with state law.

------. *Statement of the Vote of the State of California.* Official election results,
published after each regular and special state election.

State Council of Defense. *Bulletin* (1941–1943).

------. *California Defense Digest* (1941–1942).

State Relief Administration. Leigh Athearn. *Unemployment Relief in Labor Disputes*
(Los Angeles, 1939).

------. *Monthly Statistical Summary* (1939–1941).

------. *Unemployment Relief in California* (1939).

Supreme Court. *California Decisions.*

------. *California Reports.*

BOOKS AND PAMPHLETS

Allen, Robert S., ed. *Our Sovereign State.* (New York: Vanguard, 1949).

Anderson, Dewey. *California State Government* (Stanford University: Stanford University Press, 1942).

------. *Our California State Taxes* (Stanford University: Stanford University Press,
1937).

Barrett, Edward L., Jr. *The Tenney Committee* (Ithaca: Cornell University Press,
1951).

Beek, Joseph Allen. *The California Legislature* (Sacramento: California State Printing Office, 1942).

Bird, Frederick L. *Revenue Bonds* (Los Angeles: Haynes Foundation, 1941).

California State Chamber of Commerce. *Handbook of Sources of Economic Data
Pertaining to California* (San Francisco: California State Chamber of Commerce,
1941).

------. *Tabulation of Votes Upon Selected Legislative Measures by the Fifty-third
Session of the California State Legislature* (San Francisco: California State Chamber of Commerce, 1939).

California State Chamber of Commerce, Migrant Committee. *Migrants: A National
Problem and Its Impact on California* (San Francisco: California State Chamber
of Commerce, 1940).

California State Federation of Labor. *Labor Records of Senators and Members of
the Assembly 53rd Session of the California Legislature* (San Francisco: California
State Federation of Labor, 1939).

Carlson, Oliver. *A Mirror for Californians* (Indianapolis: Bobbs-Merrill, 1941).

Carrasco, H. C. *A San Franciscan Tells the Story of the Mooney Case* (published by
the Railway Employees' Committee for the Release of Thomas J. Mooney, n.d.,
n.p.).

Chambers, Clark A. *California Farm Organizations.* (Berkeley and Los Angeles: University of California Press, 1952).

Cleland, Robert Glass. *California in Our Time (1900–1940)* (New York: Knopf,
1947).

Cooley, Edwin James. *The Facts on the Proposed SRA Work Relief Program, An
Answer to the McLaughlin Report* (San Francisco: n. pub., 1939).

Correspondents of *Time, Life* and *Fortune. December 7: The First Thirty Hours*
(New York: Knopf, 1942).

Creel, George. *Rebel at Large: Recollections of Fifty Crowded Years* (New York: Putnam, 1947).

Crouch, Winston, and Dean E. McHenry. *California Government, Politics and Administration* (2d ed., Berkeley and Los Angeles: University of California Press, 1949).

de Roos, Robert. *The Thirsty Land: The Story of the Central Valley Project* (Stanford University: Stanford University Press, 1948).

Downey, Sheridan. *They Would Rule the Valley* (San Francisco: privately printed, 1947).

Duffy, Clinton T. (as told to Dean Jennings). *The San Quentin Story* (Garden City: Doubleday, 1950).

Ewing, Cortez A. M. *Congressional Elections, 1896–1944* (Norman: University of Oklahoma Press, 1947).

Farrelly, David, and Ivan Hinderaker (eds.). *The Politics of California* (New York: Ronald Press, 1951).

Gellermann, William. *Martin Dies* (New York: John Day, 1944).

Goldschmidt, Walter. *As You Sow* (New York: Harcourt, Brace, 1947).

Grodzins, Morton. *Americans Betrayed: Politics and the Japanese Evacuation* (Chicago: University of Chicago Press, 1949).

Gunther, John. *Inside U.S.A.* (revised ed., New York: Harper's, 1951).

Haldeman-Julius, Mrs. Anna Marcet. *The Amazing Frameup of Mooney and Billings* (Girard, Kansas: Haldeman-Julius, 1931).

Hopkins, Ernest Jerome. *What Happened In the Mooney Case* (New York: Brewer, Warren and Putnam, 1932).

Hurt, Elsey. *California State Government: An Outline of Its Administrative Organization* (Sacramento: California State Printing Office, 1937–1939). 2 vols.

Hyatt, Edward. *Power Prospects of the Central Valley Project* (Sacramento: California State Printing Office, 1940).

Key, V. O., and Winston W. Crouch. *The Initiative and Referendum in California* (Berkeley: University of California Press, 1939).

Lipson, Leslie. *The American Governor from Figurehead to Leader* (Chicago: University of Chicago Press, 1939).

Luck, Mary Gorringe and Agnes B. Cummings. *Standards of Relief in California, 1940* (Berkeley and Los Angeles: University of California Press, 1945).

McHenry, Dean E. *A New Legislature for Modern California* (Los Angeles: Haynes Foundation, 1940).

McLaughlin, Frank Y. *Report on the Proposed S.R.A. Work Relief Program* (San Francisco: n.pub., 1939).

McWilliams, Carey. *California: The Great Exception* (New York: A. A. Wyn, 1949).

———. *Factories in the Field: the Story of Migratory Farm Labor in California* (Boston: Little, Brown, 1939).

———. *Prejudice; Japanese-Americans: Symbol of Racial Intolerance* (Boston: Little, Brown, 1944).

———. *Southern California Country: An Island on the Land* (New York: Duell, Sloan and Pearce, 1946).

Montgomery, Mary, and Marion Clawson. *History of Legislation and Policy Formation of the Central Valley Project* (Berkeley: United States Department of Agriculture, Bureau of Agricultural Economics, 1946).

BIBLIOGRAPHY   257

The Mooney-Billings Report Suppressed by the Wickersham Commission (New York: Gotham House, 1932).

Moore, Winston and Marian. *Out of the Frying Pan* (Los Angeles: De Vorss, 1939).

Odegard, Peter H. *Prologue to November, 1940* (New York: Harper's, 1940).

Ogden, August Raymond. *The Dies Committee; a Study of the Special House Committee for the Investigation of Un-American Activities 1938–1944* (2d ed., Washington, D.C.: Catholic University Press, 1945).

One Hundred Votes; An Analysis of the 1937 Session of the California Legislature (Los Angeles: United Progressive News, 1938).

Packard, Walter Eugene. *The Economic Implications of the Central Valley Project* (Los Angeles: Haynes Foundation, 1942).

Panunzio, Constantine M., Wade Church, and Louis Wasserman. *Self-Help Coöperatives in Los Angeles* (Berkeley: University of California Press, 1939).

Peterson, George M. *Composition and Characteristics of the Agricultural Population in California* (Berkeley: University of California Press, 1939).

Philbrick, H. R. *Legislative Investigative Report* (Sacramento: n. pub., 1939).

Phillips, Senator John. *Inside California* (Los Angeles: Murray and Gee, 1939).

Public Administration Service (Chicago). *Administrative Evaluation of California State Relief Administration* (Chicago: Public Administration Service, 1938).

Rauch, Basil. *The History of the New Deal 1933–1938* (New York: Creative Age, 1944).

Scudder, Kenyon J. *Prisoners Are People* (Garden City: Doubleday, 1952).

Scully, Frank. *The Next Governor of California* (n.d., n.p.).

Sherwood, Robert E. *Roosevelt and Hopkins; An Intimate History* (New York: Harper, 1948).

Sinclair, Upton. *I, Candidate for Governor and How I Got Licked* (Pasadena: the author, 1935).

——. *I, Governor of California and How I Ended Poverty* (Pasadena: the author, 1933).

Smith, Bradford. *Americans From Japan* (Philadelphia and New York: Lippincott, 1948).

Stokes, Thomas L. *Chip Off My Shoulder* (Princeton: Princeton University Press, 1940).

Stone, Irving. *Earl Warren; A Great American Story* (New York: Prentice-Hall, 1948).

Strong, Anna Louise. *My Native Land* (New York: Viking, 1940).

Swan, John Harold, and George C. Kimber. *Liberals and Conservatives; An Impartial Analysis of the Record of the Members of the 1939 California Legislature* (Monterey: Monterey Democrat, 1939).

Thomas, Dorothy Swaine, and Richard S. Nishimoto. *The Spoilage* (Berkeley and Los Angeles: University of California Press, 1946).

Thomas, Norman. *Democracy and Japanese Americans* (New York: Post War World Council, 1942).

Thurman, V. E. (ed.). *Who's Who in the New Deal* (California edition) (Los Angeles: The New Deal Historical Society, Inc., 1939).

United States Army. Western Defense Command and Fourth Army. *Final Report, Japanese Evacuation from the West Coast, 1942* (Washington: Government Printing Office, 1943).

Voorhis, Jerry. *Confessions of a Congressman* (Garden City: Doubleday, 1947).

Wecter, Dixon. *Age of the Great Depression 1929–1941* (New York: Macmillan, 1948).

Whiteman, Luther, and Samuel L. Lewis. *Glory Roads; The Psychological State of California* (New York: Crowell, 1936).

Workers of the Writers' Program of the Works Project Administration of Northern California. *The Central Valley Project* (Sacramento: California State Department of Education, 1942).

Young, C. C. (ed.). *The Legislature of California; Its Membership, Procedure and Work* (San Francisco: Parker Printing Co., 1943).

Young, Jack. *The People Be Damned; A Record of the 53d Session of the State Legislature of California* (San Francisco: People's World, 1939).

UNIVERSITY OF CALIFORNIA BUREAU OF PUBLIC ADMINISTRATION STUDIES

(*, mimeographed; †, typescript)

Campbell, O. W. *The Status of Civil Service in California, 1937* (1937).*

Chernin, Milton. *Probation—Prisons—Parole* (1941). Supplement by John F. Duffy, Jr. (1944).*

——. *Unemployment Relief Administration, 1937* (1937).*

Culver, Dorothy C. *Legislative Reorganization* (1941).*

Culver, Margaret S. "Proposals for Legislative Reorganization" (1939).†

——. *State Fiscal Organization* (1939).*

——. *State Tax Administration* (1939).*

"Digest of Revised Health Insurance Bill" (A.B. 2172) (1939).†

Farm Wage Boards (1941).*

Harris, Arthur. *Low Cost Housing Legislation* (1937).*

Harris, Arthur, and Robert Ward. *Administrative Decisions and Judicial Review* (1941).*

Jones, Victor. *Legislature and the Budget* (1941).*

——. *Relief and Welfare Organization in California* (1939).*

——. *Transients and Migrants* (1939).*

Kerr, Clark, and Arthur Harris. *Self-Help Cooperatives in California* (1939).*

Kneedler, Grace M. *Legislative Councils and Commissions* (1939).*

——. *Severance Taxation* (1939).*

May, Samuel C. *Financial Aspects of Health Insurance* (1945).*

McKinley, John R., and Stanley Scott. "An Index to California Special Legislative Committees and Their Reports, 1937–1947" (1948).†

Rohrer, Margaret, and Kenneth Decker. *Water Resources Problems in California* (1949).*

Scneder, Fern E. *Health Insurance and Medical Care* (1939).*

Sharp, Fred. "California Horse Racing; Its Advantages and Disadvantages; Disposition of Revenue Received from Horseracing" (1941).†

——. "The Effects of Licensing Bookmakers upon Horse Racing in California" (1941).†

Staniford, Edward F. *Recent State Labor Legislation* (1949).*

State Councils of Defense (1943).*

"A Study of Administrative Expenses in the State Relief Administration" (1941).†

Thomas, Jack E. *Administrative Reorganization of the State Government* (1939).*

Thomas, Jack E. *(Continued)*

———. "Digest of Testimony and Briefs Submitted to the Assembly Interim Committee on Unemployment Relief" (1939).†

———. *Small Loan Legislation, with Particular Reference to the California Personal Property Brokers' Act* (1939).*

ARTICLES

Anderson, Paul Y. "Investigate Mr. Dies!" *Nation,* 147 (November 5, 1938), 471–472.

———. "What the Election Means," *Nation,* 147 (November 19, 1938), 527–529.

Ayearst, M. "Democratic Defeat," *Canadian Forum,* 22 (January, 1943), 297–299.

"Ballot Proposals for November, 1940," *Transactions of the Commonwealth Club of California,* 35 (October 15, 1940), 207–213.

"Ballot Proposals for November, 1942," *Transactions of the Commonwealth Club of California,* 37 (October 12, 1942), 93–165.

"Battle of November 3," *Nation,* 155 (October 31, 1942), 431–432.

Bellquist, Eric C. "Tolerance Needed," *California Monthly,* 43 (April, 1942), 8 *et passim.*

Bemis, G. W. "Sectionalism in State Politics," *Annals of the American Academy of Political and Social Science,* 248 (November, 1946), 232–235.

Benedict, M. R., and R. L. Adams. "Methods of Wage Determination in Agriculture," *Journal of Farm Economics,* 23 (February, 1941), 71–88.

Berdahl, C. A. "American Government in War-time: Political Parties and Elections," *American Political Science Review,* 37 (February, 1943), 68–80.

Bisbee, Fordyce W. "Governor Olson's Victory," *New Republic,* 98 (February 22, 1939), 76.

"California Health Insurance Plans," *Transactions of the Commonwealth Club of California,* 33 (March 28, 1939), 353–393.

"The California State Budget for 1941–1943," *California State Chamber of Commerce Bulletin,* 2:2 (February 3, 1941).

"California State Spending Plan: Budget and Special Appropriations Listed," *Tax Digest,* 19 (August, 1941), 257–258 *et passim.*

Canterbury, John B. "Ham and Eggs in California," *Nation,* 147 (October 22, 1938), 408–410.

Carlson, Oliver. "Los Angeles Grows Up," *Nation,* 146 (January 8, 1938), 43–44.

Caughey, John W. "Current Discussion of California's Migrant Labor Problems," *Pacific Historical Review,* 8 (1939), 347–354.

"Class Justice; Hearing of Mooney Case Refused by Supreme Court," *Nation,* 147 (October 22, 1938), 395–396.

Cline, Paul. "The Los Angeles Mayoralty Recall Election," *The Communist,* 17 (November, 1938), 1019–1027.

"Central Valley Power," *Transactions of the Commonwealth Club of California,* 40 (October 7, 1946), 133–220.

"Compulsory Health Insurance?" *Transactions of the Commonwealth Club of California,* 35 (May 27, 1941), 423–470.

Cottrell, Edwin A. "Twenty-Five Years of Direct Legislation in California," *Public Opinion Quarterly,* 4 (January, 1939), 30–45.

Creel, George. "California's Elephant Boy," *Collier's,* 117 (June 8, 1946), 20–21 *et passim.*

Davenport, Walter. "California Scrip Tease," *Collier's*, 102 (October 15, 1938), 12–13 *et passim*.

———. "Sinclair Gets the Glory Vote," *Collier's*, 94 (October 27, 1934), 12–13 *et passim*.

Davis, Neill. "Who Won the Budget Battle—and Why," *Building-Loan Journal*, 12 (July, 1939), 81.

Dennis, Gene. "Some Questions Concerning the Democratic Front," *The Communist*, 17 (June, 1938), 534–540.

Dilliard, Irving. "Can the Republicans Win?" *New Republic*, 107 (September 7, 1942), 276–278.

"Election Doldrums," *New Republic*, 107 (October 5, 1942), 412.

"EPIC of Upton Sinclair," *Nation*, 139 (October 31, 1934), 495–496.

Fensel, A. C., and A. O. Lefors. "The State Budget: $552,570,135 Spending Proposal Analyzed," *Tax Digest*, 19 (March, 1941), 77–79.

Fuller, Helen. "Voting for Victory," *New Republic*, 107 (July 6, 1942), 21–22; (September 7, 1942) 282; (October 12, 1942) 465; (October 26, 1942) 544.

Fuller, Varden. "Population and Politics in California," *Nation*, special Western supplement (September 21, 1946), 29–32.

George, Harrison. "Class Forces in California Agriculture," *The Communist*, 18 (February, 1939), 156–162; (March, 1939) 269–273.

Gibson, Phil S. "The Governor's Budget," *Tax Digest*, 17 (April, 1939), 116–117 *et passim*.

Gifford, L. D. "How Big Was the SRA?" *Tax Digest*, 19 (July, 1941), 234–237.

"Governor Olson in Hot Water," *New Republic*, 102 (June 3, 1940), 746.

"Governor Olson Will Carry on Fight to Bring People Water and Power at Cost," *California Highways and Public Works*, 17 (October, 1939), 4.

Hathaway, Clarence A. "The 1938 Elections and Our Tasks," *The Communist*, 17 (March, 1938), 208–219.

"Highlights of the 1941 Legislature," *California State Chamber of Commerce Bulletin*, 2:5 (July 1, 1941).

Ickes, Harold L. "My Twelve Years With FDR," Part VI, *Saturday Evening Post*, 221 (July 10, 1948), 32–33 *et passim*.

"Income and Expenditures of Government in California, 1900–1942," *Tax Digest*, 21 (February, 1943), 52–69.

Klein, Herbert, and Carey McWilliams, "Cold Terror in California," *Nation*, 141 (July 24, 1935), 97–98.

LaFollette, Philip F., Elmer A. Benson, and Frank Murphy, "Why We Lost," *Nation*, 147 (December 3, 1938), 586–590.

LeBerthon, John L. "The Pacific States Savings and Loan Squabble," *News Letter and Wasp*, 83 (March 10, 1939), 2.

Lee, John C., and Ralph F. Shawhan. "California Votes on Utopia," *Saturday Evening Post*, 211 (November 5, 1938), 8–9 *et passim*

Lefors, A. O. "California's State Spending Plan: Budget and Special Appropriations Listed," *Tax Digest*, 19 (August, 1941), 257.

———. "Legislative Highlights," *Tax Digest*, 19 (July, 1941), 221–222.

"Legislative Summary—1941 Session," *Western City*, 17 (July, 1941), 27–29.

Lyons, Eugene. "Lament for Ham-and-Eggs," *American Mercury*, 49 (January, 1940), 95–97.

McHenry, Dean E. "Cross Filing of Political Candidates in California," *Annals of the American Academy of Political and Social Science*, 248 (November, 1946), 226–231.

———. "The Pattern of California Politics," *Western Political Quarterly*, 1 (March, 1948), 44–53.

———. "Urban vs. Rural in California," *National Municipal Review*, 35 (July, 1946), 350–354 *et passim*.

McWilliams, Carey. "California and the Japanese," *New Republic*, 106 (March 2, 1942), 295–297.

———. "California Pastoral," *Antioch Review*, 2 (March, 1942), 103–121.

———. "Civil Rights in California," *New Republic*, 102 (January 22, 1940), 108–110.

———. "Earl Warren, A Likely Dark Horse," *Nation*, 165 (November 29, 1947), 581–583.

———. "Ham and Eggs," *New Republic*, 100 (October 25, 1939), 331–333.

———. "Japanese Out of California," *New Republic*, 106 (April 6, 1942), 456–457.

———. "Joads on Strike," *Nation*, 149 (November 4, 1939), 488–489.

———. "La Follette Hearings: Final Sessions," *New Republic*, 102 (March 25, 1940), 400–403.

———. "Moving the West-Coast Japanese," *Harper's*, 185 (September, 1942), 359–369.

———. "Strange Doings in California," *Nation*, 160 (February 10, 1945), 152–154.

———. "Warren of California," *New Republic*, 109 (October 18, 1943), 514–517.

———. "What's Being Done About the Joads?" *New Republic*, 100 (September 20, 1939), 178–180.

Marshall, Jim. "The Problem People," *Collier's* 110, (August 15, 1942), 50–52.

"Men Under the Moon," *Time*, 32 (October 24, 1938), 12–14.

"Migratory Labor: A Social Problem," *Fortune*, 19 (April, 1938), 90–100 *et passim*.

"Mr. Dies Goes to Town," *Nation*, 147 (September 3, 1938), 216.

Moley, Raymond. "California Talks Back," *Newsweek*, 16 (September 9, 1940), 64.

———. "Chaos in California," *Newsweek*, 15 (April 15, 1940), 72.

———. "Three Governorships," *Newsweek*, 20 (October 19, 1942), 88.

"The Nation's Honor Roll for 1939," *Nation*, 150 (January 6, 1940), 6.

Neuberger, Richard L. "Ballot Poison for Labor," *Nation*, 147 (October 29, 1938), 444–446.

"A New Constitution and a One House Legislature," *Transactions of the Commonwealth Club of California*, 30 (May, 1936), 197–248.

"Next Week's Elections," *Nation*, 147 (November 5, 1938), 469–471.

"No Cause for Panic," *Nation*, 147 (November 19, 1938), 525–526.

"November 1939 Ballot Measures," *Transactions of the Commonwealth Club of California*, 34 (October 24, 1939), 83–118.

"Olson Out," *Time*, 40 (November 16, 1942), 19.

"Olson's Luck," *Time*, 34 (June 3, 1939), 10–11.

"P. G. & E. is a Private Utility and a Good One; Case History of California Water-power and Politics," *Fortune*, 20 (September, 1939), 32–40 *et passim*.

Peirce, John M. "California's Special Session: Work of Legislature Reviewed," *Tax Digest*, 18 (July, 1940), 221–222 *et passim*.

———. "The New State Budget," *Tax Digest*, 17 (March, 1939), 77–80 *et passim*.

————. "What Does the State Owe: Debt, Deficit, and Cash Deficiency Defined," *Tax Digest*, 18 (May, 1940), 153 *et passim*.

"Politics on the West Coast, Land Where Third Term Means Less Than Power or Pensions," *Fortune*, 21 (March, 1940), 40–53 *et passim*.

"Possibilities of the Election," *New Republic*, 97 (November 16, 1938), 31–32.

Radin, Max. "Legislative Pardons: Another View," *California Law Review*, 27 (May, 1939), 387–397.

————. "Popular Legislation in California," *Minnesota Law Review*, 23 (April, 1939), 559–584.

————. "Popular Legislation in California: 1936–1946," *California Law Review*, 35 (June 1947), 171–190.

Riley, Harry B. "California's Deficit Wiped Out: Red Ink Era Ended March 31," *Tax Digest*, 20 (May, 1942), 150–152.

Rubinow, Sidney G. "What's Wrong With State Relief?" *Transactions of the Commonwealth Club of California*, 35 (February 18, 1941), 403–406.

"Saga of a Convict." *Newsweek*, 13 (January 16, 1939), 14–15.

Schneiderman, William. "The California Elections," *The Communist*, 21 (August, 1942), 602–609.

————. "The Democratic Front in California," *The Communist*, 17 (July, 1938), 663–666.

————. "The Election Struggle in California," *The Communist*, 17 (October, 1938), 919–926.

"Shasta Dam Power Distribution (A Progress Report)," *Transactions of the Commonwealth Club of California*, 34 (March 26, 1940), 233–274.

Sinclair, Upton. "Future of EPIC," *Nation*, 139 (November 28, 1934), 616–617.

"State- or County-Control of Relief Moneys and Administration," *Transactions of the Commonwealth Club of California*, 35 (February 18, 1941), 385–421.

"State Revenue Totals $345,000,000: Receipts up 15% Over 1940–1941," *Tax Digest*, 20 (December, 1942), 414–417.

Stevens, Alden. "100,000 Political Footballs," *Nation*, 153 (July 19, 1941), 52–53.

"Surprise in California," *Time*, 40 (September 7, 1942), 29.

Swing, Raymond Gram. "Last Look at the Campaign," *Nation*, 139 (November 7, 1934), 529.

Symes, Lillian. "After EPIC in California," *Nation*, 142 (April 22, 1936), 509–511.

————. "California, There She Stands," *Harper's*, 170 (February, 1935), 360–368.

————. "Our American Dreyfus Case, A Challenge to California Justice," *Harper's*, 162 (May 19, 1931), 641–652.

Taylor, Frank J. "Man With a New Broom: California's Governor Warren," *Saturday Evening Post*, 216 (August 7, 1943), 22–23 *et passim*.

Taylor, Paul S. "Central Valley Project: Water and Land," *Western Political Quarterly*, 2 (June, 1949), 228–253.

"The $30 Every Thursday Plan Pro and Con," *Transactions of the Commonwealth Club of California*, 34 (October 3, 1939), 43–82.

Tickle, Edward H. "A Senator Looks at California: The People Pay for Government," *Tax Digest*, 20 (May, 1942), 154–155 *et passim*.

"Tom Mooney Goes Free," *New Republic*, 97 (January 18, 1939), 297.

"Tory Relief in California," *New Republic*, 102 (June 17, 1940), 812–813.

"Trimming the State Budget: Work of Legislative Economy Bloc Told," *Tax Digest*, 17 (July, 1939), 221–223 *et passim*.

"22 Years After," *Time*, 33 (January 16, 1939), 18.

"U. S. A. Goes Republican," *Life*, 13 (November 16, 1942), 33–40.

"Upton Sinclair's Victory," *Nation*, 139 (September 12, 1934), 285–286.

Vale, Rena M. "Stalin Over California," *American Mercury*, 49 (April, 1940), 412–420.

Velie, Lester. "Secret Boss of California," *Collier's*, 124 (August 13, 1949), 11–13 *et passim*; (August 20, 1949) 12–13 *et passim*.

Villard, Oswald Garrison. "Issues and Men: Los Angeles Kaleidoscope," *Nation*, 138 (March 21, 1934), 321.

Weihofen, Henry. "Legislative Pardons," *California Law Review*, 27 (May, 1939), 371–386.

"What the Election Means," *New Republic*, 97 (November 23, 1938), 57–59.

Winter, Ella. "Hollywood Wakes Up; Political Activity Among Screen Writers and Actors," *New Republic*, 93 (January 12, 1938), 276–278.

UNPUBLISHED THESES AND DISSERTATIONS
(University of California, Berkeley, unless otherwise noted)

Angel, Arthur Desko. "Political and Administrative Aspects of the Central Valley Project of California" (Ph.D., University of California, Los Angeles, 1944).

Brazil, Burton Russell. "Voting in California, 1920–1946" (M.A., University of California, Los Angeles, 1948).

Burke, Robert Eugene. "Cross Filing in California Elections, 1914–1946" (M.A., 1947).

———. "The Olson Regime in California" (Ph.D., 1950).

Caplan, Jerry Saul. "The CIVIC Committee in the Recall of Mayor Shaw" (M.A., University of California, Los Angeles, 1947).

Casey, Jack Tull. "Legislative History of the Central Valley Project, 1933–1949" (Ph.D., 1949).

Chambers, Clarke A. "History of the Associated Farmers of California, 1934–1939" (M.A., 1947).

———. "A Comparative Study of Farmer Organizations in California During the Depression Years, 1929–1941" (Ph.D., 1950).

Croutch, Albert. "Housing Migratory Agricultural Workers in California, 1913–1948" (M.A., 1948).

Davis, Alten Bigler. "The California State Council of Defense" (M.A., 1949).

Donley, Wilfred George. "An Analysis of Building and Loan Associations in California, 1920–1935" (Ph.D., 1937).

Donnelly, Raymond Edward. "The Health Insurance Movement in California, 1938–1948" (M.A., 1949).

Dresdner, Edith Claire. "The Dies Committee Investigations, With Special Reference to Labor" (M.A., 1947).

Estep, Harold Alva. "Rights, Privileges, Interests, Duties, and Authorities under the California State Civil Service Act" (M.A., 1941).

Faustman, Stanley Paul. "Pressure Groups and the California State Relief Administration" (M.A., 1942).

Finch, L. Boyd. "The Direct Primary in California, 1926–1948" (M.A., Stanford University, 1940).

Frizzell, Alice Joy. "Some Economic and Political Aspects of Water Resource Development in Central Valley of California" (M.A., 1949).

Fuller, Levi Varden. "The Supply of Agricultural Labor as a Factor in the Evolution of Farm Organization in California" (Ph.D., 1940).

Goodall, Merrill Randall. "Administration of the Central Valley Project" (M.A., 1942).

Goodman, T. William. "Culbert L. Olson and California Politics, 1933–1943" (M.A., University of California, Los Angeles, 1948).

Gruenberg, Howard. "The California Apprenticeship Council" (M.A., 1941).

Jensen, Don. "The Development of the Health Insurance Movement in California" (M.A., 1939).

Kerr, Clark. "Productive Enterprises of the Unemployed, 1931–1938" (Ph.D., 1939).

Larsen, Charles Edward. "The 'Epic' Movement in California Politics, 1933–1934" (M.A., 1945).

McGrath, Edward Gorham. "California Labor Legislation Concerning Industrial Disputes, 1941–1947, with Special Reference to 'Hot Cargo' and Secondary Boycott" (M.A., 1948).

McHenry, Dean E. "The Third House: A Study of Organized Groups before the California Legislature" (M.A., Stanford University, 1933).

Parker, Zelma E. "History of the Destitute Migrant in California, 1840–1939" (M.A., 1940).

Pedersen, Richard Foote. "Governor Earl Warren As Seen Through His Speeches" (M.A., Stanford University, 1947).

Rice, Richard Brewer. "The Manzanar War Relocation Center" (M.A., 1947).

Thomas, Jack Eugene. "Small Loan Regulation in California" (M.A., 1939).

Thompson, Homer Bartlett. "An Analysis of Voting Behavior in San Francisco, 1936–1946" (M.A., Stanford University, 1947).

True, William. "Some Aspects of the Conflict over Central Valley Project Power" (M.A., 1949).

Unger, Gritter. "An Analysis of Housing Legislation in California" (M.A., 1944).

Williamson, Mary Helen. "Unemployment Relief in Kern County, California, 1935–1940" (M.A., 1941).

Wolf, Marcie Hancock. "The Pardoning Power of the Governors of California" (M.A., 1943).

Wood, Samuel Egerton. "The California State Commission of Immigration and Housing; a Study of Administrative Organization and the Growth of Function" (Ph.D., 1942).

NEWSPAPERS

Berkeley *Daily Gazette*

EPIC News (Los Angeles)

Los Angeles *Daily News*

Los Angeles *Evening Herald-Express*

Los Angeles *Evening News*

Los Angeles *Examiner*

Oakland *Post-Enquirer*

Oakland *Tribune*

People's World (San Francisco)

Sacramento *Bee*

Sacramento *Union*

San Francisco *Call-Bulletin*

San Francisco *Chronicle*

San Francisco *Examiner*

San Francisco *News*

index

Adams, Loreta, 84
Agricultural wage boards, 73, 86–87, 90–91
Ahlport, Brodie E., 145
Allen, Don A., 102, 121, 145–147
Allen, Lawrence: in Ham and Eggs movement, 16, 26–27, 107–108; on Olson, 112; supports Warren in 1942, 221
Allen, Sam Houston: in SRA, 92–93, 129–137; on Patterson slate, 141
Allen, Willis: in Ham and Eggs movement, 16, 24, 26–27, 107–109; on Olson, 112; heads slate, 142–143; supports Warren in 1942, 221
Altgeld, John Peter, 55
American Federation of Labor (AFL). *See* California State Federation of Labor
American Federation of Musicians, 131, 213
American League for Peace and Democracy, 131
American Legion: and Dies committee testimony, 29–30; opposes unicameral legislature, 175; sponsors California Joint Immigration Committee, 203
American President Lines, 140
Anderson, H. Dewey: opposes anti-labor initiative, 31; and Olson's fiscal program, 38, 64–65, 154; SRA administrator, 38, 79–93; resigns, 93–94, 128, 162–164; on Wakefield, 137
Andreas, Godfrey A., 103
Apprenticeship Council, 73.
Armstrong, Barbara, 176
Armstrong, Thomas, 162
Assembly, composition and organization: 1939, 44–45, 61; 1940, 120–123; 1941, 149, 151–152. *See also* Legislature.
Associated Farmers of California, 19, 30, 74, 79
Atherton, Edward N., and Associates:

Philbrick report, 71–72; SRA report, 128–129
Atkinson, Maurice, 62; oil bill, 116–118, 122–123, 150
Auditor-general, 174

Bainbridge, Sherman J., "The Voice," 16, 107–108
Bakery Wagon Drivers Union, 39
Ballou, Walter T., 93, 94, 137, 145
Bancroft, Philip, 31–33
Bank and corporation franchise taxes, 64, 70, 155
Bashore, Lee T.: investigates SRA, 81–82, 130, 136; 146, 192–193
Beesemyer, Gilbert H., 184
Behrens, Earl C., 130, 143.
Bellquist, Eric, on Japanese evacuation, 203
Bennett, F. Ray, 125–126, 154
Benson, Elmer A., 34
Berkeley *Gazette:* on Olson appointments, 40
Billings, Warren K.: and Preparedness Day bombing, 49–57; seeks pardon, 50, 51; Mooney pledges aid, 55, 57; sentence commuted, 58, 233
Board of Pilot Commissioners of San Francisco Harbor, 46
Board of State Harbor Commissioners, 61, 63
Boddy, Manchester: on 1938 elections, 14, 18, 21, 27, 31; on Dies committee, 30; on 1940 elections, 141, 146; on 1942 elections, 214, 225, 231
"Bookie" bill, 75–76
Borough, Reuben W., 18
Bourquin, M. Mitchell, 17, 25
Bowron, Fletcher: mayor of Los Angeles, 35, 205–206, 227
Breed, Arthur H., Jr., 189
Bridges, Harry, 29, 63, 149
Briggs, George A., 185–186

May, Samuel C., 176, 188
Mellen, James W., 149
Mellinkoff, Helen, 178–179
Mental institutions, 69, 180–181, 215, 233
Merriam, Frank F.: governor, 2, 4, 9, 156, 229–230, 232; Olson on, 1938, 11, 12, 13, 19, 20, 25, 26, 27, 35, 169–170; career, to 1938, 23; campaign for renomination, 1938, 24; opposes Ham and Eggs plan, 27; campaign for re-election, 1938, 28–35, 213; and Mooney case, 51–52; fiscal policy, 64; and Philbrick Report, 71; and SRA, 78–79, 86, 88, 93; and "Proclivity Affair," 170–171; and governmental reorganization study, 173; and Advisory Pardon Board, 184; and parole policies, 220
Metzger, D. Jack, 89, 172, 203
Migratory workers: SRA and, 86–87
Miller, Eleanor, 103
Millington, Seth: "economy bloc" assemblyman, 67–68; sponsors gift tax, 70; opposes Donnelly lobby bill, 72; and Garrison revenue bond bill, 99; opposes Pierovich revenue bond bill, 102; opposes Atkinson oil bill, 118; nominates Garland for speaker, 121; on SRA investitgating committee, 130; endorses Garner slate, 1940, 142; and 1941 budget, 153–154
Milne, E. J., 179
Mittelstaedt, R. E., 188, 190
Moffitt, James K., 144–145
Moley, Raymond: on 1940 presidential preference primary, 142; on Democratic party in California, 231–232
Mooney, Rena, 48–49
Mooney, Thomas J., summary of case, 48–53; in 1938 elections, 15, 39, 52–53; Olson pardons, 27, 36, 53–56, 149, 233; death, 57
Mosk, M. Stanley, 123–126, 144–145
Motion Picture Democratic Committee, 27
Murphy, Daniel C., 14, 18, 20, 21, 28, 32, 52
Murphy, Frank, 30, 34
Murphy, J. A. ("Foghorn"), 149
Mutual Assistance Act, 195
Myhand, Peter, P., 101, 132, 219

Nation: on Mooney pardon, 56; on Ham and Eggs plan, 110

National Conference of Law Enforcement Officers: anti-sabotage bill, 157
National Council of Defense, 187–188
National defense migration, select committee investigating (Tolan), 204–205
National defense program: Olson and, 135, 138, 152, 187–201
National Reclamation Association, 105
National Youth Administration, 132
Native Sons of the Golden West, 203
Neblett, William H., 2, 4, 15, 20, 28
Nelles School for Boys, 179–180
New Deal: Olson on, 1938, 12, 36; Republicans on, 1938, 28; Olson on, 1939, 41, 43, 1940, 139; 1942, 207, 215–216, 225, 228; Republicans on, 1942, 219, 230–231
New Republic: on Mooney pardon, 56
Newsboys bill, 161
Newspapers: in 1934 elections, 4; 1938 elections, 27; Olson on, 1939, 43, 74; on Olson inaugural address, 1939, 43–44; on Olson, 1939, 77; on Ham and Eggs plan, 1939, 110; on usury acts, 1939, 115; in 1942 elections, 214, 215; on Olson, 231. *See also* names of newspapers
Neylan, John Francis, 24
Nielsen, Roy J., 99, 148
Nimmo, Ray E., 29–31
Nisei: evacuation, 201–206
Nolan, Edward, 48–49
Noral, Alexander, 83

Oakland *Post Enquirer. See* Hearst newspapers
Oakland *Tribune:* supports Atkinson oil bill, 118; on plan to oust speaker Peek, 120
O'Connor, J. F. T., 14, 17, 20, 27
Odell, Robert S.: and seizure of Pacific States Savings and Loan Co., 169–173
O'Donnell, John H., 103
Office of Civilian Defense, 198
Ogden, Father August Raymond, S. J.: on Dies committee, 29–31
Ogden *Standard,* 6
O'Hare, Kate Richards, 182
Oil conservation: Atkinson oil bill, 116–118, 122–123, 150
Oil taxation: Olson recommends severance tax, 64; opposed by Seawell, 65; Assembly rejects, 70
Oil, tidelands: Olson heads investigation, 1935–1937, 9–10; Olson oil bill, 1937–

Oil, tidelands—*Continued*
    1938, 10, 19, 26; proposition 4 (initiative), 1936, 9; State Lands Act, 1938, 10; Hichborn on, 10; Olson on, 1938, 25, 26; Olson on, 1939, 42–43
Old age pensions: Olson on, 1938, 12, 25, 36, 40; 1939, 41–42, 65, 112; 1940, 119; Republicans on, 1938, 29; Olson veto, 75; Assembly refuses to increase, 108–109; in 1942 elections, 213, 220–224. *See also* Townsend Plan; Ham and Eggs movement
Olson, Culbert L.: birth and career in Utah, 6–7; chairman, Democratic state central committee, 1934–1936, 4, 6, 8; state senator, 1935–1938, 6, 8, 10; special assistant U. S. attorney general, 1935–1936, 9–10; U. S. Senatorial ambitions, 1937, 10; in presidential preference primary, 1936, 10; candidate for nomination for Governor, 1938, 11–23; on Ham and Eggs plan, 1938, 16–17, 25–27; 1939, 108–112; campaign expenditures, 1938, 18, 20, 25; Democratic candidate for governor, 1938, 23–35; elected governor, 1938, 33–35; plans his administration, 36–47; inaugural address, 1939, 40–44; tries to withdraw Merriam appointments, 1939, 46–47; supports Peek for speaker, 1938–1939, 45; collapse and illness, 59–60, 231; appointments to Board of State Harbor Commissioners, 61, 63; budget and tax program, 1939, 63–70; effort to regulate lobbyists, 71–73; and State Relief Administration, 77–95; and Central Valley Project, 96–106; and special sessions of Legislature, 1940, 91, 119–136; and "Dictograph Case," 123–126; supports Roosevelt for third term, 139–143, 148; feud with Patterson, 1940, 143–145; becomes Democratic national committeeman, 1940, 139, 143; mentioned for vice-president, 1940, 144; "purge" campaign, 1940, 145–147; first biennial message, 1941, 152–153; budget and tax program, 1941, 153–156; and national defense program, 187–201; feud with Warren, 194–199; and Lt. Gen. De Witt, 195, 200–201, 204; and Japanese evacuation, 201–206; candidate for reëlection, 1942, 207–229; debate with Warren, 225–226; defeat, 226–229; significance of

his administration, 230–233
Olson, Dean, 7
Olson, Delilah King, 6–7
Olson, John, 7
Olson, Kate Jeremy, 7, 68, 231
Olson, Richard: son of Culbert L. Olson, 7; supports Kenny for chairman, 1938, 24; private secretary to Olson, 38, 40; difficulties with Legislature, 60–61, 63, 74–76; lobbies for Pierovich revenue bond bill, 102; mentioned in recall campaign, 149
Olson oil bill, 1937–1938: 10, 26; defeated, 33–34
Olson recall committee, 149–150
Oregon Commonwealth Federation, Olson addresses, 139
Osborne, Sidney, 200
Osborne Society, 179
Owens, Roy G.: in Ham and Eggs movement, 16, 109–110, 111; candidate for governor, 1942, 217, 218
Oxman, Frank, 49–50

Pacht, Isaac, 183–186
Pacific Gas and Electric Co., 48, 96, 99–100, 104–106
Pacific States Auxiliary Corporation, 170–171
Pardons (Olson): Mooney, 48, 53–55, 233; "Stockton 18," 168; all applications turned over to the Advisory Pardon Board, 184; Republican charges, 1942, 219, 221
Parole: of mental patients, 180–181; of Beesemyer, 184; of King, Ramsay, and Connor, 212, 221; Republican charges, 1942, 219–221, 233
Patronage problem: facing Olson, 1938, 35, 37–38, 78; in SRA, 78–79, 80, 92–95, 162–164, 168; at Chino prison, 185–186; 207; Republican charges, 1942, 213, 219–220, 232
Patterson, Ellis E.: career, to 1938, 22; candidate for lieutenant governor, 10, 22, 24–25, 27–31, 52, 84; lieutenant governor, 33, 45–46, 60, 63, 118, 176, 182; supports Ham and Eggs plan, 1939, 108–109, 111; heads left-wing slate, 140–143; feud with Olson, 143–145; defeated for U. S. Senate nomination, 147–148; candidacy for reëlection, 1942, 209, 218, 224; defeat, 227
Peck, Lydell, 218
Peek, Paul: speaker of the Assembly,

1939, 45; appoints committees, 61; supports memorial to lift Spanish embargo, 62; favors revenue bond bill, 1939, 100, 102; advises Olson on special session of Legislature, 104; and Atkinson oil bill, 116–117; ouster from speakership, 120–121; appointed secretary of state, 122; and 1940 elections, 140–142, 145–146, 148; candidate for reëlection, 1942, 209; nominated, 218; defeated, 227

People's World: in 1938 elections, 18; on SRA "purge," 86

Personal property brokers. *See* Usury

Phelan, James D., 1

Philbrick, Howard R.: report on legislative corruption, 71–72; director of motor vehicles, 72; and "Dictograph Case," 123–126

Phillips, Herbert L.: on 1941 budget, 154; on Olson and SRA, 1940, 164; on 1942 primary result, 217; on 1942 election, 228

Phillips, James H., 102; usury act, 113–115; 180

Phillips, John, State Senator: on SRA, 89; on Ham and Eggs plan, 1939, 110; investigations of SRA, 128–129, 133–138, 162–164; plan for county administration of SRA, 164–168; bill to reform prisons, 184

Picketing. *See* Labor legislation

Pierovich, A. L.: revenue bond bill, 1939, 101–104, 122–123; appointed superior judge, 76

Plant inspection service, 200–201

Plunkert, William J.: in 1938 elections, 18; opposes anti-labor initiative, 1938, 31; ouster from SRA, 84–86, 94

"Point Lobos" (Ship) Murder Case": 212, 221

Pomeroy, Harold: policies in SRA, 79, 83–84, 86–87, 93; in Associated Farmers, 79

Porter, Langley, 181

Power, electric. *See* Utilities, public

Preparedness Day parade, 1916: bombing, 48–49, 57

Presidential preference primaries (Democratic): 1932, 2, 8, 14; 1936, 5, 10; 1940, 139–143

Price, Archie, 21

Price, David, 85

Prison reform, 181–186, 215, 220, 233

"Proclivity Affair," 170–171

Production-for-use: Olson supports, 1935, 8; 1938, 12, 36, 38, 40; 1939, 42, 78, 80–81, 89; San Francisco *News* on, 1939, 43; Los Angeles *Times* on, 1939, 44; Dewey Anderson on, 1939, 79, 83; San Francisco *Chronicle* on, 1939, 79; Assemblyman Bashore on, 1939, 82; C. L. Preisker on, 82; Chambers on, 94; Governor's Commission on Reemployment advocates, 127; Olson on, 1940, 127, 133, 134; Phillips committee opposes, 134; Olson on, 1941, 152–153; 1942, 215

Progressive party: formation, 2; 1934 election, 4; 1938 election, 14, 15, 31, 53

Pro-rate commissioners, 46

Prostitution, 200

Public ownership. *See* Utilities, public

Public utilities. *See* Utilities, public

"Purge." *See* Legislature

Qualifications Commission, 211

Quinn, Irwin T., 189, 192–193

Quinn, James H., 227

Radin, Max, 211–212

Raker Act, 105–106

Ramsay, E. G., 212, 221

Real, Charles, 213

Recall (of Olson): threats, 112, 139, 149–150, 164

Reconstruction Finance Corporation, 40

Reemployment, Governor's Commission on, 80–81, 91, 127

Reilly, George R., 223, 229

Relief. *See* State Relief Administration

Republican National Convention, 1936, 211

Republican party of California: supremacy in 1920's, 1; Olson on, 11, 19–20, 25–26, 65, 74, 76–77, 123, 146, 195, 215–216, 226–227. *See also* Elections; Republican state conventions

Republican state conventions: 1938, 25–28; 1942, 219–220

Revenue bonds: Central Valley Project Act, 1933, 97; Garrison revenue bond bills, 1935–1938, 12, 19, 33–34, 42–43, 98–100; Nielsen revenue bond bills, 1935 and 1937, 99; Pierovich revenue bond bill, 1939, 101–104, 122–123; bills die in committee, 1940 and 1941, 104–105, 120, 153

Rich, William P., 151, 155, 156

Richards, John R.: Chairman of Governor's Commission on Reemployment, 81, 91, 127; appointed director of finance, 127; recommends Rubinow for SRA Administrator, 135; resigns, 136–138, 154; charges on SRA, 162–164; supports Kenny for governor, 1942, 208

Richie, Paul A., 50–51, 141

Rigall, Frank, 49

Robbins, Wesley E., 120

Robertson, Alfred W.: supports Peek for speaker, 1939, 45; 1940, 121; Democratic state chairman, 1942, 224, 228–229

Rolph, James, Jr.: candidate for governor, 1918, 2, 210; governor, 23, 97, 156, 185, 207–208, 230

Rolph, James, III, 112

Roosevelt, Franklin Delano: nominated for president, 1932, 2; fails to support Sinclair, 1934, 4; carries California, 1936, 5, 10; and 1938 elections in California, 14, 21, 28; Olson visits, 1938, 25, 40; opposes Ham and Eggs plan, 1938, 21, 28; 1939, 110; on Dies committee, 30; and Central Valley Project, 98, 102, 104; favors Atkinson oil bill, 118; 1940 campaign in California, 139–143, 146, 148; seizes North American Aircraft Corporation plant, 159; and Japanese evacuation, 204; Olson on, 1942, 207, 215–216; statement on adjournment of partisan politics, 213, 219, 224; tries to secure Creel support for Olson, 1942, 222; administration losses, 1942 Congressional elections, 229

Rosanoff, Aaron J.: director of institutions, 39; trouble at Whittier State School, 178, 180; reform of mental institutions, 180

Rosenthal, Ben: administration floor leader in Assembly, 62, 67, 76, 176–178

Rowe, Paul H., 123–126

Rowell, Chester, 150, 176–177

Rubinow, Sidney G.: SRA administrator, 135–138; fired by Olson, 138; charges on SRA, 162–164

Saadi, Mitchell, 84

Sabotage: Anti-Sabotage Act, 1941, 157, 195

Sacramento *Bee. See* McClatchy newspapers.

Sacramento Citizens Non-Partisan Committee, 146

Sacramento County Grand Jury investigation of the legislature, 1937–1938, 15, 19, 24, 71–72, 75

Sacramento *Union:* on Olson's inaugural address, 44; on State Guard appropriation, 192

Sales tax, 155, 214, 224

Samish, Arthur H.: supports Hatfield for governor, 1938, 24, 34; and Philbrick Report, 72

San Francisco *Call-Bulletin. See* Hearst newspapers

San Francisco Chamber of Commerce, 97

San Francisco *Chronicle:* on Commonwealth-Progressive Federation, 10; on Olson's inaugural address, 44; on Mooney case, 51; on production-for-use, 79; Herb Caen quoted, 85–86; on SRA appropriation, 1939, 88; on ouster of Rubinow, 137; advocates reelection of Garland as speaker, 1941, 152; on SRA, 1940–1941, 163, 164; on seizure of Pacific States Savings and Loan Co., 172–173; on State Guard, 194; on Japanese in California, 1942, 204; on appointment of Max Radin to State Supreme Court, 211–212; on Olson, 1942, 214, 217; on 1942 elections, 228

San Francisco *Examiner. See* Hearst newspapers

San Francisco Junior Chamber of Commerce, 60

San Francisco Labor Council, 32

San Francisco Legal Aid Society, 113

San Francisco *News:* on 1938 elections, 14, 26, 27; on McDonough contribution to Olson campaign, 1938, 25; opposes anti-labor initiative, 31; on Kenny, 1938, 208; on Olson's inaugural address, 43; on production-for-use, 43; supports Donnelly lobby bill, 72–73; on Olson veto of grand jury bill, 75; on SRA appropriation, 1939, 88; supports Garrison revenue bond bill, 100; supports Pierovich revenue bond bill, 103; special supplement on Olson administration, 110; opposes tax cuts, 1941, 155; on SRA, 1940, 164; on SRA, 1941, 167; supports Warren, 1942, 214; sponsors

State Relief Administration
(1939)—*Continued*
tion, 80; patronage problems, 78–80,
92–95, 162–164; case loads, 81; investigation of, 81–85, 89; appropriation, 82, 88–91; Olson and, 77–95;
headquarters moved to Los Angeles,
92, 94–95; Anderson administrator, 38,
79–95, 136; Chambers administrator,
94, 136; report of Governor's Commission on Reemployment, 127
State Relief Administration, 1940: relief
rolls rise, 119, 127–128; appropriations, 119, 129, 131–136; and "Dictograph Case," 123–126; Board of Personnel Standards and Appeals appointed, 128; actions, 135, 137, 163;
investigations of, 128–131, 133–138,
162–164; abolition of Los Angeles
County headquarters, 130–131; county
administration bill, 132, 134; Chambers resigns, 135; Rubinow administrator, 135–138, 162–164; Wakefield
administrator, 137–138; patronage
problems, 130–131, 135–138; defense
emergency relieves problems, 138;
Richards and Rubinow charges, 162–
164; newspaper comment on charges,
163–164
State Relief Administration, 1941: appropriations, 153, 162, 165–166; San
Francisco *News* on, 155, 167; county
administration bills, 164–168; rolls
continue to drop, 164–165; Olson vetoes county administration bill, 165;
Legislature adjourns without appropriation, 166–167; abolition, 167–168;
Los Angeles *Times* on, 167; Olson and,
165–168; "Stockton 18," 168, 212;
property given to State Guard, 192;
issue in 1942 campaign, 213–214
State Relief Commission: function, 79;
strike policy, 87
State Retirement Life Payments administrator, 110
State Supreme Court: and Mooney case,
49, 50; recommends commutation of
Billings' sentence, 58; on Tenney Act,
157; upholds Fletcher State Guard
Act, 194; Radin appointment rejected,
211
State War Production Board, 223
State Water Project Authority, 96–98,
100–102, 104–105
Stephens, James, 184

Stephens, William D., 49–50
Stephenson, Dwight W., 137
Stewart, Fred E.: approves cut in State
Board of Equalization funds, 67–68;
and ouster of Speaker Peek, 120, 174
Stimson, Henry L., 204
"Stockton 18": Olson pardons, 168; Max
Radin and, 212
Stockton *Record:* on Olson's inaugural
address, 43–44
Stone, Irving: on Olson-Warren feud,
195–197; on Warren as attorney gen-
eral, 211
Strikes: San Francisco waterfront, 1934,
23; Kern County cotton pickers, 1938,
83; Madera County cotton pickers,
1939, 87; Westwood lumber workers,
1939, 211; Inglewood, North American
Aircraft Corporation, 1941, 159
Strong, Anna Louise: on San Francisco
Labor Day parade, 1938, 52; on SRA
"purge," 86
Sturzenacker, Carl, 20
Swan, John Harold, 203

Tatum, C. C. C., 149–150
Taxation: Olson program, 1935, 8–9;
Olson program, 1938, 12, 38; Anderson on, 38; Republican assemblymen
on, 1938, 45; Olson program, 1939,
42, 64–70, 76; Olson program, 1940,
119; Garland on, 122–123; rejected
by Legislature, 134; Olson program,
1941, 152, 155–156, 213–214; initiative to abolish income tax, 213–214,
216, 224, 227; Warren pledges, 1942,
213–214–223
Taylor, Ralph J., 19
Temple, Shirley: Dies committee testi-
mony on, 30–31, 35
Temporary National Economic Commis-
sion, 138
Tenney, Jack B.: left-wing assemblyman,
46, 62; on SRA investigating committee, 129–131; Olson seeks to purge,
145, 146; committee investigating un-
American activities, 156–157; supports
Warren, 1942, 222
Thorp, James E., 103
Tickle, Edward H., 154–155
Timmons, Rosamund (Rose Segure), 85
Tolan, John H., 204–205
Tomasini, Teodoro Antonio, 20
Townsend plan: Olson on, 1935, 9, 16;
Republicans on, 1938, 29